LIVE AND LET SPY

BRIXMIS – THE LAST COLD WAR MISSION

STEVE GIBSON

note all of these 'shy' organisatio[n] globally - are all controlled by the same elites. The goons working at National level - in the main - do not yet know this fact. yet!!!

'See but don't be seen.
Hear but don't be heard.'

First published in 1997
This edition published in 2012

The History Press
The Mill, Brimscombe Port
Stroud, Gloucestershire, GL5 2QG
www.thehistorypress.co.uk

British Library Cataloguing in Publication Data.
A catalogue record for this book is available from the British Library.

ISBN 978 0 7524 6580 7

Typesetting and origination by The History Press
Printed in the EU for The History Press.

Contents

Foreword

This is a book of two parts. For those wanting to read an action-based first-hand account of 'licensed' spying operations behind enemy lines, the story remains unchanged. For those who want a case-study in intelligence's fundamental relationship with power and politics, then the additional new chapter – 'Reflections' – charts a route from the mutually assured destruction strategy of the early Cold War years to the contemporary context that Western nations are constructing for themselves post-1989.

This book was originally conceived by Stevyn Gibson as a personal story. It was intended as an individual account of a private experience set down for the record. The addition of the final chapter is a continuation of that personal experience. The new chapter cradles the original story in an analytical framework that pays tribute to the role of intelligence – Brixmis specifically – in 'winning' the Cold War. Yet, it also demonstrates the Cold War origins of today's debilitating political context in which intelligence now finds itself operating.

The new title – *Live and Let Spy* – perfectly conveys the paradox of spying on, while at the same time liaising with, the 'enemy'. Agreeing, mutually, to spy upon each other worked as a pressure release valve and in its own small way contributed to preventing the Cold War going hot. Clearly Brixmis did not contribute to this happy outcome alone; the aggressive acquisition of information replicated across a myriad of different agencies, across the electromagnetic spectrum, across all collection categories, and by all sides contributed to a peaceful coexistence amidst the broader conceptual notion of nuclear Armageddon. But, getting drunk with the 'enemy' goes a long way to humanising and de-demonising them.

Live and Let Spy reflects upon this historical role of intelligence in building confidence and providing verification. In the realist search for geo-political equilibrium – to live and let live – intelligence plays an important part in demonstrating that one power will not remain supine in the face of another wishing to exert their power. In the absence of perfect systems of trust then intelligence will necessarily act in order to preserve the live and let live condition by filling in some of those gaps that trust cannot plug. Thus, the necessity of intelligence as a function of government remains extant.

Yet, *Live and Let Spy* also argues that, while Cold War warriors fought a tyrannical and ruthless version of Communism abroad, they remained ignorant of – and lost – an ideological battle at home. That battle saw government and business come to dominate the expectations of their populations in the post-WWII world. This political ideology was fuelled by the construction of a convenient 'enemy' abroad, while utilising the Cold War's Game Theory and Freudian-based public relations management to tame the irrational, self-serving, unconscious nature of individuals at home. Gibson argues that in doing so, liberal democracies traduced power to construct regimes of vacuous politics and 'negative' freedom, absent of purpose, meaning, and moral autonomy. Intelligence became complicit and so aligned in this progression such that, by 2003, it supinely offered a version of truth to power that power demanded to hear.

The author has come full circle from the energetic, enthusiastic, and effective military 'spy' to the more thoughtful and sceptical academic that age and experience confers. The result is insightful and challenging. He notes that, in a sense, liberal democracy seems to be completing the reverse circle. Western polities now offer a watered down version of the interfering, intolerant, controlling, and authoritarian government that they were initially set against rather than anything freer. It is not too bizarre to contrast the secret East German state that the author was immersed in with the intrusion, monitoring, and surveillance that citizens of Western nation-states now endure. The one operated through fear, repression, and violence. The others are notably 'lite' on repression, yet still stifling and mistrustful. Worse, the West is turning its back on the Enlightenment project and a 'positive' pursuit of freedom that had inspired it before the Cold War. Explicitly, he argues that power is increasingly managerial and interfering. The decline in the role and influence of intelligence upon an enlightened purposeful politics is implicit. If intelligence cannot now point that out, then intelligent people should.

It is said that scepticism is the first step on the road to philosophy. This book reveals how things are not always as they seem; and, that what happens at the soldier's 'desperate edge of now' can bear little relation to the intentions of their political masters at home. In particular, the 'Reflections' chapter is a powerful challenge to received wisdom. With the benefit of hindsight and sceptical inquiry comes a realisation that, in part, much of what the author was led to believe, and some of what he was told, was simply wrong! Gibson reflects that it takes the passage of time to recognise that one is misled by power. Worse still that, unwittingly and unconsciously, one may have contributed to that deceit; that construction of a reality designed as much for a domestic audience as any other. Thus, *Live and Let Spy* is not only a personal account of a Cold War spying agency – Brixmis – but also a means to articulate some of the consequences of that experience at a philosophical level for both the individual and the society from which that individual came from. It asks the question – how intelligent is intelligence really? But most importantly, it is a warning to cherish scepticism as a precursor to free will, toleration, and a genuinely enlightened purposeful politics.

Richard J. Aldrich
Professor of Political Science and Director – Institute of Advanced Study,
University of Warwick

Acknowledgements

I am most grateful to the following people, who helped in varying degrees towards the completion of this edition – *Live and Let Spy* – and the original edition – *The Last Mission*: Colonel Crispian Beattie CBE, Graham Geary BEM, Colonel Stephen Harrison MBE, Group Captain Mark Knight, Master Aircrew Ray Parnell, Master Air Engineer Bob Hamilton, Ian Passingham, Paul Seagar, Major General Peter Williams CMG OBE, Ernie Wilson, Colonel Nigel Wylde QGM (all former Mission members); other members of the Brixmis Association; Dr Peter Boyden (National Army Museum, London); Dr Bill Durodie (Chatham House); Bernd von Kostka (AlliiertenMuseums, Berlin); Ian Houghton (*Sunday Times*); Mike Biggar; Ant Edmondson; Paul Lewis-Isemonger; and finally Jo de Vries and Paul Baillie-Lane (The History Press) for bringing this edition to publication, and Sarah Bragginton and Jonathan Falconer (Sutton Publishing) for the original edition.

BALTIC SEA

Rügen Island

● Rostock

● Greifswald

● Wismar

● Schwerin

Stettin ●

● Hamburg

IGB

River Elbe

POLAND

River Oder

● Neustrelitz
● Mirow

● Buchholz
● Wittenburg

● Rheinsberg

IGB

● Neuruppin

Klein Behnitz ●

● Schoenwalde

● Gardelegen

Potsdam ●

Berlin

● Zossen Wünsdorf

WEST GERMANY

● Letzlinger

Berlin Corridor

● Storkow

Helmstedt ●

Magdeburg ●

EAST GERMANY

● Jüterbog

● Lübben

● Dessau

● Herzberg

● Gollmitz

● Cottbus

River Neisse

IGB

River Saale

● Halle

● Falkenberg

● Leipzig

● Meissen

● Haufeld

● Colditz

● Görlitz

Erfurt ●

● Weimar

● Dresden

Zittau

Crawinkel ●

● Moenchenholzhausen

● Zehla-Mehlis

● Karl Marx Stadt

● Jena

● Zwickau

● Rudolstadt

IGB

● Plauen

● Marienburg

CZECHOSLOVAKIA

IGB

DDR LOCATIONS

0   150 km

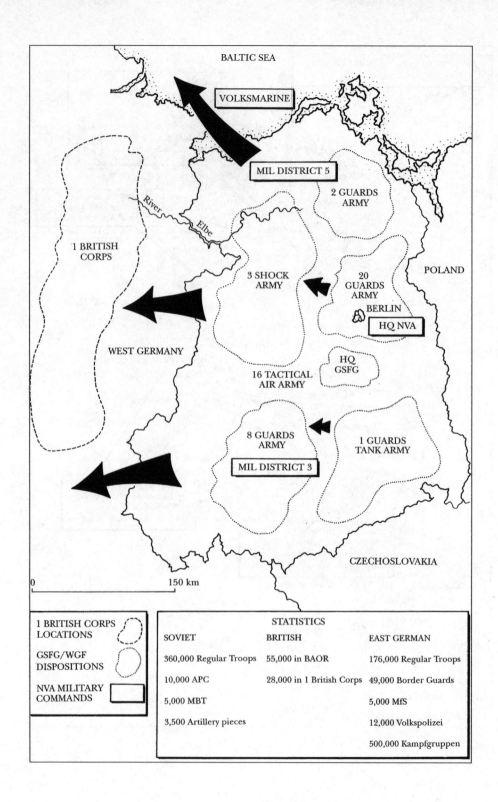

BALTIC SEA

VOLKSMARINE

MIL DISTRICT 5

2 GUARDS
ARMY

1 BRITISH
CORPS

River

Elbe

POLAND

3 SHOCK
ARMY

20
GUARDS
ARMY

BERLIN

HQ NVA

WEST GERMANY

16 TACTICAL
AIR ARMY

HQ
GSFG

8 GUARDS
ARMY

1 GUARDS
TANK ARMY

MIL DISTRICT 3

CZECHOSLOVAKIA

0   150 km

1 BRITISH CORPS
LOCATIONS

GSFG/WGF
DISPOSITIONS

NVA MILITARY
COMMANDS

STATISTICS		
SOVIET	BRITISH	EAST GERMAN
360,000 Regular Troops	55,000 in BAOR	176,000 Regular Troops
10,000 APC	28,000 in 1 British Corps	49,000 Border Guards
5,000 MBT		5,000 MfS
3,500 Artillery pieces		12,000 Volkspolizei
		500,000 Kampfgruppen

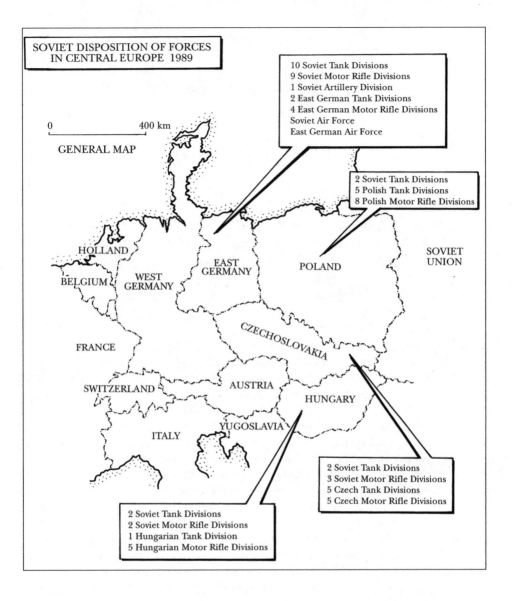

SOVIET DISPOSITION OF FORCES
IN CENTRAL EUROPE 1989

10 Soviet Tank Divisions
9 Soviet Motor Rifle Divisions
1 Soviet Artillery Division
2 East German Tank Divisions
4 East German Motor Rifle Divisions
Soviet Air Force
East German Air Force

2 Soviet Tank Divisions
5 Polish Tank Divisions
8 Polish Motor Rifle Divisions

0   400 km

GENERAL MAP

HOLLAND
BELGIUM
WEST
GERMANY
EAST
GERMANY
POLAND
SOVIET
UNION

FRANCE
CZECHOSLOVAKIA

SWITZERLAND
AUSTRIA
HUNGARY

ITALY
YUGOSLAVIA

2 Soviet Tank Divisions
3 Soviet Motor Rifle Divisions
5 Czech Tank Divisions
5 Czech Motor Rifle Divisions

2 Soviet Tank Divisions
2 Soviet Motor Rifle Divisions
1 Hungarian Tank Division
5 Hungarian Motor Rifle Divisions

Introduction

I kept six serving serving-men
They taught me all I knew;
Their names are What and Why and When
And How and Where and Who.

Rudyard Kipling
The Elephant's Child

From September 1946 to December 1990, for 365 days a year without a break, a single British Army unit operated behind the Iron Curtain throughout the entire Cold War. This very small, highly specialised and intensively trained group openly collected intelligence against the Warsaw Pact forces based in East Germany. Well beyond the safety of their own front lines, from the Baltic coast to the Czechoslovakian border and from the Inner German Border (IGB) to the Polish frontier they operated unarmed, using Soviet identity cards and in full view of the enemy. Accommodated, fuelled and fed by the Soviets, accredited with an East German bank account, forced to employ East German Stasi agents as staff and working from a watched house in Potsdam, they routinely monitored the composition, strengths, technology, morale and training of the hundreds of thousands of Warsaw Pact troops stationed in East Germany. They would be the first British military personnel to report from the ground that the Warsaw Pact had mobilised against Nato in Europe. Often at enormous risk to their own safety these men were themselves regularly watched, followed, rammed, beaten and shot at during the course of their function as the eyes and ears of the intelligence community beyond the Iron Curtain.

On 16 September 1946, following the division of Germany into the four allied controlled zones and in accordance with Article 2 of the Agreement of the Control Machinery in Germany 1944, Soviet and British Commanders-in-Chief exchanged Military Liaison Missions. The 'rules' of exchange, encapsulated in the Robertson-Malinin agreement, gave licence and flexibility to the, then, new unit. The organisation was titled the British Commander-in-Chief's Mission to the Group of Soviet Forces of Occupation in Germany, shortened not surprisingly to Brixmis and known generally as the Mission. An equivalent Soviet organisation was similarly ennobled and shortened to Soxmis. Both Missions' objective was to maintain liaison between the staffs of the two Commanders-in-Chief and their respective military governments, unhindered and with full diplomatic immunity. Both also had hidden agendas. The fundamental ingredients for a legitimate spying operation had been set in place.

That there was a need to spy rapidly developed out of the early mistrust created between the Soviets and their Western Allies in the immediate postwar struggle to resolve the Germany question. The tacit acquiescence of the Western Allies to the division of Germany and Berlin, its microcosm, was merely rejoined by the bullying, intransigent and frustrating Soviet Union. Germany became the fulcrum of Soviet leverage against the West and the focal point of tension, disagreement and bitterness that was ever the Cold War. Mistrust fuelled suspicion and suspicion had to be satiated. The Mission was ideally situated and, with additional special training, its operatives could answer the questions that face to face encounters and direct questioning between politicians and diplomats could not. Such questions ranged across all aspects of Soviet involvement in the German Democratic Republic (DDR) from industrial output to the latest tank design. The Mission's answers gave a comprehensive picture of the day-to-day state of Warsaw pact forces (Soviet and East German), their capabilities, their effectiveness and their readiness for war. At every

The lucky number 7 myth is dispelled. This tour vehicle was deliberately rammed by a URAL 10-ton truck from the East German Army. It climbed the bonnet and front right-hand side, its momentum carrying it almost completely over the car. The tour NCO was trapped in the wreckage with a badly broken leg and torn ligaments, while the tour officer and driver escaped with shock and heavy bruising. It was one of the sixty or more routine incidents that year. Ironically, unlucky number 7 was recovered by lucky number 13.

major political crisis, from the Berlin Airlift in 1948, through the building of the Wall in 1961 to reunification in 1990, the Mission was able to give military analysis and reaction to internationally significant events as they occurred on the ground.

The Mission's intelligence gathering activities were conducted in three-man, vehicle-borne patrols. These patrols quickly became known as 'tours' in order to disguise any hint of implied aggressive reconnaissance operations. They lasted from two to seven days and covered all manner of military (Army, Air and Naval), industrial and civilian targets that were considered relevant. Anything that tours could see, touch or hear was consumed for the intelligence community. They talked, listened, removed and recorded in an effort to construct the intelligence picture on a would-be enemy. Tasked by all the major intelligence agencies in the Western world, the Mission product was promulgated to its customers for further analysis, comment and wider disposal as seen fit. Simultaneously, Soxmis undertook the same task for the Soviet Union in West Germany. This curious mirror image, coupled with its unique diplomatic status, conferred upon the Mission – in theory if not in practice – a respect and tolerance that allowed it to operate as it did.

Replicated in April 1947 by sister units from France and the USA and mirrored again by two further equivalent Soviet units operating in the respective allied zones of West Germany, Brixmis worked throughout the next forty-four years to maintain channels of communication between the British and Soviet Commanders-in-Chief. When negotiation in the political and diplomatic spheres became difficult, non-existent or even forbidden, there was always an avenue for messages to be conveyed through Brixmis. At the same time the Mission exploited to the full its unique geographical, political, diplomatic and military position in order to observe and comment upon all matters pertaining to the Warsaw Pact in East Germany through its alternative role of intelligence gathering.

The special operatives chosen to carry out these curiously juxtaposed roles of liaison and observation were drawn from all parts of the armed forces. With language ability, driving expertise, military service in the SAS and 14 Company Northern Ireland together with a range of specialist technical skills from lock-picking to photography, among many others, they were asked to operate beyond the front lines drawn up at the end of the Second World War, beyond the assistance of the most forward Nato reconnaissance units and into the heart of Soviet-controlled East Germany. They played a small but significant role in the eventual defeat of Communism as it threatened the West, an integral part in bringing the Cold War to an end and, after the fall of the Wall in 1989, ultimately witnessed the final breakdown of the social, economic and political order that hitherto shackled much of eastern Europe.

This book is a firsthand account of some of the Mission adventures undertaken by the author under the code name 'Red 41' and points to their significance in the never-ending intelligence game that characterised the history of the Cold War. It is not the full story. There are still several stones unturned and several more that will have to remain so. Furthermore, one person's experience is a mere reflection of the cumulative experiences that Brixmis tourers down the years have witnessed. They have something more precious than any book could ever reveal; they have done it themselves and done it for real. Therefore this book is not for those very few, although many of them have helped write it, but an insight for those who ask how, why, when, where, what and who . . .

CHAPTER ONE

The Stuff of Touring

THE RULES OF TOURING

Rule One	–	There are no rules.
Rule Two	–	Think sneaky 'cos sneaky's best.
Rule Three	–	Beware the wandering Sov, 'cos he's the one that's going to fuck you.
Rule Four	–	Write it down now. You'll forget it later.
Rule Five	–	The truth is a very powerful weapon. There is nowhere to go from the truth.

'Kiiiitt!'

The word was shouted; drawn out, extended on the 'i' for a good two seconds and ended with emphasis on the 't'. The word 'kit' was the Mission's battle cry and it deserved to be emphasised. That such a small word could galvanise an entire crew was astonishing. 'Kit' was shorthand for military equipment and the main road between Buchholz and Schwerin was exploding with it. This was the third column of the morning.

'HIP-C. Red white outline sixteen, figures one six. Red star markings on tail. It's Sov.[1] He's seen us.'

Pete Curran spotted it. He had taken over lookout as Geoff and I prepared for the vehicles coming towards us on the road.

'Seen. He hasn't got comms[2] with these other guys or he would have stopped them already. Pete, you keep an eye on him. If he lands then we'll think about moving. I don't want to be flushed out just yet. Geoff, you keep calling.'

Having Geoff Cotter as tour NCO was like having Electric Light[3] and Research[4] along with you. A part-time tourer and Intelligence Corps NCO, his main job

---

[1] Sov: slang for Soviet or Soviet troops.

[2] Comms: communications.

[3] Electric Light: computer section within Brixmis responsible for compiling databases of all Soviet and NVA equipment, troops, barracks and installations within the DDR.

[4] Research: the Brixmis section responsible for collating all the side numbers, VRNs, target files and personality files prior to feeding them to Electric Light.

The infamous HIP-C red white outline 16 being photographed as it returns to Potsdam.

back in Berlin was helping to run the inventory of all Soviet equipment held in the DDR. As part of Research, his job was to feed collated intelligence on all these vehicles into the database operation. If you gave Geoff a Soviet vehicle registration number (VRN) he would know which unit it came from and where. It was like asking someone to identify the unit and location of a British Army vehicle based solely on its number-plate. Only there were at least five times as many vehicles and registrations to remember in the Group of Soviet Forces in Germany (GSFG) or Western Group of Forces (WGF) as they had recently renamed themselves since the Wall came down.

Geoff was a little rusty on the calling. He knew what the kit was and he could read the Cyrillics but the speed had to be there too, particularly for the number of vehicles that were passing us. Pete Curran, Royal Corps of Transport corporal and driver for this tour, was helping him out, checking our security and changing film for me. Cameras were moving in a production line, a closed loop between him in the front taking out the spent cartridge and loading a new roll and then back to me taking the photos; one every two seconds or less, as the vehicles rolled past. The frequency of the vehicles was too quick for me to handle it alone. We were stationary so his hands were free but never too far from the ignition. The kit was streaming past in hundred-plus vehicle columns. I had all three cameras working the 85-mm lens. Pete was also responsible for keeping main lookout for narks[5] or any attempt to block us from the passing columns. The latter was very unlikely as we were in a near-perfect observation post (OP). The columns were travelling south from Schwerin back to Buchholz. As they passed through the little village we were in, they had to negotiate a 90 degree left-hand bend. This bend was joined by a minor road coming into it from the right. Vehicles on the main road had priority over the minor road so there was no need for them to stop. They just swept round the corner. All the better for us.

There was a single reggie[6] on the bend. He stood on the far side of the junction on the grass verge, first to make sure the column followed its designated route and second to stop any civilian traffic coming up the minor road. In the fork formed by the two roads a small collection of houses had sprung up, no more than seven or eight, which constituted the sum total of the village dwellings. The Mercedes Geländewagen, or 'G-wagon' as it was better known, was concealed up a short narrow alleyway created by the gaps between the houses. Out of the left side we had a three-quarter view of the vehicles as they slowed to make the turn and a view of them disappearing away from us to our front.

There was an 8-ft wall immediately to our left, concealing us from the view of the approaching columns. Several gaps and passageways between the buildings gave us options out to the right and back behind us. The houses were all two-storey buildings, not very high, and although there were not many of them inhabiting this bleak little meeting spot of routes, they concealed us very well and gave us excellent views out. It wasn't a particularly prosperous or important communications junction. History hadn't blessed it or blighted its inhabitants with development. It was yet another dreary, paint-free, sleepy little hamlet in the flat open agricultural plains of the north-west DDR, centred on a road junction that proved to be a major landmark for military traffic heading north out of Potsdam or south back to it. There was no one around in the village. They were all out working by now, so there was no attention drawn by locals either staring at us or coming to talk to us.

Regrettably, there was no cover from the view of the helicopter above. It was uncommon to be observed from the air during a road move. However, it was normally only an inconvenience and rarely a deterrence. Frankly, without landing, whoever was on board the helicopter could do little about us. They were unlikely to have comms with many vehicles on the ground and would therefore find it difficult to target anyone onto us.

---

5 Narks: Stasi teams involved in anti-Mission surveillance operations. Licensed to provoke and entrap tourers. Often violent.

6 Reggie: Regulator/traffic regulator. Soviet troops were not issued with maps for road moves. At every junction where a decision had to be made there would be a regulator to direct traffic. They were put out before road moves, left for days on end and picked up as the column returned. As such they were tell-tale signs of movement and regularly befriended without compromising them.

It was the first day of February 1990, a clear, bright but very cold day. We had been in the OP for about four hours having spotted the reggies being 'put out' at about 6 a.m. It wasn't this particular reggie that had caught our attention initially but it was this one who had influenced the choice of OP. He seemed singularly uninterested in us as we drove past him. That, together with the fact that it offered good cover and an excellent shot of the targets as they slowed for the bend, made it the junction we would watch.

We had firkled[7] our way back into the hamlet across country, out of sight to him on our final approach into the OP. He couldn't see us now for the houses. As far as he was concerned, if he had registered us at all, we were long gone down the road. The drivers of the vehicles couldn't see us either because we were positioned out of sight as they approached the turn. As they drew level with us they were concentrating on making the turn and as they rounded the corner we were behind them looking at their rear ends. The vehicle commanders, those who were awake on these long route marches across East Germany, were too busy making sure their vehicles turned without damage to notice us. If any of them did choose to glance behind as they cornered they would have had to have been very quick to take in a G-wagon backed into the shadows, understand who it was and then take the decision to stop their vehicle and have the column apprehend us. The ensuing snarl-up would have given us ample time to exploit the confusion, take one of the side alleys right, out to the adjoining main road and away, returning to this or another OP at a later time for a different column. The other option would be to simply pull forward, turn left and join the main road travelling against the flow of vehicles, the advantage here being that we would not have lost any vehicle shots while moving. It was a great OP. It had good escape routes and was almost fully concealed from the target. The helicopter was just a nuisance but it was distracting and upset the calm. It gave us one more thing we could have done without worrying about.

There was a break in the columns. We moved forward 10 metres beyond the wall to give ourselves a clearer view up the road to our left and allow a precious few extra seconds lead time to prepare for approaching vehicles. The odd East German civilian vehicle came past. One of them saw us in our slightly more exposed position. We waved and they waved back.

It was customary practice for tour crews to wave at anyone and everyone. Over the years a huge psychology had been built up around waving. First, it was a friendly gesture and generally put people off their guard. By waving to them, it made them think twice about exactly who you were: then you were gone before they could react. Second, it took the onlookers' gaze away from activity inside the G-wagon to the top two corners of the front windscreen. This detracted from the more suspicious work going on inside the vehicle, whether it be the tour officer taking photographs, the video set up on the pole, or facial gestures and signals that could be read and interpreted by other more careful observers. All hand signals, indications of direction and equipment adjustments were done below

---

[7] Firkle: commonly used slang for stealthily working a way around a target either on foot or in a vehicle without being seen.

Waving and smiling was practised on the very youngest members of the DDR . . .

. . . until they become graduates of our course!

the dashboard. Third, the reaction to a wave told us a lot about the wavers. If an East German civilian waved back with a full smile it meant that they knew who you were, had probably seen you before, knew what you did and wished you the best of luck in stuffing the Sovs at their own game. If it was a rueful smile or a slightly forced sheepish grin, it meant the same but without the good luck. Rather, it meant, 'I know what you are doing but I can't do anything about it'. If there was no reaction it usually meant they didn't have a clue who you were or what you were doing and why the hell were you waving at them in the first place. Much the same reaction you might get from waving at someone you don't know. They would probably spend the next few days trying to work out who it was.

We waved at everyone, from Soviet officers to East German schoolchildren. We particularly concentrated on the children. We waved at them long and hard, forcing them to wave back at us. Most didn't need prompting. They loved it. Some of the tour NCOs had red noses in the tops of their tour bags ready to whip on every time we passed a group of schoolkids. It made them roar with laughter. We knew that they were being indoctrinated against us at an early age so we figured the sooner we tried some psychological adjustment ourselves the better. Furthermore, it would irritate any Sovs or hard-nosed East Germans when we could get their kids to smile as the adults shook their fists. The wave was a very powerful weapon. This simple gesture could get ordinary people on our side, deflate the authorities who witnessed it and also prepare the kids for future generations of pro-Mission touring.

Inevitably there was a converse reaction. Some Soviet and East German soldiers would respond aggressively. The slower ones would wave first and then shake their fists once they recognised who we were, making us howl with laughter. East German civilians who shook their fists were either part of the establishment or narks. The narks had their own peculiar set of reactions to the wave. They either violently returned the gesture, using the expressive Western single digit sign that gave them away as having been privileged enough to watch too many American films, or they would look away as though they hadn't seen us at all.

The latter were particularly amusing and we had a very satisfying way of getting our own back on them without resorting to violence. We might be quite innocently and legitimately pulled up next to them in a traffic queue in town. Despite frantic waving and knocking on windows they would completely ignore us. It wasn't that they were intensely shy but rather they preferred to respond with the ostrich or shop assistant routine, whose premise is, 'if I look away they can't see me'. It was sometimes quite hilarious as everyone around looked on at the scene of three British soldiers waving like mad at the car next to us, the occupants of which, possibly in their own home town, were trying like mad to ignore us and hoping that the traffic would move quickly for them. The onlookers would then quickly work out who they were and who we were, which was fine by us. The MfS[8]

---

[8] MfS (Stasi): Ministerium fur Staadtsicherheit – Ministry for State Security. The secret police of the East German government, together with informants numbered 20,000. They worked against Mission crews, in collaboration with KGB, GRU and Spetsnaz. They undertook the dirty work against tours. Their authority was not recognised but their potential to frustrate was rarely underestimated.

Breaking and entering into one of the many underground bunkers scattered across the DDR. The vast majority were linked by an elaborate and extensive underground telephone system and thus had enormous intelligence potential.

or 'Stasi', from where the narks came, were hated by the overwhelming majority of their own people but rather depressingly also greatly feared.

Narks never waved back. They were too serious and self-important for that and certainly not clever enough! This, together with the fact that they usually travelled two or four up in a vehicle, dressed like Black Spy in *Mad Magazine*'s Black Spy Versus White Spy with short black leather jackets and blue jeans, made them easy to spot at close quarters. But they were good at their job in other respects. They had incriminating evidence of tourers and they forced reactions from us that prevented us from doing what we were supposed to be doing. They photographed us at every opportunity and occasionally they took a shot that could be used against us in tit for tat complaints when our Soviet counterparts in West Germany, Soxmis, had been caught themselves. It was a big game. The word reciprocity had significant meaning for us. If the anti-Soxmis White Mice[9] unit in West Germany gave our Soviet counterparts a hard time then we were sure to feel an equal and opposite response the other way. The Stasi worked closely with the Soviet

---

[9] White Mice: nickname for the combined Intelligence Corps/Royal Military Police operation working against Soxmis in West Germany.

*One of the many nark teams in attendance. It is hardly sophisticated surveillance but they were mak-
ing their point. Their car and number-plate would be recorded for future tourers to check against.
The tour crew would remain unprovoked.*

Different car, different number-plate, same effect.

GRU[10] and KGB[11] intelligence services as well as their Spetsnaz[12] troops. They were able to call for, coordinate, and set up anti-Mission ambushes that usually involved extreme violence. These incidents were few and far between, invariably coinciding with events on the world stage, mirroring the Cold War as it was played out in the larger political arena.

The occupants of the passing car were locals, probably off to fill up at the garage down the road or coming home after a night shift at the local shoe factory in Buchholz. Pete created a cigarette from his never-ending supply of roll-ups and baccy, opening the window a touch to let the smoke out. I never allowed people to smoke in the vehicle apart from Pete. He performed much better as a result and his pouch tobacco was pleasant to smell, unlike the packet cigarettes some of the other guys used.

'So far we've had sixteen Guards Tank Division (GTD), two Guards Tank Army (GTA) and ninety-four Guards Motor Rifle Division (GMRD), Boss.' Geoff had already worked out the unit designators. They were returning from exercise and Buchholz was their home garrison. I would never have known exactly which units we were observing without looking it up. That was normally Geoff's job back in Berlin when a crew returned with the information. I would have been aware what the composition of the unit was and I could probably have hazarded a guess at the unit but I was still relatively new to the game to predict it exactly. From the number and type of vehicles, I would have been aware that the wheeled column was a support unit to a tank division, but Geoff's extra detail allowed me to pinpoint where the main vehicles would be coming off the tac-route[13] to get back to the barracks or at which railway ramp their fighting vehicles would be off-loading possibly later that evening. It saved us tripping round all the possible combinations until we stumbled on it.

'We've still got this bloody helicopter with us, Boss,' said Pete. In the confines of the vehicle and under these exceptionally close operational conditions, we dispensed with the formalities of 'Sir', 'Staff' and 'Colour Sergeant'. The officer called the NCO and driver by their christian or nickname. The officer was called Boss. Leadership was based entirely on experience and ability in this environment. Titles were not important.

The helicopter was shadowing the convoys as they travelled down the main road. It was probably a divisional or possibly an army commander watching his troops move. He'd spotted us and we were bugging him as much as he was bugging us. The people in the helicopter were almost irrelevant. It was the helicopter itself that took on the persona of the hunter. Because we could hardly make out the crew or passenger faces we couldn't really determine their intentions. It wasn't necessary, the body language of the helicopter was doing that for us.

---

10 GRU: Soviet Military Intelligence.

11 KGB: Soviet foreign intelligence, loosely equivalent to British MI6.

12 Spetsnaz: special forces group with their own role in war but working with GRU and KGB to ambush and detain crews caught spying. Similar to SAS and US Delta Force.

13 Tac-route: tactical route. Usually off-road tracks leading directly from barracks to Emergency Deployment Areas (EDAs). Regularly used for training and exercise purposes.

Dropping to about 50 ft off the ground, it hovered over the road junction. The co-pilot, or more likely the senior officer passenger, gesticulated furiously at the reggie, pointing in our direction. The reggie was doing his best to avoid any contact. He probably knew there was a high-ranking officer in there and was studiously ignoring him, hoping not to get involved. We could make out four in total in the cockpit and assumed there would be more in the hold. The door to the hold was open and with the bins[14] I could see someone crouching in the doorway. The reggie, who couldn't see us anyway so wouldn't have been able to understand what the waving and pointing was all about, continued to ignore them. We withdrew further back into the alleyway ready for the next column as it came into view about a kilometre away. We tried to disregard the antics of the pilot and concentrate on getting the cameras ready.

'This guy is not going to give up. He's really pissed at us, Boss.'

The helicopter moved towards us, now about 30 ft off the ground and doing what can only be described as a cross between a peacock fan dance and a scorpion striking stance. His nose was pointing down and towards us, the back end up in the air waving from side to side. He was hovering over the road only 20 metres to our front and perilously close to the line of tall poplar trees that bordered the road. He looked like a giant wasp with a bad attitude. He came forward, dangerously close to the buildings that we were sheltering behind. A rope was dropped out of the side hold door. That was enough for me. They were clearly not happy and were going to do something about it.

'Bollocks! Time to go please, Pete.'

I didn't know who or how many were in there, or even if it was a feint, but we couldn't operate with this attention and I certainly wasn't going to have them rappelling out onto the top of the vehicle.

'Get out before the column, turn right down the minor road and we'll work our way back.'

We drove straight out onto the junction we were observing and turned half right down the joining minor road. The reggie, prompted by the sight of a military vehicle, raised his magic 'pajalsta' stick[15] to try and direct us left. Slowly but surely he realised who we were, put two and two together with the helicopter and lunged at the vehicle, but far too late. Pete, anticipating such an attempt, neatly manoeuvred the vehicle around him in a sidestep that an All Black fly-half would have been proud of. The helicopter swung away up the road to the approaching column. Unless he was in comms with them or he physically put down in front of them there was still nothing he could do.

'150, turn left down the track to your front. Trip. Into the wood and we'll firkle our way back to take the column on the side.' The wood we had entered paralleled the road that the columns would travel on after they had made the turn. The front of the wood was about 40 metres from the road. We threaded

---

[14] Bins: commonly used slang for binoculars.

[15] Pajalsta stick: used by traffic regulators to denote direction of travel for convoys. Pajalsta being the Russian for 'please'.

our way to the front, square on to their direction of travel. This was fine for me with the imagery, I merely swapped to a 180-mm lens but it was too far for Geoff to make out the number-plates without bins. He either had to wait for the vehicles to go some way down the road past him to his right, getting their rear plates, or look to his left back to the junction as the vehicles turned left towards us and at our 10 o'clock position. Letting them pass would put the imagery out of 'synch' with the calling, making it more difficult for him back in Berlin. I'd already used 38 rolls of film at 36 or 37 frames per roll, which meant a minimum of 1,300 vehicles for him to identify alone that day. He didn't need it made any harder.

We just got out to the front of the wood in time for the first vehicle to round the corner. Geoff chose to call at the junction rather than letting them go past him. Very wise. He then had the second chance as they went past him, if there were one or two he didn't recognise it allowed either Pete or myself to call them.

'Christ, he's back again.'

The HIP-C red white outline 16 swooped into the open space between us and the column on the road. He must have guessed we wouldn't leave and it was just a matter of time before he spotted us again. The foliage at that time of year was minimal and offered little protection from view. He was almost at ground level now, facing us and slowly advancing. Two Sovs jumped out of the hold at the side, bounced up from a near 10-ft drop and motioned the first column vehicle to pull off, pointing purposefully towards us and the wood line that we were backed into. It carried straight on, ignoring or not understanding the signals. However, the BTR-80[16] behind him got the message and swung off violently towards us.

'Straight out Pete. Go, go, go! Join the road and we'll take the column on the move.'

Pete launched the vehicle into the open ground between us and the road. It was about the width of a football pitch. The helicopter spotted us leaving. The Sovs on the ground directed more vehicles onto us in an effort to close us down. Two more jumped out from the other side of the helicopter and ran towards us. The helicopter pilot was going mad. The passenger in the copilot seat was shaking his fist at us. Pete dodged round the men on the ground, giving them a wide berth and in doing so avoided the BTR which had emerged from the blind side of the helicopter. He was forced to swing round in a wide loop to get behind us.

It wasn't him that was the immediate threat. The HIP came straight for us still at ground level and swung violently up to avoid a collision. It passed a couple of feet overhead, his landing gear nearly skewering the G-wagon but at the last moment rising parallel to the windscreen as if deflected by a force field around the vehicle. The noise was deafening and the downwash rocked the vehicle. The G-wagon was a solid beast weighing nearly 3 tons and very difficult to dislodge.

'Stop and face him,' I shouted at Pete.

Pete spun the car round to rest and looked at me. He had been doing his best to get away. The two guys on the ground were a good 30 metres away and the BTR was still making his turn. I was furious at having been flushed from an OP for a second time and furious at this helicopter's antics. It was highly dangerous

---

[16] BTR-80: armoured infantry personnel carrier.

Close detail of a HIND-E revealing a range of technical details from weapons and communications aerials to markings and designators.

and could easily have resulted in loss of life for us or for him. I threw the cupola open in the top of the roof and took aim with the 180-mm. The wheels came terrifyingly close to the vehicle again as he made another pass. He pulled up sharply but slightly further away. I made it very clear that I was photographing him and for an instant I caught the recognition in his face that he knew he'd pushed us too far. He'd frightened the hell out of us and he knew it but I could also see that he was suddenly aware of the consequences of his actions, not to mention that I was putting it on the record with the camera.

Whether it was the camera or the abrupt stop, I'm not sure. Either way the communication between our two respective vehicles was clear. I pulled my camera lens in flush with the top of the G-wagon as he went over the top of us for a third time before backing off. Several rapid shots of the undercarriage, at no more than 3 or 4 metres range, later revealed rivets and openings previously unknown.

'Get in Boss, we're off.'

Quite rightly Pete had decided that now was not the time to mess around but to get the hell out of there. We rejoined the road having missed only five or six vehicles in the excitement and took the rest of the column on the nose. In the mirrors we saw the HIP having to put down to pick up the dismounted passengers as well as take the opportunity to remonstrate with the reggie and BTR driver for their inability to close us down. Geoff had kept quiet

Nine 'reggies' on the Herzberg junction. Trying to work out what would happen next was the art of 'regiology'. How many convoys were they monitoring? Which direction were they travelling in? How could you cover all the possible options without missing anything?

throughout the whole short episode and merely exclaimed 'Shit' as we rejoined the road and ran the column. The whole incident had lasted no more than two or three minutes.

'Get on with the calling,' I chided him.

I swapped lenses back to the 85-mm and continued to snap away. Pete had managed to save his roll-up in the excitement and was puffing away contentedly. He was a really cool customer. Geoff carried on with the calling and we ran the column to the end before moving to another OP for the next column.

* * *

'Turning off coming up in 200. Trip please, Martin.'

The road was deserted. We made sure of that before pulling out of the vehicle lay-up. It was late spring. Consequently, the wait in the lay-up had gone on until 10 p.m. before it was fully dark enough to revisit the target. The designated turn-off loomed up, highlighted against the darker frontage of the wood line.

'OK. Kill the lights, Ernie. Pull off. Let's listen up.'

We pulled off left into the wood that flanked the left-hand side of the road. Ernie Wilson toggled off the master light switch and pulled up 30 metres along the dirt track. There would be no external lights showing on the vehicle. All headlamps were isolated from the controls and the brake lights would be isolated from the brake pedal. A brake light could be seen a mile off at night and in this flat land possibly a good deal further. All other lights were disabled so that there

Liaison crossed with the art of regiology included befriending them, feeding them and, in the process, taking information off them. Captain Stephen Harrison (on the left) exemplified this skill!

would be no possibility of accidentally flicking on indicators, reversing lights or sounding the horn as the car was being flung around by an animated driver. The rear door window was blacked out on the inside with a permanently drawn curtain and painted over on the outside with drab olive green for good measure. The turn-off was no more than the opening of one of many fire-breaks regularly spaced at kilometre intervals throughout the whole wood. The track had been cut by the Forstmeister (head ranger) as a safety precaution against rampaging fire in this massive expanse of mixed deciduous and evergreen woodland.

I pulled my side curtains across left and right windows in the rear to contain the map reading light. The light was little more than a pinprick on a stiff but flexible extension, like a bendy ruler bar, illuminating a very small circle of the map resting on my lap. The Mercedes Geländewagen, one of fifteen in the fleet, was a vehicle that had been finely tuned over the past few years for silent running, both audibly and visibly.

'Tracks are one way, Boss. They didn't come back this route.'

We cranked the windows open for a final listen. The target was a further 1,200 metres down the track. We had to stop not just to listen but also to give us a few minutes to become accustomed to the dark after travelling on the road with lights on. The next move would be in the dark. There was no moonlight to help and the forest we were about to cut through had been closely planted, making it even more difficult to see and navigate through.

'Can you hear them?'

The question did not require an answer. A moving tank makes a distinctive noise. The gas turbines of a T-80 emit a high-pitched whine that crescendos into a roar similar to a jet engine as it moves away. The sound is very directional, coming or going away as its back end, housing the power-pack, either swings towards or away from you. A T-80 coming towards you with its rear exhaust shielded by the hull is as quiet as a pussy-cat tiptoeing on all fours. As it goes past you, exposing the back end, it's like a lion roaring in anger. The Sovs had managed to camouflage the noise as well as the appearance. If an infantryman, squatting in his hole in the ground, survived to hear the change in volume then he would be a very lucky person indeed.

The other tank fleets, the T-60s (62 and 64) and T-72s, were all diesel. They made a much more conventional throaty engine sound and were generally much louder all round. The sound, being less directional, made it more tricky to determine their movement. It was also difficult to distinguish from the noise alone which diesel varieties they were. Although the T-80 had become quieter, once detected it was readily discernible. These were diesel engines we could hear and definitely tanks but which sort and what they were doing up here required further explanation.

Five minutes elapsed. I conferred with Martin on the map for routes in, routes out and in this particular case the presence of a small stream on our immediate right-hand side once into the chosen OP we were making for. The stream and the railway track to the front of the OP meant that it was a one-way-in, one-way-out option and therefore more easy to become trapped.

'It restricts our way out, Boss, but on the other hand it will stop anything coming for us other than on foot or in one of the tanks themselves and they're very unlikely to want to hurtle the tanks around these woods at night. There's no way they know we're here. We'll keep it that way. Go in, do the biz, back out and away.' Martin Brain was an enthusiastic tour NCO, a Royal Artillery sergeant and still relatively young for the Mission. He was keen to try anything and that suited me down to the ground. But I would still take the rap for any incident.

I had to be sure that there was no other course of action before committing the crew to a balls-up[17] approach. It was the Chief of Mission's maxim that nothing in the DDR was worth dying for. It was the tour officer's responsibility to ensure that only a sensible level of risk was undertaken. Unfortunately, there was no measurably prescribed level of sensibility beyond which the risk could not go. It was simply left to the tour officer's judgement out on the ground. At the end of the day there were no rules. If it worked then it must have been right and the proof was more in the accomplishment than in the untried theory. The Missions had already lost two officers, one French, one American, killed deliberately in the pursuit of their duties and both in the last five years. There had been many notable hospital cases and countless very near misses. There was no need to boost these statistics unnecessarily.

I had to consider whether the gain would outweigh the risk. It wasn't always the case that getting caught or being observed might produce a violent response. Invariably the reaction was completely unpredictable. Sometimes we were mistaken for a Soviet vehicle and the reaction would be a cursory wave and complete indifference. On other occasions the speed of reaction was too slow and too predictable to be effective against us. More often than not we chose the time and the place to conduct operations. But every now and then the scales would be

---

[17] Balls-up: as in risky rather than a cock-up!

tipped against us and we would be forced to corner ourselves in order to achieve objectives. It was much more the time wasted and the raising of the profile of a particular target than the being caught, that was to be avoided. Furthermore, if caught, then the danger that all the intelligence we had gathered so far might be forcibly removed from the vehicle was even more concerning. The ramifications were far too worrying to countenance. Violence in all its forms was a constant worry but the risk of being ineffective as an intelligence gatherer was more motivating.

If they were bog-standard tanks loading on to a train or out-loading from one then the Mission had probably seen them somewhere before. But I couldn't work out why they were in this particular part of the DDR. On balance I thought it was worth investigating further and, furthermore, we could do with the practice!

We had visited this railway loading ramp on our way up to Schwerin earlier that day, really as a matter of routine rather than expecting to find anything. It hadn't been visited for a good while and therefore deserved a call. At best we might determine from a litter sweep or an examination of track and tyre prints whether or not it had been used recently. At worst it would be an opportunity to check the ground for going, likely OPs, the state of the ramp and track, new construction and so on, in order to update the target file for future tours. As luck would have it (Ops[18] would put it down to inspired tour planning) there had been signs of activity before we got anywhere near the ramp. A TATRA had dropped off a bunch of NVA[19] at the mouth of the same fire-break we were now sitting on, some eight hours ago. We chanced upon them, our arrival in the afternoon coinciding with theirs. We observed them walk down the track and moved on to find out what they were up to. They didn't see us. Having threaded a circuitous route down what passed for the main road to the station on the other side of the wood, we watched them arrive at the ramp. They lounged around, clearly indicating that they were here for some time and intent on performing some sort of loading or out-loading act. Given that this road was the only way in and out for vehicles and therefore the likely route for loading or unloading then it would certainly be off limits to us. But why had these guys been dropped off at the main road and not been taken all the way down to the ramp? Were they trying to conceal the fact that there was a move in the offing or were they local and knew it was probably quicker on foot than taking the twisty road to the ramp that we had just used? If they were local, which their knowledge of the forest, or this particular track at least, seemed to suggest, then it was likely that these were the drivers and commanders come to collect. Therefore it was more than likely to be an off-load at the ramp than an out-load. But why NVA and why this remote station? We couldn't make sense of it and it therefore required fathoming.

---

[18] Ops: Operations/Operations officer. Responsible for the direction of the ground-based touring programme. Ultimately responsible for the overall touring schedule on a tri-mission basis.

[19] NVA: National Volks Army: East German People's Army. Together with the East German Air Force, a significant, efficient and highly reliable force trained and equipped by the Soviets. Not recognised by the Missions but targeted, observed and recorded by them, nevertheless.

We took the opportunity, while watching them, to check available lighting for night photography and a likely OP from which to take it. Which way any artificial light was likely to shine was critically important for the Modulux.[20] The ramp had one lamppost positioned at the end away from the slope. It was preferable for the light to shine away from us towards the target rather than reflect back towards us and flare out the tube. To a large extent this predetermined the area for a night OP if imagery was critical. If it was an off-load then we would have to take them as they arrived on the train. The sheer size of the equipment on top of their respective flatbeds[21] would block any available light from the station but the single ramp light would be shining directly down on them. If they were out-loading then they would go on to the flat-beds one at a time, be better illuminated and allow us greater flexibility as to where we shot them. The light was workable for both options. We counted the number of railway staff at the station, noted their beats and their apparent level of interest in these guys. Finally we identified a possible OP given what we had seen and what we anticipated happening.

This ramp was set at the end of a spur line off the main Berlin–Schwerin railway line, in the middle of a huge forest with a long twisty access road in and out to the main road that looped around the forest about 4 kilometres away on the far side as we were placed. The road-rail crossing had a single light and no barriers. An old Prussian-style wooden building served as the railway station itself but looked more like a traditional timber-framed farm building in need of some repair. The station building was set on the other side of the line to the ramp. The forest came up to the edge of the line, the edge of the access road and almost up to the station itself. The only clear area was immediately around the ramp, where equipment was parked up ready for loading onto a train or formed up prior to departing *en masse* by road. Apart from that, it looked as harmless as Hansel and Gretel's gingerbread house! The soldiers loafing at the ramp were all armed, the final clue that there was an equipment move afoot. We retired gracefully without being seen to plan an alternative route in, to watch the proceedings unfold.

Current activity always took precedence over the tour plan unless specifically directed otherwise. All subsequent targets would be rearranged or missed out depending upon what happened now. Current activity was important because in its most dramatic form it might be part of some larger operation. When put together with other tour observations, Sigint[22] and satellite imagery, patterns emerged which could range from routine training exercises at unit level to divisional or larger exercises. On the other hand it needn't just be exercise.

It was Brixmis who observed the first signs of the Berlin Wall going up in 1961, were able to alert the allied military governing authorities and test the resolve of

---

[20] Modulux (Mini-Modulux): Image intensifying (II) devices fitted to cameras for night photography. Worked on the principle of passively using what light was available rather than actively creating light such as infrared (IR) spotlights.

[21] Flatbed: a low open freight platform onto which equipment can be loaded or driven for transport by rail.

[22] Sigint: signals intelligence e.g, listening in to radio messages.

Loading kit on to rail flats was not always straightforward! This BMP, side-number 636, has overshot. The soldiers display a classic indifference: 'It wasn't me, Guv, honest!'

the Khruschev-backed fledgling DDR. Nothing was done and the obscenity that divided families in their own houses was erected over night without challenge. Ian Wellstead, a legendary Brixmis tour officer of the day, observed the first blocks being mortared together and could have kicked them down himself had he been given the nod, but the politicians of the day let it go unchallenged. It was Brixmis in 1968 who observed the invasion of Czechoslovakia from the deep south-east of the DDR, a potential repeat performance into Poland against Lech Walesa throughout 1980–1 and it was Brixmis in 1989–90 who was observing without invitation and therefore impartially, the scale and validity of politically agreed troop reductions throughout the Western Group of Forces. It was not unreasonable to claim that the Missions were the eyes and ears of Nato, its most forward troops already on the ground, committed, sacrificed and deep inside enemy territory even before the proverbial balloon went up. We were fighting a Third World War before it had been officially declared.

Pulled up in the track we were going over it again on the map. All of this information already existed on the target file back in Berlin and we had gone through it meticulously, able to commit the target map to memory with routes in, routes out, likely OPs, problem areas, fields of view, sentries' fields of fire and so on. But there was nothing like a final recce to give you confidence that no fences or barriers had suddenly gone up since the last visit, right across a likely escape route. In this case there was little or no change. We were not expecting the ramp to be occupied so now it was imperative to be sure where we were going, how we were going to do it and what we were going to do.

'OK, you ready to go, Ernie? Do you need PNG?'[23]

'No, Boss, I'm nearly there.'

'Martin, I've got the map to take us to target, you take us away when we leave, prematurely or otherwise. Doors locked, windows up. 200 metres, Ernie, stop and cut. Let's go.'

It was a familiar routine. All windows were wound up while on the move. Needless to say having an unlocked door would be doubly awkward! There were too many other things to do when the vehicle was moving to have to wind up windows if you were jumped: reading the map, juggling cameras and controlling the vehicle were consuming enough. The last thing we would need if trying to leave forcibly was a Soviet or East German soldier hanging on by his fingertips jammed in an open window, or worse still, trying to rip you out if you left a door open. Narks we could be a little more robust with but they were unlikely to tackle us without backup. They were not the military enemy, nor did we actively target them, but they were a nasty devious organisation who operated along the same lines as us. We had to work round them rather than against them in order to get the real intelligence that we were after. At least the soldiers were only doing their job. It wasn't their fault that they were on the wrong side and badly misguided. They were just people taking orders and as such were treated with enormous respect. There was nothing personal against them and certainly no hate for them. We, too, were just doing a job and unfortunately for them that required shafting them whenever the opportunity arose.

---

[23] PNG: Passive Night Goggles – image intensifying (II) equipment to aid night vision.

We rolled forward quietly and stopped 200 metres further into the wood. Ernie cut the engine. The windows were cranked in the front and we paused to listen. More audible now, but still not visible, the vehicles were clearly manoeuvring in the open area adjacent to the ramp. It still remained unclear if they were loading or off-loading. It was important to know. Was this an outside unit come to exercise in the area or a unit from the area leaving to exercise elsewhere? Either way it was a strange occurrence because although this was a well-known East German military district it was very much the preserve of the local Soviet regiment. It was very unusual to see NVA here.

'400 metres and stop, no need to cut, route out is reverse to the main road and away right. Trip please, Martin.'

'Thanks, Boss!' Ernie had probably worked out for himself that going forward to the station and saying hello to the sentries was not my preferred option but it gave me confidence that we were absolutely clear what we would do if we were bumped there and then.

'You just keep your eyes on the road behind as well as ahead in case anything comes up our chuff,' added Martin. It was this sort of sharp banter that helped keep a lid on rising apprehensions.

We always tried to avoid going into an occupied target. It was always the last option. Invariably it meant having to reveal yourself and this in turn might reveal routes and OPs you had used, allowing them to be set up for ambush in the future. But in some cases there was no alternative to the direct approach if you needed the intelligence. It was rarely practised on an installation or barracks unless you were sure of your ground or the intelligence was absolutely guaranteed to be worth the risk. It was more feasible on training areas and among equipment deployments because there was always the option of using the open ground or the route the target vehicles themselves had come in on. We normally had the distinct advantages of speed and surprise in those situations to achieve it. The only thing we wouldn't know is whether or not the route would be blocked by their vehicles. It was a rarely practised option because it was asking for trouble and it sullied the integrity of the intelligence gathered: they knew you knew. On the other hand there was nothing that knocked people off balance more than actually driving right at them and through them.

Anticipating Ernie's next question, I added, 'If we have to go forward to the ramp this track joins the road just left of the crossing light and we'll join it going left away from the crossing. But we'll need to cross the lines to do it. It's only single track.'

The atmosphere in the G-wagon was relaxed, Martin was smiling and Ernie was smirking. This was pretty routine stuff so far. We were still 500 or 600 metres away from the ramp at the next stop. There was no need to turn off the engine, the tanks were louder now and they would certainly mask the very slight noises we were making. Nevertheless, the mood began to change with the increasing volume of noise coming from the target. They couldn't hear us, we were certain of that, but equally we found it difficult to hear anything approaching us. We were close enough now for a response. The anticipation of what might happen was enough to concentrate the mind considerably.

Martin adopted his customary bracing position, leaning right forward on the edge of his seat, one hand on the front of the dashboard, the arm straight

A typical air tour operating at the perimeter of an airfield. The tour officer is photographing with the 1,000-mm lens out of the cupola. The tour NCO is spotting and identifying the aircraft for the benefit of the tape. The driver, in this case Stan Matthews, is keeping a lookout for security.

to brace the rest of the body, the other hand clutching the tape recorder in his fist, the base of his fist holding down the 1:50,000 strip map ready for our withdrawal to the next target. He was scanning forward and back, loathe to use the PNG unless he absolutely had to. Once you put the PNG up to your eyes you increased your night viewing capability enormously but when you lowered them you lost your natural night vision immediately. The same was partially true of the Modulux. The eerie green hue of the image intensifier screwed up night vision. Fortunately with the camera it was only in one eye. With practice it was possible to keep one eye open maintaining night vision while taking photographs with the other. Ernie shifted in his seat, unclipped his safety belt for full movement and gripped the steering wheel a little more tightly.

Between the three of us we probably had over 200 tours under our belts, but the adrenalin rush as you closed in on the target was always present. It was a reasonably common experience that towards the end of your time in the Mission you tended to take more risks as you became more and more confident of the ground, the equipment available to you and the crew's respective abilities to get you out of a situation either by talking, driving or navigating. There was no doubt that the danger increased the closer one got to a target and it was this overwhelming fear that either motivated tourers or broke them. There was an occasional tourer who simply couldn't perform once out on the ground. By and large, selection procedures determined who on balance would be suited to these operations but doing it for real and training for it made men react very differently indeed.

We paused briefly at the 400-metre mark. '50 metres turn right, small track. Trip.' It was good practice to issue directions one stage at a time. There was nothing more infuriating for a driver to be told three moves in advance. We'd gone through the route well away from here earlier this afternoon and again briefly as we paused on leaving the road. Ernie had a good mental picture of the map in his mind but he had enough to concentrate on without remembering lefts, rights and straight-ons delivered at once.

The track opening was barely visible against the forest wall, only becoming obvious after we passed it. Ernie reversed up slightly to make the turn. We could no longer see the tyre tracks so Martin quickly used the PNG to confirm that they went straight on where we were turning off. It would not have been too clever to follow them in and find a TATRA looming up in front of us.

'50 metres the track turns sharp left back towards the ramp and it's 200 metres on the nose. Trip.'

'Roger.'

We were very much alert now. Martin and Ernie were scanning constantly while I kept bobbing my head up and down from the map to the outside, continually checking position.

'The way out remains backwards, there is no forward now unless something comes up behind us.'

'Roger.'

The continuous chatter between all three seats was deliberately calm and businesslike, similar to the constant communication between aircraft crews and air traffic control – clipped, succinct and clear.

We manoeuvred very slowly into the final OP, which effectively marked the end of the little track that we were following. It looked as though the only vehicle or people to have used this particular route in were probably previous mission vehicles. It certainly wasn't on the 1: 50,000 OS, merely marked in on the 1:25,000 target map made up by ourselves. The vehicle was just tucked inside the edge of the wood where it fronted on to the railway line. In front of us to our right and on the other side of the line was the ramp, a simple brick and concrete construction in some disrepair, rising up level with the flat-beds allowing the vehicles to drive on to them. It was a side-loading ramp, rather than an end loader. The railway line ran on for a further 200 metres to the right where the empty flatbeds had been shunted having disgorged their load. The track ran on into buffers but we were unable to see that far. The train's flatbeds continued to our left for about 50 metres, at the head of which was the locomotive. The whole train was stretched in front of us, effectively creating a barrier. If we were forced to go forward here we would have to run parallel to the train before being able to cut across the line. Not a great option to get so close to the rolling stock and the troops on top.

'T-72s, one, two, three . . . I count eighteen, Boss. What do you reckon?'

'Agreed. I only see one side-number[24], it's three-figure, not easy to read. Two, zero, three. It's pretty vague.' Soviet side-numbering was invariably three numbers, sometimes two but never four. Four-figure side-numbers were reserved for the NVA.

The NVA soldiers we had seen earlier were taking the tanks off the flatbed and parking them up in the open area adjacent to the ramp. They'd just about finished the process but the noise was still loud enough for us to have to talk above it to make ourselves heard. They were no more than 30 metres away. We were peering out from the cover of the wood into a dimly lit area of the ramp. It would have been difficult for them to see beyond the curtain of light that framed their activity towards us, even if they knew we were there. The light was good enough for some sharp definition with the Modulux. I caught the one single side-number that was visible. It seemed as though all the others had been removed.

'They're definitely unloading and they're definitely Sov. So why the NVA? Hello, who's this then? On the platform, Martin, seen?'

'Seen.'

A Soviet officer, senior lieutenant, tank epaulettes on the black backing of his tunic lapel, was standing on the platform with a couple of NVA officers in attendance watching the unloading procedure.

'I think they're handing them over, Boss.'

That the NVA were equipped by Moscow was well known. Knowing how, when and with what was not so well known. The T-72 was very much a mainstay of the Soviet tank fleet, if no longer state-of-the-art following the introduction of T-80. This little gem of a sighting told us several things. The side-number would tell us which Soviet unit was now upgraded with T-80, the location of the ramp told us which NVA military district was being upgraded with T-72 and with both bits of information we would now know the very latest state of the orbat[25] of the respective Warsaw Pact units ranged against the West along this sector of the front line. Ops would probably be picky and want to know where the current T-62s and 64s were being held that the T-72s were replacing. They were never satisfied, but that would be someone else's job. This was a very nice night's work indeed.

'There's more Easties over to the right, Boss. What can you see with the Modulux?'

Silhouetted at the back end of the ramp were a dozen or so East German soldiers. I used the Modulux to get a better view of them.

'I reckon they're the drivers to take them away.'

'We've got company, Boss. Your 3 o'clock. They've not seen us but they look as though they're wandering this way for a fag. Rule three applies.' He turned round

---

[24] Side-number: the number on the side of a fighting vehicle, aircraft or helicopter. Usually three figures for Soviet ground vehicles and four figures for NVA ground vehicles. Usually two- sometimes three-figure numbers with varying colour schemes for aircraft. These numbers, together with their location and association with VRNs, helped to determine their place in the orbat.

[25] orbat: order of battle – the organisation and hierarchy of military units.

and grinned. I swung the Modulux to my hard right. There were a group of five or so jumping the stream, hands in pockets reaching for cigarettes and lighters. The flare in the II tube as one of them lit up told its own story. They were not 20 metres away.

'That accounts for all the drivers anyway. Time to go Ernie, please. Back up to the fire-break and away. Martin, you've got the map, I'll keep a watch on these guys.'

Ernie started up and moved out backwards. He had to use his mirrors to thread a way back through the close cover.

'No reaction from them. They haven't heard us. Well done. Keep going.'

Even at 20 metres, with the noise of their own tank engines behind them, they wouldn't have heard the G-wagon glide away.

'150 metres and then the sharp left.' Martin tripped the meter.

'OK, we're clear of them.' Ernie increased the pace from nudge to walking.

'50 metres and we come to the fire-break.'

It seemed to be taking forever, but it was a tricky 400-metre reverse without lights in the dark and with rear-view vision only by wing mirror. Backing into the forest and completing a three-point turn without knowing the ground and in this visibility wasn't worth it. We'd come down the path, we could go back along it. Furthermore, if something did come in behind us, then we would be facing forward, the best way to make any escape.

As we approached the opening that we had nearly missed on the way in, a single headlight shattered the dark from our hard left, oscillated slightly and moved towards us, gathering pace as it did so.

I leaned forward closer to Ernie.

'Reverse, reverse, reverse!' I exclaimed in his ear. I didn't want him to think twice about it.

'Go, go, go!' Martin shouted simultaneously as he turned to look at the approaching vehicle.

There was no panic in the vehicle but things happened very quickly. I'm not sure who saw the vehicle first. Ernie had floored the accelerator by the time Martin had spoken. Martin reached across and flicked on the master switch and put all the lights on. There was no point in not being able to see fully now.

'All the way. Don't let him get to the opening before us,' I urged Ernie on. He hadn't hesitated at all. As soon as the light came on he had made up his mind in an instant what to do. We hadn't discussed this particular option but it was the best choice. The vehicle was coming towards us but on the very track that we were trying to get away on.

'It's a bloody motorbike and sidecar on the fire-break.' Martin had identified the single headlight that was now approaching us, perpendicular to the track we were on. He'd obviously heard a vehicle move and was investigating. Going forward would mean that he could come up behind us. Driving forward into the ramp with a motorbike on our tail would certainly alert the other sentries. The bike was about 40 or 50 metres from the opening that we were making for. We were about 20 metres away but already moving. The plan had been simply to reverse out on to the main track, left hand down, back end towards the ramp and then drive out forward the way we had come in. That wasn't possible now. The motorbike was on course for the same opening and we would knock him clean off if we reversed into the fire-break.

The tour officer's back seat in the G-wagon. Behind him is a spare wheel and side nets containing bed rolls and other equipment. The Modulux is on his lap, a strip map on his left. An RAF navigator's briefcase containing binoculars, aide-mémoires and other material can just be seen bottom right.

'Reverse all the way.' It was a clear instruction to ensure that Ernie's mind was made up and that we didn't try for the turn round with a bike in the way. Ernie swung right hand hard down into the path of the oncoming bike but away from him, continuing our rearwards motion as he negotiated the turn. The sidecar was now to our front but following us as we continued up the track in reverse.

'Shit! They must have put guys out after we got in. He was in the right place at the right time and must have wondered what was coming out of the woods.'

It was a statement of the bleeding obvious. Martin looked hard at me.

'Really, Boss!'

I shrugged my shoulders.

We were reversing up a narrow fire-break, certainly not two cars width, at about 30 m.p.h. with a motorbike and sidecar chasing us only metres from our front bumper. Ernie wound down the window, lurching the G-wagon from side to side as he took his left hand off the steering wheel to do so. He stuck his head out and floored the accelerator again, now that he could see properly. He clamped his right forearm firmly across the steering wheel and jammed his right elbow into the rim. This allowed him to reverse back quickly without snaking. Fortunately, all fire-breaks were cut clinically straight, allowing him to perform this driving stunt more easily. The G-wagon in reverse was an impressive beast, easily capable of 50 m.p.h. The track was churning up a cloud of dust, putting it straight into the motorcyclist's face. But he wasn't giving up and attempted to get round us wherever he thought he could.

'Don't let him get round, Ernie.' Another statement of the obvious. If he got round the back of us he would simply slow up and stop. The route back to the ramp was probably alive now, the commotion of bike, car and headlights leaping around the forest tracks would have alerted them. Once again the fortunes of the crew were left to the skill of the driver. Martin, with his head darting in and out of his window, gave Ernie 'touch left, touch right' commands to alter the path of the G-wagon and prevent the bike from passing down one side. It was a gutsy performance by the bike rider. The sidecar passenger on the other hand was clearly petrified, holding on for grim death as his driver lurched forward, almost touching our front bumper, or attempting to lunge into the dark down the side of us. The whole scene was lit up by our own headlights, illuminating the dust as it billowed out in front of them. The full beam plus spotlights would certainly stop him from seeing our number-plate if not blind him from seeing the road, but it didn't seem to deter him.

He kept on coming. Ernie jerked the vehicle from side to side the full kilometre length of the track at about 40 m.p.h., finally bursting out onto the main road where he was able to J-turn[26] through 180 degrees from reverse to forward and away. The motorbike burst out onto the road behind us. He may very well have caught a glimpse of the number-plate but he was unlikely to have distinguished the number or its tiny Union Jack. The bike stopped immediately. He'd done his bit and he knew he was no match for us on the main road.

It was the most incredible piece of driving skill that I had ever witnessed. It was like a ride on a fairground, with the exception that one slip might have put us into a tree, or worse, in a collision with the mad motorcyclist pursuing us only 2 or 3 metres from the front of the vehicle. We left the area that night. It wouldn't have been worth trying to follow the tanks now. That would have been red rag to a bull. We'd seen enough and there'd been enough excitement.

It was always useful, if not prudent, to stop after one of these near misses and talk it through. Sometimes they were terrifying incidents and for a new tourer it was quite often enough to paralyse them into inaction. Once you had experienced a close shave it became instinctive to want to get away and the methods by which to do it became practised events. The Ashford course put tourers through these precise drills but it was never quite the same as the real thing. We pulled over some good twenty minutes driving time away from the scene and had a brew.[27] Martin and Ernie were very experienced tourers. We were sure that we had done the right thing. There had been no other way in and the intelligence was worth the risk. Nevertheless, we ran over how we might have approached it differently. We were certainly taken by surprise at the suddenness of the bike's appearance and quite shaken at the drive that followed but we didn't over-analyse it.

'Did you not manage to set the video up, Boss? Too busy for you?' Ernie ribbed me. We had a good laugh about it and moved on to a Z-platz.[28]

---

[26] J-turn: spinning the car through 180° in a deliberate move to escape and evade.

[27] Brew: coffee break, also an opportunity to watch known military lines of communication for any movement.

[28] Z-platz: a secure place to sleep, most of the time.

* * *

'Kiiiit.'

Jim Edgerton had spotted them. He lowered his bins and stuffed them into the tour bag on the floor between his legs and grabbed the tape recorder held between his knees. He was ready. He looked impatiently at the driver, Buncie, followed by a half glance into the back of the vehicle to check if I was set up. I threw my brew out of the window and started checks on the camera equipment.

Paul Bunce, 'Buncie', had been getting some shut-eye while the two of us watched. He was knackered. He'd been driving virtually non-stop since we left on Friday. It was now late Sunday morning. Friday night, the first night of the tour, saw us watching the northern loading ramp in Halle. Trains had been loading with Sov kit all night. We suspected it was 27 GMRD and we reckoned that we had caught them as they were moving out on exercise.

The out-loading had continued throughout Saturday so we had repeated the ramp watch for a second night. Friday night had been a great success. We observed four full kit trains leave the ramp at almost regular two-hourly intervals. They were untarped[29] and completely open to us. We'd taken VRNs, side-numbers and vehicle profiles without missing one. Routes in and out of our OPs had been clear and we'd made them without detection. During Saturday we completed routine sweeps of all local barracks to confirm what we suspected, that 27 GMRD was on the move. Two of the barracks were deserted apart from the customary sentries in their towers at all corners of the installation and on the gates.

It was late August so the routine end-of-year exercises were about to start. This was probably the first one. The exercise season, a bit of a misnomer since it was more or less incessant, began with low-level training in the spring immediately after troop rotation from the Soviet Union had been completed. It built up in scale to late autumn when Divisional- and then Army-level exercises took place. The Mission had already completed Operation Troika[30] for the year. The troops were in country. Now we were watching them undertake their first combined operations exercises.

Military rail movement ceased during the day, giving way to commuter and freight priorities. Military rail movement was invariably programmed for the small hours, partly due to the priority system and partly for reasons of security and secrecy. Movement under cover of darkness was regularly practised and now firmly established by the Mission as a normal part of Warsaw Pact plans

---

[29] tarped/tarpology/untarped: the draping of tarpaulin over equipment to disguise its true designation. Tarpology was the art of recognising equipment under tarpaulin from the tell-tale lumps and bumps that would protrude. Often Brixmis vehicles would be tarped in detention situations to prevent them from seeing any military activity going on outside the vehicle. This was illegal and in summer highly dangerous as temperatures underneath soared to well over 40 degrees.

[30] Operation Troika: the systematic observation of incoming and outgoing conscripted Soviet troops within the DDR.

The appearance of a T-64 bursting out of the wood and onto the road in front of you may be well planned, but also unnerving nevertheless!

for transition to war. It suited us too. The cover of darkness gave us similar advantages. We took a couple of hours kip on the Saturday afternoon prior to returning to the ramp watch that evening. Saturday night did not go so well.

It started ominously with an East German railway official, probably one of the station workers, walking past us on his way to the evening shift. The look on his face told us that he wasn't happy with us being there. Assuming that he would pass on the information to the Sovs on the ramp, no more than his duties expected of him, we moved to a second OP. Now they would know we were about and we would have to start working to get what we wanted. It was always a difficult task trying to balance getting the best view of the kit and yet maintain the most secure position.

Halle main station was right in the middle of a built-up area of the city. During the day traffic was incessant and people thronged the streets. We were able to mingle freely with the traffic. For the most part people either ignored us or didn't even recognise us for who we were. They probably registered us as yet another military vehicle. When we turned off the main street and threaded our way through little alleyways and across waste ground, we were careful to watch for narks but invariably we were totally ignored.

The prevailing culture helped our cause. East Germans simply didn't ask the sort of questions that we might ask of strange activity in our own public places. They also thought twice about getting involved, partly through apathy and partly from a fear of tangling with the authorities that might complicate their already difficult lives. They had many more pressing difficulties looking after themselves without taking on additional burdens. There were vast numbers of military, quasi-military and police organisations set up specifically to deal with suspicious activity. Furthermore, there were the huge numbers of state workers, Kampfgruppen, whose jobs obliged them to watch for and report on Mission personnel. Their vast network consisted of railway personnel from signalmen to train drivers, from postmen, bus and tram drivers to civil servants and factory workers. They all had to report us in. They would deal with it. The average East German lacked a sense of awareness that has been forced upon Britain and to a lesser extent on some other Western countries by the activities of terrorism. It all combined to create a culture that worked in our favour most of the time.

The traffic was useful cover. The hustle and bustle on the street made our watchers think twice about the course of action open to them. On the other hand, a successful apprehension in broad daylight, with an audience for approval, was a most useful show of strength. By night the civilian traffic was replaced by Vopo[31] patrol cars and Stasi saloons, the streets occupied by night-shift workers and drunks. A self-imposed curfew descended. It became sinisterly quiet and dark.

The choice of OP invariably necessitated taking risks that included toughing out a stay for as long as possible before being forced to move on. It took about fifteen minutes to get round to the other side of the ramp from the first OP and

---

[31] Vopo: Volkspolizei: The East German civilian police. Often incorporated to try and detain us but with little success. They were not recognised by the Missions and were more of a nuisance than anything else.

carefully into position in the second without being observed. We just made the first column moving onto the ramp.

A battalion of T-80 tanks plus support vehicles moved into the loading area, about 40 or 50 metres away from us. The light onto the loading ramp was good. I snapped away with the Nikon F3 fitted for the low-light levels with the Modulux image intensifier. It made the camera nearly 2 ft long and heavy enough to warrant breaks from continually supporting it. The Modulux enhanced the available artificial light, creating an image in the lens of varying shades of green and white.

We were stationary on a cobblestone road tucked into the bushes, side on, facing down the slope. Behind us the road continued upwards at an incline before flattening out, turning sharply right and forming a bridge over the railway line that these flatbeds would eventually be pulled out onto. The way forward down the slope was momentarily blocked by the incoming tanks. The escape route out, while the way forward was blocked, was to reverse over the bridge to a T-junction and swing down either one of the roads that was free. We would literally cross that bridge when we came to it. When the tanks passed through we would be able to get out forward again. All this detail was constantly assessed and reassessed between the three of us in the vehicle. At any one time Buncie knew where he had to go to get away.

The train loaded in just under an hour and a half; thirty-one T-80, fifteen BMP-1s, 2s, a KSH and a score of BTR-60 variants. As it pulled out we also left for a safer spot away from the ramp before returning about an hour later. There was no point staying in one place. It made sense, having been seen once, to keep on the move. We found a deserted spot on the edge of the city where we stopped for a brew and went through all the ramifications of being spotted in the first OP. It wasn't good practice to return to a location that we had already been seen in, although it had the better light and less complicated escape routes. The second OP was still uncompromised and so on balance we decided to push our luck and return to it for one more train before having to find a third.

A third OP would mean having to move away from the station and find a road crossing over the line where the light was good enough for both identifying the equipment and photographing it. A further complication would be the moving train itself, picking up speed in excess of 40 m.p.h. depending how far from the station we had to go. The combination of speed and light made the photography more tricky than back at the ramp. The equipment might possibly be tarped for the journey and sentries may have been posted along the train, less preoccupied with loading as they were now and concentrating more on their job of security.

Halle was a difficult station. In the centre of an urban conurbation, occupied by tens of thousands of soldiers, its own police force and Stasi secret police, not to mention a well-manned railway station, it would be difficult not to be spotted at some stage. The advantages of taking the equipment in the floodlight of the station as it rolled onto the flatbeds and thus obtaining the best conditions for identification and imagery were too great. We returned to the OP on the cobble road overlooking the line. It was single-car width, barely wide enough on the bridge to get our Geländewagen through. We checked escape routes, this time deciding to face up the slope for a getaway, rather than have to negotiate it backwards.

Conditions were extreme. Winters got down to -30°C, which had to be slept out in. Summers sent temperatures inside the vehicle to +40°C, which couldn't be left unattended.

A second column approached the loading ramp. It must have been 3 a.m. on Sunday morning, over two hours since the last column and well over three hours since being scrutinised by the railway worker. We could hear them miles away as they clattered their way through the cobbled streets. They were mostly BMP from one of the mechanised infantry brigades belonging to 27 GMRD. They had drivers and commanders only. The full compliment of infantrymen that would normally sit in the back of these tracked armoured personnel carriers were conspicuously absent. Sometimes the kit trains had passenger compartments attached. Cattle wagons we would probably call them. They would transport the full complement of troops together with their vehicles rather than split them up and drive them across country. It would have been more difficult if they were all here. They would have wandered around the station, bored and looking for something to do. You could bet that one of them would have wandered towards us and stumbled upon us quite innocently. If it was only drivers and commanders then they would be too busy organising the loading. However, it wasn't to be.

Almost immediately the vehicles halted, one of the commanders got out and organised some of the others to spread out along the ramp. He sent a group of four in the direction of our last OP. The railway official had told them. Two of them were sent across the line towards us, more by luck than judgement on his part. Either way the effect was the same. Although it was unlikely that they could see us we had to move again before they stumbled on to us.

The two coming towards us saw the vehicle move, adjusted direction on to us and started to climb the fence on to the road. They still couldn't be sure who we were. Coming out of the light their night vision would be severely limited and there were no identifying lights on our vehicle to help them. I could see that they were both armed. We pulled over the bridge and turned left away from them. I took passing shots of the last vehicle in the convoy. Now it was going to be more difficult. The two soldiers resumed their search. We could have been any passing vehicle in that light.

The rest of that night and early morning, we took a third and final kit train by darting in and out of the station from parallel side roads, using the bridge as well as the alleyways off the main street as they approached the station. We stayed no more than three or four minutes at each place, keeping on the move all night, patching together a jigsaw of all the separate glimpses of equipment to create the whole trainload. By the end of the evening we had tied up several Vopo cars that had been called in to find us, playing an ever increasingly dangerous game of cat and mouse. As the night wore on, more agencies were drafted in to see us off. We chased the last train to the main sidings on the outskirts of the city, waiting for it to be switched to its final line out of Halle in order that we could determine whereabouts in East Germany it was going next. This was vital for further tasking, enabling another tour to observe the unit training at its final destination.

It was about 6 a.m. before we left the ramp, retiring gracefully to a spot outside Halle installation number 261, the only other barracks that still seemed occupied. We were high up on an overlooking hill just under a kilometre away. During the course of the night we had become quite a nuisance. We elected to keep well away now before pushing our luck too far. This installation was on the very edge of the built-up part of Halle with residential blocks of flats not 500 metres from their front gate. The hill we were on was the excavated spoil from the development.

'They're coming out of the main gate turning right,' Jim continued. Paul was alert instantly, adjusting his seat ready for the off.

'That's not the way to the ramp. Shit! They're moving by road. Buncie, get ready to move.'

I leaned forward with the tour map and anticipated their likely routes with Jim. The column pulled out of the gates and disappeared from view into a dip that was created over thousands of years by the River Saale cutting through the land it snaked across. It comprised entirely of wheeled vehicles and so less in need of a ride on a train to their final destination. From our position they were too far away for decent imagery, yet far enough away for us not to be seen.

I knew the route they were crossing well, if not in the course of the last few hours then certainly in previous tours to Halle. The concrete road out of their barracks forded the river, almost impassable in spring, and led out to the local training area. Once committed across this bridge the going became difficult like any training ground anywhere. Severely undulating tank routes and tussocky scrub were the main features. The road ran alongside it. If you strayed off the concrete road then you were in a Mission-restricted area and liable for a hard time from any one of the major Soviet units exercising there. In Soviet eyes it was a forbidden area to us. For us it was precisely where we should be. For all their public May Day parades in Red Square and East Berlin they exercised their latest and best kit in private. Our job was to get among it.

The concrete road came to a T-junction about 100 metres after fording the river. Left took it back into town crossing a more substantial bridge further down stream, right eventually joined up with the main public road, the F6 out of Halle to Bernberg. We couldn't simply chase them and overtake them, that would be suicidal, given our recent activity. Every Sov in Halle was probably aware by now that a Mission car was operating. We would have to get ahead of them and make it look as though we just happened to be coming the other way. We could have taken them from a long-range OP but the ground was so open that we would have had to be a long way off to remain undetected and once again that would detract from the imagery. Furthermore, I wanted to be coming back into Halle for a final look at the ramp to see if we should be expecting more.

'We'll watch them from here to see which way they go at the T-junction. If it's left then maybe they're taking a longer route round to the ramp. If they go right then they're definitely going out of town by road and we can take them on route 6 on the nose.'

This was simply a trigger OP chosen in such a way that the target would have to commit to one of two or three routes very quickly. Once committed we could predict exactly where they were going, create enough time to anticipate them and get ourselves into a better position to take them. They probably weren't going to the ramp. That left the training area or somewhere further afield. Given what we had seen the previous two nights the latter was most likely.

'This looks a good stretch of road, Boss.' Jim pointed to a stretch of route 6 that was long and straight.

'We can get round there quite easily without having to go past the ramp again. I know that road, it's quite open, plenty of room to manoeuvre and lots of ways out.'

'OK. You take us there if they go that way, I'll get us back to the ramp if they go the other.'

'They've turned right, Boss, they're moving this lot by road, definitely.' Buncie had watched them reappear and followed them to the junction.

They'd committed themselves. We knew where they were going now. Unless they did something out of character we would be seeing them again.

'OK, let's go.'

Paul eased the vehicle away from the OP and joined the road that they had moved out on. Instead of following them we turned right away from them, past the flats and back into town taking a fairly circuitous route to get to the north of the city before turning back south-west. Jim knew this city like the back of his hand. I didn't interfere with the map reading, I didn't need to. Not only was he a most competent soldier, he was also exceptionally bright and had the rare distinction of being an interpreter for the Mission as well as a tour NCO. He spoke French, German and Russian better than me and rather dispelled the myth that the Parachute Regiment was full of the less intelligent end of the army's manpower intake.

'200 metres, junction, our priority, take the right. Trip.'

Jim reset the trip meter. Each vehicle was fitted with an accurate trip meter to aid navigation. Every junction or key landmark was 'tripped'. It wasn't always necessary but it was good practice. Things happened in-between one marker and another to change your course and occasionally we had to retrace our steps.

The less distance you had to retrace the better. Furthermore, if you could follow this procedure when the going was easy then you had a chance when it was dark or when you were being chased. Distances are difficult to gauge in a vehicle at night or in a vehicle that is moving much faster than you would normally travel. Also, when you see a turning or a landmark that is not on the map, it throws you sufficiently that you've probably travelled another 300 metres before you work out the explanation for it. The error then becomes compounded and the map and the ground start to play tricks on you. The trip meter was a lifesaver. We didn't stop for the junction. We had right of way.

'400 metres. Crossroads. Go left.'

'Roger,' responded Buncie.

We were travelling at about 80 m.p.h. out of town. The road was straight, the lie of the land flat and we rapidly left Halle behind us. We were closing on a Trabbie[32] approaching the crossroads ahead of us.

'Clear left,' said Jim.

'Clear right,' said Paul.

'Reggie on the right, sitting down. He hasn't seen us. But he is facing the way we're going.'

'Good sign.' Jim turned, grinned and rubbed his hands together with anticipated excitement. That was about as animated as Jim got. The reggie meant that we had picked the right route for the column and that they had still not passed this point. Buncie swung the vehicle into the oncoming lane and without slowing down overtook the Trabbie on the junction, turning left in the process and proceeding down the new road still in the oncoming lane. The G-wagon took the corner with a slight tilt but hardly moved from the intended line. They were fantastic cars; under-armoured, finely tuned and fitted out in our own workshops with all sorts of extra gadgets from infrared searchlights to long-range fuel tanks and a bank of switches that could shut down lights, change configuration to replicate a Trabbie or illuminate a target like Oxford Street at Christmas. We passed the traffic regulator on our right as we turned. He didn't look up or acknowledge us in any way. He looked shattered. How long had he been there? What had we missed already?

'OK, they should be on the nose now about 3 or 4 k away.'

'They're up ahead, Boss. I think I can see them already.'

They were moving fast. The slightest delay on our part and we would have missed them completely.

My camera was up to my face, the Kevlar body resting on my cheek, while I maintained a watch on the approaching convoy ready to react to anything they might do. I chose not to set the video. From first sighting it didn't look as though there was much of interest to warrant replicating the 'stills' with video.

The first vehicle in the column appeared in view, not surprisingly it was a UAZ-469[33] leading the rest.

---

[32] Trabbie: the ubiquitous East German Trabant car.

[33] UAZ-469: the ubiquitous Soviet jeep. Curiously similar to the G-wagon.

The UAZ flashed its lights, to warn us that a column was coming.

'Stupid bastard thinks we're one of them,' said Jim.

The G-wagon had a very striking resemblance to the UAZ series of vehicles. It was a jeep shape with an angular, square body and front lights set in a similar pattern. But on closer inspection the G-wagon was larger all round. Paul flashed back in acknowledgement. Pretending to be one of them would prolong the sham just that little bit longer. All the time we were closing in it gave them less time to react. If we could get past the front vehicle then we would have passed the one crew that was likely to stop and do something about us.

'OK, Paul, nice and steady now.'

Buncie slowed the vehicle down to about 30 m.p.h.; the convoy would be doing about 50 m.p.h. maximum. He put the car on the extreme outside of the lane to maximise the angle of visibility on to the vehicle registration number. Jim would have to read it off and I would have to ensure that it was in focus while the whole vehicle filled the frame: 500 metres and closing. There was still no reaction from the lead vehicle. They'd probably been up all night themselves preparing for the move. They may not have been expecting attention so soon into their road trip. As we closed senses sharpened, ready to react to the unexpected. Any tiredness had disappeared long ago as the adrenalin pumped round the body during the high speed drive out of Halle. The thrill of bagging more kit consumed us: 250 metres and still no reaction.

'OK, Paul, ways out are across the field to our right. There are some tracks right beyond the wood line to our front but not until. Any one's a goer should you need it.'

'Roger, Boss.'

Several seconds later we were on them. Paul slowed the vehicle down further, 'UAZ-469, two up, swords on black, 59 23 EK. BTR 60-PB 138. Again 139. 1KSh 140.'

Jim was bolt upright, his body completely taut, shouting at the windscreen in front of him and yet showing virtually no outward emotion for the oncoming vehicles to see. His left hand clutched the tape recorder down in his lap. His right hand raised in a friendly submissive wave that you might do when acknowledging it was your mistake on the road. He barked out the detail of each vehicle that came past. As it went by he whipped his head round to record the contents of the rear and back to the front again for the next vehicle. Paul slowed as much as he could without causing suspicion while trying to give both Jim and myself the maximum time to take each vehicle, Jim identifying it and calling the registration or side-number, me photographing it. All the time we were watching for an aggressive or unexpected reaction from any one of the oncoming vehicles.

'KAMAZ 4310. 27 34 EK, nothing in the back. Again 28. Again, 67 34 EM, Again 68, again 69.'

The vehicles were well spaced out at about 30-metre intervals. This gave two maybe three seconds between each vehicle and each description. The column stretched away as far as the wood line well over a kilometre away. As we got further down the line the vehicles became more bunched. Jim's calling quickened and became louder as he raced to get all the detail. Because he spoke Russian he could get the VRN noted quicker than a non-Russian speaker.

'Boss, the UAZ has pulled off.'

Paul had been watching the rear for anything coming up behind us and had noticed the UAZ come out of the column and stop in the oncoming lane. Whether he was just stopping to observe progress or whether he was coming back for us I wasn't prepared to deal with until he committed himself.

My camera was working quicker now as the vehicles got closer together. I had set up all three bodies with 100 ASA film and simply moved the 85-mm lens from one to the other. I was trained to change bodies in less than two seconds, thereby not missing a single vehicle. With three cameras on the go I had an absolute minimum of 108 shots before having to change a film. Sometimes a roll would give you an extra shot if you only wound it on two frames at the start rather than the safe three. I always tried to get thirty-seven shots from one roll. It gave you that little extra advantage before having to change film with the left hand and work a camera with the right.

'Keep an eye on him and let me know if he follows.'

I continued to frame the oncoming vehicles to get three-quarter profiles and VRNs. I changed bodies to the second camera as the film ran out on the first.

'Changing camera,' I shouted from the back to be heard on the tape. It would help Jim later when he was coordinating imagery with his calling.

When the second film ran out I started to change film in the first camera and continued photographing with the third. The first film came out. I shoved it under my leg, barely taking my eye off the view through the windscreen. The vehicles were more bunched up the further down the column we went, only 15 or 20 metres between them and some of them almost on top of each other.

'Steady, steady, they're getting tighter.'

Jim was shouting into the tape. The activity in the vehicle was furiously busy but quite routine. From the outside it looked very calm. All directional signals were made below the dashboard to avoid being seen. The two in the front seats waved with their respective outside hands in friendly greeting to the oncoming vehicles. I was well over to the off-side of the vehicle, pressed as far back into the seat as the body and camera angle would allow. It was invisible from outside the vehicle. Both of my side windows had curtains drawn across them and I photographed through the front windscreen. Cameras were being juggled on my lap in the back, film was dropped among them as it became used up, Jim was shouting faster to keep up with the vehicles passing us and Paul was adding ones that he couldn't get out quickly enough. The activity was short, sharp and frenzied, everyone's individual roles meticulously working together to achieve the objective.

Thirty minutes previously we had been sitting having a coffee, Paul catching up on some kip. Now this explosive burst of activity, fused with the danger and excitement of mixing with a column of Sov fighting vehicles, was pumping adrenalin round the body keeping us awake and highly alert. About 150 metres in front of us a BTR-60 command vehicle pulled out of the line as if to overtake and ducked back in again. Two seconds later it pulled out all the way and held the lane only 50 metres away. He'd spotted us or had been alerted by the lead vehicle, it was entirely probable that these two vehicles had comms between them. Either way it was very clear that he was coming for us. There was no time to say anything and again very little need to. It was not uncommon to be rammed and Paul was ready for it. You could guarantee every few tours that somebody would have a pop at you. It was completely illegal in the rules of the game. Unfortunately, not everyone interpreted the rules in the same way. Rammings were uncommon, largely due to the evasive skills of our own drivers, averting attempted rammings from becoming the real thing.

Paul wrenched the G-wagon over to the right, down a slight embankment towards the open field. We passed round the BTR's front near deck as it continued to lunge forward, trying to ram us off the road. It passed down the embankment behind us. The near miss looked like a complicated stunt manoeuvre for a Royal Tournament display. As it tried to come after us it must have stalled or broken something as it met the bottom of the embankment square on.

We rejoined the road at the next field entrance. The BTR remained stranded. We continued to take the column on the nose, the last vehicle appearing before the wood line where we turned sharply right and away from them, virtually a whole regiment in the bag. The last vehicle in the column had its rear canopy open and in the back was the familiar sight of reggies asleep or smoking, having been picked up one by one along the route. The man we had passed half asleep back at the junction would be picked up shortly and we would return to the ramp to check for more kit trains. As it happened, we remained in Halle that night continuing to play the cat and mouse game as the final units of 27 GMRD deployed. We extended the tour into a fourth day until we were content that no more trains were forthcoming.

CHAPTER TWO

Selection

'We've got company behind.'

'Well spotted. What are you going to do about it?'

'Get away from them.'

'Why? Are you doing anything wrong?'

'Not yet.'

'So what's the problem? Keep them there where you can see them and start looking for others. Don't alert them to the fact that you know they're there. We're nowhere contentious. Don't let them bug you and don't let them block you. What's your grid reference?'

I had lost my place on the map during this ten-second exchange and the excitement of spotting my first narks.

'We're just coming up to the bridge over.'

'Hmm. How far to the target?'

'Pass,' I mumbled to myself and then wished I hadn't alerted him to the fact that I was concentrating more on these guys behind rather than the target coming up. There was a pause.

'About 2 kilometres.'

'Now what's your grid reference?'

Another 10 seconds and we were a further 300 metres down the road and even further away from the last point I was really sure of. I was waiting for a clear reference point on the ground to match with the map. The further we went from my last good checkpoint the less sure I was and the quicker the error was being compounded as we covered more ground. Being followed, thinking about routes to the target and constantly checking the camera equipment did not help the map reading. All had to be done equally proficiently.

It was still dark at this time in the morning. We were aiming to be on target by first light, using the cover of darkness to get in position then waiting for natural light to maximise the imagery opportunity. It was the third and final day of this particular tour and the effort of concentration was getting to me. The previous two nights we'd scrutinised local barracks and watched railway lines until about two in the morning. It wasn't so much the short hours of sleep but the continual decision making required every single waking moment that was knackering. So far I had survived my Army career on the 'so what' technique, familiar to all ranks of the armed forces, where the next course of action is established by asking the question 'so what?' Here, it was 'what if', 'then what', 'what next' and 'why', 'how', with 'who', 'when' and 'where' thrown in for good measure.

The bridge over the railway line came up. I knew where I was.

'967 388. 1½ kilometres to target. We should start to think about routes in and these guys behind us.'

'OK. They're obviously bugging you. Let's lose them. You've got the map.'

There were several techniques for losing narks, depending upon the circumstances. In town it was relatively easy. Performing a box routine, where you basically turned left, left and left or right, right and right at every opportunity, allowed you to complete a square, bringing you up behind the car you were following. Town provided many aids to getting away. Incorrect signalling, use of the traffic lights, even drawing attention to the tail by pointing at them sometimes embarrassed them off especially if the locals started to take note.

That was fine if it was a single tail and your intention was merely to let them know that you were aware of their presence. If there was more than one tail or if their intentions were more than just surveillance, then speed, a thorough knowledge of the area and excellent navigation skills under pressure were essential. In the countryside the best option was to take them where their vehicles couldn't follow. East Germany was largely made up of either huge areas of open, endless and flat arable farmland or vast wooded areas. Interspersed between the two were towns and cities linked by the road system. Roads of the standard we were used to in Western Europe were few and far between. There were several key autobahns but even these were concrete and most were in bad repair. The majority of roads we used were simple dirt tracks, dusty enough in summer to locate a moving vehicle 3 or 4 kilometres away, wet enough in spring or autumn to sink a vehicle up to the tops of its wheels and piled at least a foot high with snow every winter. This was not the sort of country where a Trabbie, Wartburg or even four-wheel drive Niva, one of the more modern in the nark inventory, could easily compete with a G-wagon.

The narks' aim was first to compromise us, second keep us away from targets and finally set us up for other agencies. Theirs was not an easy job. First they had to find us. They could follow us from the Glienicke Bridge when we crossed over into East Germany or they could follow us from the Mission House when we left Potsdam. But they didn't all work from Potsdam, they didn't have the range or the cross-country ability that we had and even they had finite resources. If they insisted on following us from the outset then if we couldn't lose them with a turn of speed or a cross-country route then we could simply choose to drive round until they ran out of petrol. It simply wasn't practical, precise or logical on their part. In order to compromise us they had to photograph us to provide proof. The proof necessitated a shot of the vehicle with number-plate clearly visible, preferably a face of the tour officer or one of the crew members and all that in front of an obvious piece of Soviet military hardware or property that we were interested in. It was a very tall order indeed. Setting us up was easier for them. They observed any routine or pattern and punished it severely whenever they could. The Soviets were more than happy to take on the work and effect capture of a Mission crew.

'Trip. 130 metres turn left. Track.'

Buncie hit the accelerator pedal hard. We'd been travelling at a steady 30 to 40 m.p.h. There was never a need to break speed limits if you didn't have to.

Travelling fast merely served to highlight you against all the other vehicles. Furthermore, a chance sighting or a brief glimpse might never have occurred if moving too quickly. It was difficult enough to predict where military activity might be. The slower you moved the more chance you would have to find it or run into it. Installations and barracks would always be there but vehicles and exercising troops could pop up anywhere.

We were also extremely safety conscious. The number of road accidents that the Missions were involved in over the course of forty-four years was minimal. Travelling fast, by definition, increases the likelihood of accidents and however much they might be another person's fault they were not good publicity for the Missions. More importantly they delayed a crew from its real objectives and allowed the Soviet authorities to make something more of them than was warranted. There was a time and a place for fast, aggressive driving. It was reserved for when you were in the shit or when you were engaged on a target. It was simply unnecessary and counter-productive otherwise.

The vehicle soon reached 70, 80 m.p.h. The narks behind us responded and confirmed their presence. Their intention was clearly more than surveillance.

'What's the registration? What sort of vehicle? What colour? How many up?'

'Right,' was my response.

Buncie flashed a glance behind at me.

'I meant right as in I get the picture, not turn right.'

'How are we going to lose them? Are we still proceeding to target or do you want to draw them away first?'

This was getting out of control. There were too many things to think about: where we were now, where we were going, these idiots behind, not to mention the cameras and the job we were supposed to be doing.

'Come off the track now and head for that copse on the skyline across the field.'

'Roger.'

Buncie flung the vehicle off the farm track and straight into a stubble field. There was hardly a change in the ride of the vehicle. The G-wagon was built for speed and comfort and a little step like this hardly registered. The car behind clattered down the small drop that marked the boundary between the rough track and the stubble but they still came after us.

'At the wood keep going round it on the right-hand side where we'll come back to another track. Get on the track going left.'

'Roger,' Buncie responded again. Graham said nothing.

The speed didn't drop as we launched up the slope to the skyline. Fortunately, the light was getting better as dawn started to come through. Soon there would be many more vehicles out on the roads, particularly in this farming area, and we would have to be careful how we drove. We slowed slightly to corner round the copse. The chasing car must have anticipated what we were doing because it shot off to the left, taking the obstacle from the other side. I checked the map quickly. No wonder he anticipated us. To the right the road was a dead end into farm buildings. I had no choice but to go left and they knew it. We emerged the other side, flat out towards the track, the chasing car converging on us from the other side of the copse. It was too open for them to be able to block us but it was not sufficiently difficult going for us to lose them.

'Don't let them get in front. 200 metres, take a left on to the main road. Trip.'

We got onto the track first and ahead of them. They had to slow to avoid ripping out the sump on the verge.

'We're going into the next village. We'll try and lose them there. OK, left here and straight on. After the telephone box take a right followed by the first right, and the next first right. We'll do a hollow box to try and shake them off and back out of the village down this main road we're on now.'

The telephone box stood out well, giving Buncie plenty of time to plan the turn. He'd already switched off the lights so there were no clues to be had by the guys behind. He stamped on the brake at the last possible moment, holding the hand brake with his right hand and swinging the wheel with his left, using the flat of his palm to keep the motion going. The vehicle turned the corner with little difficulty. It felt as though it should lurch right over but the suspension, its extra weight and extra-wide wheel base kept it solid on the ground. The chasing car had little time to anticipate and couldn't safely make the turn, it had got so close behind us. It shot past, screeched to a halt and then spun through 180 degrees to come back at us.

'OK. It's a black Mercedes, four up, all male, two in the front and two in the back. Civilian. Couldn't get the front number-plate.'

'Photograph?'

'Shit!' The camera was in my hand but I hadn't used the opportunity of a broadside to get a shot at it. Too late. We were back up to 40 m.p.h. I concentrated on the map.

'First right, which should be 80 metres, then the next first right which should be 150 metres, then . . .'

'One at a time, one at a time. You'll confuse the hell out of him.'

'Roger. 80 metres. Trip. Turn right.'

Just as we made the first right the pursuing narks loomed in the wing mirror. Buncie accelerated again and we made the turn easily before they finished the stretch. The map couldn't foretell what happened at the next right. It was blocked off by roadworks. I'd boxed us in.

Buncie didn't stop. He lifted the vehicle over the kerb, around the roadworks, across the front of the adjoining property and back onto the road. The pursuing vehicle followed, and was lucky to get on to the pavement over a dropped section of kerb. I hadn't spotted the option but Buncie wasn't going to wait for me to make a different call. He was either helping me out or was not going to be embarrassed by waiting to be told to get on with it. The pursuing car rocketed past us on the pavement, taking advantage of our slowing down to drop back on to the road, and was now ahead of us. His brake lights came on and he started to slow up in front of us. Having them in front was not good, particularly if there was another car in the chase. Now they could control the pace. I did not want to be stopped.

'J-turn now and back out the way we came in.'

Buncie slammed on the brake, flicked the automatic gearbox into reverse and backed up towards the roadworks. With the flat of his hand he span the wheel hard left-hand down, into the driveway of another property which had a single-strand electric fence running at knee height around it. As he braked, hard enough to rock the G-wagon on the spot, he flicked the automatic back into drive and accelerated away. It was one smooth continuous movement. As we spun away I took a shot of the rear of the nark vehicle, getting the full number-plate and vehicle make. We manoeuvred back around the roadworks and away. As we left we must have caught the strand of fencing, spreading it across the road. I saw it get caught up in the pursuing axles as they followed our manoeuvre out. We left the village and pulled up about 4 kilometres back down the road and waited. There was no sign of them.

'OK. Well done.' Graham turned round.

'We got rid of them, that's the main thing. But don't let them bug you. Don't react to them. Keep your eye on the main objective. If you're not doing anything they can use against you, like reckless driving or being on target, then carry on as normal. Remember what their aim is and what your aim is. Now let's get on with the target. Take the next left and back across the training area.'

The chase had been exciting and given me quite an adrenalin buzz. I was well awake. But I wasn't scared or frightened partly, I'm sure, because I didn't know the full consequences of being detained and partly because this was only training on Salisbury Plain. I knew I had to perform in order to get through the Special Duties course but somehow I knew the real thing was going to be very different.

'Let's sort ourselves out for a brew and some breakfast. We've missed being in place by first light so we'll approach a different way. Up that hill, Buncie, and we can get a good watch down on to the main tac-route across the plains.' This was the first of three tours conducted on the course. Graham Geary, an experienced tour NCO, already several years with the Mission, together with Paul Bunce, an equally experienced tour driver, were instructing as much as assessing my learning and assimilation from mistakes. They would only pass me if they thought they could subsequently work with me for real.

Sidbury Hill is a well-known landmark to most soldiers in the British Army. We approached it from a track below, up through a straggly copse using a well-covered approach to get ourselves on to the top without being spotted. There was some white mine tape attached to a wooden post, blowing in the wind at the entrance to the approach. As a Royal Engineer I put it down to some untidy night work that was missed during clear-up.

We started the ascent up the slope. It was quite steep and difficult going even for the G-wagon. There was an almighty thud on the back of the vehicle as what I assumed to be a log kicked up against the back. Then there were several thuds in quick succession and suddenly on all four sides soldiers, roughly dressed in Soviet uniforms and brandishing pick helves, surrounded the vehicle. I saw one land on my side door. They surrounded the vehicle, putting two men on the bonnet, two round the back and two on each side. We couldn't move without running them over. They ran to each door and tried to open them but they were all locked. They checked the windows to see if they could get a finger in. I noticed shovel blades with which they could have forced a window down had there been a gap.

The suddenness of their arrival was quite alarming, momentarily throwing me off balance. One minute we were haring around the countryside, the next we were off for a brew and belated breakfast when we were jumped by what appeared to be a bunch of hooligans in full flight, thoroughly enjoying themselves. There was no doubt that they were taking this seriously. I recalled

Graham and Buncie checking their doors just before the ascent up the hill. The bastards had set me up. Fortunately, my two back doors were locked so they couldn't get in. I stashed the cameras, binoculars, maps and all other evidence of being up to no good, just in time. A 'Soviet' officer in full dress uniform appeared out of the bushes and motioned me to wind my window down.

'Not a chance,' I mumbled inside the vehicle. 'What do you want?' I shouted in Russian through the window to him.

'What are you doing here? This is a Mission Restricted Area, therefore you have no business here.'

'I am a member of British Military Mission accredited to GSFG and we are transiting through to the next town.'

'Why don't you use the road?'

'Because I am a keen bird-watcher and there is a very interesting specimen in this wood that caught my eye.'

'You're lying.'

He had a point but it was time to cut the crap. 'I demand that you fetch the local Kommandant and explain on what grounds you have detained this vehicle.'

Miraculously, the Kommandant, a full colonel, appeared from the bushes and proceeded to pursue a different line of questioning, accusing me of spying, using cameras and that his men had seen them.

'That is not the case.'

'You have been observed driving recklessly around the local area and that is inconsistent with your status.'

Status. It was a key word. I'd forgotten to identify myself and more importantly confirm who he was.

'I demand to see your identity card,' I said to him.

He held it up to the window. I studied his pass and satisfied myself that it was genuine.

'I am Colonel Alexei Farenov, Kommandant of the local area, and I am not satisfied as to your identity.'

I pressed my Tour Pass flat against the inside of the window. Every tourer was issued one. Apart from identifying us, it stipulated how we were to be dealt with and conveyed an authority to travel in the DDR as well as a degree of immunity guaranteed by the Soviet Commander of GSFG to whom we were directly accredited. It wasn't working. One of the 'Soviet' soldiers busied himself with removing the offside wing mirror and I pointed it out to the Kommandant indignantly. He completely ignored it. I wound my window down slightly, sufficient for a pick helve to be jammed in. The Kommandant glanced at the soldier responsible but didn't ask him to remove it.

I wasn't sure what was more worrying, the implied threat of violence or the realisation that the Kommandant, who was our only official link in this tenuous chain of quasi-diplomatic immunity, couldn't give a stuff about the rules of the game. I was quite sure that if I had left my window or door open prior to his arrival one of them would have got in and ripped me out. That I could have lived with. That the Kommandant wasn't going to play by the rules was a more disconcerting and salutary lesson. There were no rules out in the DDR. Events did not follow a set sequence. Plans changed or went wrong. The unexpected always happened. There was no such thing as a certainty. Mental fatigue affected judgement. Day in, day out, night in, night out, the pressure was unrelenting. Time for decision making became scarce. Sleep was rationed harshly by your own self-discipline and all the time there was the constant demand to achieve objectives and perform beyond what you thought you were capable of giving. These incidents were designed to give you a hint of what might occur.

I discovered later that, on the previous course, one of these fake set-ups had got out of control and the Paras, playing the role of Soviet soldiers, who could always be relied upon to play their part to the full, actually set about an officer they had managed to drag out of the vehicle before they were called off. Twelve months later, when I came back to instruct the course with a year's touring under my belt and a greater understanding of what it meant to be 'detained', I realised that, despite the amateur dramatics, it was the psychology of the situation that was most worrying.

Suddenly you were in a situation where the niceties were stripped away, the link to reality and civilisation cut and the rules replaced by new ones. It was very difficult to train for the real thing because the real thing was as varied as the incidents themselves. Mission history was littered with beatings, rammings, incarcerations and, sadly, sometimes even deaths. Detentions were as varied as there were numbers of detentions. Sometimes they were amicable and lasted a couple of hours. Sometimes they were hostile and crews were incarcerated for days. Sometimes they were used to gain evidence against the Missions or as a quid pro quo to barter against equivalent Soxmis detentions. Our only sure means of defence was to avoid being seen in the first place. If seen, not to be detained. If detained, to keep your wits about you and get out with the minimum fuss possible.

The quasi-diplomatic status conferred upon Brixmis in 1946 under the auspices of the Robertson-Malinin agreement carried only as much weight as the prevailing diplomatic atmosphere. The more practical difficulty with detentions was that however long and however difficult the event it was time lost that should have been used getting on with the job. Being rammed, detained, chased off or shot at were all wasted time, taking you away from the mission you had been set. It was extremely unprofessional and fortunately only occupied a small part of our working time, but it had to be trained for.

Finally the Kommandant produced a piece of paper known as the Akt on which it was stated that I had been spying against a Soviet installation and that if I signed it I could be on my way. I refused to sign it and demanded to be on my way anyway. Signing any Soviet document was tantamount to writing your own *persona non grata* chit. They could put anything on there. Surprisingly, it had happened in Mission history that a tour officer had been caught out by signing an incident statement. Having made it work once they kept on trying it.

Just as suddenly as they appeared the make-believe Sovs retreated and the Kommandant took his cap off, motioning me to wind down the window. Graham nodded that it was all clear. I wasn't sure. 'Your Russian is good enough. Very formal, but some Kommandants will like that from a junior officer. If you've got something more original than bird-watching. . . . They've heard that one before. What about looking for unmarked graves of allied soldiers or simply proving routes commensurate with the agreement? Best really just to get to the point in a situation like this. They know what you're up to. What they need is proof, not necessarily to hold against you but for later to make a point in defence of something Soxmis does to us, or against the Mission in difficult negotiations or perhaps against you later when they've had enough of you. It'll be filed and used again somewhere. What you mustn't do is give them any proof, either physically or verbally. If you're not using the kit then stow it out of sight. If accused of anything then deny it. Don't sign the Akt or anything that might incriminate you. If you are asked to follow the Kommandant away from the scene of the detention and back to the Kommandatura[34] then make sure you don't get led through Permanently Restricted Area (PRA) without stopping him and informing him that you are aware of being led through, against your wishes, but with his permission. At the Kommandatura don't let the vehicle out of your sight and leave at least the driver or preferably driver and NCO in the vehicle. Always watch for damage to the vehicle or anything that you can pick up on back at the Mission when it's debriefed. The Tour NCO will keep the tape running and if you can get a photograph without being seen then all well and good. The doors were locked and windows were up so that's a start but don't rely on it if they're intent on getting in.'

I'd forgotten I'd just conducted the whole exercise in Russian. It was almost instinctive now.

The next target was an RAF ammunition complex situated close to a main railway line for ease of out-loading in transition to war. It had its own spur line joining the main line direct from the ammunition storage bunkers. The task was to measure the length of the spur and confirm whether or not it was single or double track. The length of the spur line would give an indication of how many flatbeds could be backed down it and therefore how much ammunition could be out-loaded per train, how many trains per day and so on. If it was double track then in theory the out-load could be much greater. We wanted to be there for first light in order to be around for shift change. The narks and detention had changed the schedule somewhat.

Shift change is a most vulnerable period for any organisation. The people clocking off, keen to get away, skimp over the detail of the night before. Those coming on are not yet fully alert and more interested in where their next cup of tea is coming from. This installation was guarded by a mix of police, MoD Security and servicemen. Again quite a vulnerable combination in some circumstances, where communications between different agencies break down through sheer rivalry. It's readily exploitable.

The installation was split in two by a private road, running parallel to the spur line. At each end of the road was an unmanned barrier and guard post. The guard post was empty and the barriers up for the shift change, allowing a quicker exchange of cars between on-coming and off-going shifts. Both complexes were

---

[34] Kommandatura: Regional Soviet military headquarters in the DDR responsible for the day-to-day running of their military region ranging from dealings with the press to security. They were also points of contact between GSFG and Mission crews when crews were detained. Ultimately obliged to preserve our integrity and the spirit of the Robertson-Malinin agreement, their performance was variable!

high fenced round the perimeter and completely separate from each other. Halfway down the road there was another guarded gate entrance, one for each half of the installation. Behind the fence dense vegetation restricted views in. Inside and beyond the entrance to the western compound, the left-hand one as we were looking from our OP, was the security headquarters. The spur line was inside the fence for the majority of its run in this western-most compound. It wasn't marked on any OS maps and the target file had only indicated that there was such a line. This was a real nuclear warheads storage depot.

The target file recorded that the last crew to visit the installation didn't get a measurement. We could see the start of it, and assuming it did nothing more complicated than run in a straight line, I decided it would be a simple matter of running the road between the two compounds, tripping the distance from the start to the exit point and on to where it joined up with the main railway system. It looked quiet enough for a run past. Easy if no one else had been there before!

'OK. Doors and windows. Ways out are forward first and back if necessary. There are no ways off to the side. No turning into the compound by mistake. We'll take it nice and slowly to observe the state of the track. I want to get a photograph of the single or double lines. Trip on my word. OK, let's go.'

We had pulled up some 200 metres away from the installation into an OP that looked down the central private road. We'd checked both ends to ensure that the barriers were up and unmanned. We went through our approach and because it was such a relatively simple operation we took the opportunity of revising the next target and the best route to it from where we were.

We moved off nice and slowly. I was slightly tense after this morning's surprises and yet really quite ready for anything now. We drove straight into the dividing road. 'There's the start. It's double track, nice and slow Buncie, I just want to get a good shot through the crap. OK. Trip now and out the other end.'

No sooner had we gone into the road than an unmarked but obvious police car pulled up behind us and blocked the way out. We'd gone right into the trap.

'Here we go again. Where did he come from?'

Buncie didn't need to be told to put his foot down to make for the other end, which made me think that this was no set-up to test me. But the far end was similarly blocked off. As we passed the security headquarters an MoD police Land Rover pulled out behind us.

'OK, slow down; let's see what they want.'

The Land Rover pulled up behind us and out got a couple of MoD policemen and a police sergeant.

'It's you lot again. Right, you Sir, are under arrest.' He pointed to me.

'You drive this vehicle into the compound and stay in it.' He pointed to Buncie and Graham.

I looked at Graham and Buncie but they had clearly not anticipated this. This was genuine.

Personnel on courses such as these, of necessity, had to be issued with 'get out of jail free' cards. They gave us a certain latitude with the police if caught by them for suspicious behaviour. They lasted only for the duration of each exercise and were issued with the strictest of warnings on how to use them and how not to abuse them. Northern Ireland was a major headache for the police. The last thing they needed was a bunch of apparent hooligans like us running around the countryside acting suspiciously and unable to identify ourselves. These policemen were not amused. It was a serious affair to them. HM Forces identity cards alone were not sufficient guarantee of proof. Our 'get out of jail free' cards were issued by the police themselves, serialised and signed by a high-ranking police officer. Now seemed to be an appropriate time to use them!

I got out of the vehicle and was escorted by the arm into the security headquarters. There was another G-wagon parked in the compound. Their team was clearly undergoing the same treatment. It dawned on me that the only reason we had been caught was probably because of them. They had probably been trapped the same way. I was impressed with their speed of reaction and also how they appeared to come from nowhere. It wasn't until later that I was told by the other crew that they were the second team through this target and that the first team with Keith, the SAS NCO, was the first team here and had managed to get through in the way that we had planned. The police had seen them but weren't quick enough to react before they were gone. But they did set up an ambush for each subsequent vehicle. We were the third through it that morning.

It was a very valuable lesson for work in the Mission. Speed and surprise usually worked once, but rarely twice. A second and certainly a third run in such a short space of time would be severely punished. Next time I would not have the 'get out of jail free' card.

I was put in a small room and left there. The walls were only hardboard and plaster. I could hear everything going on. My name was being read down a telephone to be checked against their own records. The room had a chair and a desk and that was it. As I was marched in I noticed a map of the place above the head of the main reception desk. I looked through the keyhole to see if I could see it. It was barely visible above the head of the guy who was checking my documents. I could make out a scale but couldn't read it. The railway line was clearly marked and so I memorised the length of it ready to check the scale when I left. No reason not to take advantage of my situation, I thought. If they were going to bring me into the heart of their security system then there must be something in here worth remembering.

Eventually I was let out, and sure enough, I had to go to the desk to sign for my 'get out of jail free' card again. I took every opportunity to chat to the guy while looking above him at all the detail that was printed on the map. I was able, virtually, to reproduce it later when I got back in the car. The whole procedure took an hour and a half. Another valuable lesson learnt: getting caught wasted time. We moved on rather sheepishly.

How did I get involved in all this? I thought back to my first real knowledge of the existence of this unit called Brixmis. It was 1987 when I met Chippy Wood who was the training officer in the Royal Engineers' amphibious regiment in Hameln. He was known to have had a colourful background in some exotic posting that we weren't allowed to talk about. He had been a Tour NCO with the Mission from 1972 to 1975. So I asked him what the story was and what they did.

'They won't call you Sir. It's all first-name terms. It's very claustrophobic because you eat, sleep – if you get any – and live in your vehicle. It's relatively dangerous and very tiring. You've got to be able to fit in and cope with the pressure.'

Sometimes a violent approach was impossible to avoid. When cornered it was neither clever nor rewarding to get involved physically with the Soviets. Staff Sergeant Graham Geary is accosted by Major Nikonov and manages to resist retaliation.

It was extremely trying on the patience but mixing it would only give them ammunition. If you couldn't turn at least three or four cheeks then you would become fair game for subsequent provocation and ultimately useless.

'But what exactly do they do?'

'You can guess what they do. They spy. How they do it is another matter.'

I was looking around the Army for something to do. I was twenty-seven years old and rapidly coming to appreciate that the higher up the promotion tree one progressed, the more quickly one was put behind a desk and asked to fly it. All this realisation at the relatively junior rank of captain with two years' seniority and the sum total of nearly four years in the Army was a touch premature but I felt that time was running out for a real-life posting to come my way. I had to find it myself.

My first and thoroughly enjoyable posting as a Troop Commander with the Royal Engineer Harrier Support Force saw me travel from Germany to Belize. It was cut short to take on the Regimental Headquarters Troop back in Ripon, covering for the unexpected move of its officer to other duties. It carried with it the tasks of Regimental Signals Officer, Regimental Intelligence Officer and many other general gophering duties but actually very little meaningful responsibility.

RHQ Troop was the dumping ground for the unfit, the difficult, the indebted and the incapable. The most important thing that I seemed to be doing was managing the soldiers' welfare. Fortunately, the outgoing officer, probably realising the intense frustration I was about to suffer, booked me in for the Regimental Intelligence Officers' Course at Ashford in Kent, shortly after I took on the job. It was a very enlightening course at that age but served only to prompt more questions than answers. It further increased my frustration on return to Ripon when it was made very clear that the last thing the regiment needed was an enthusiastic intelligence officer. Fortunately, some five months later, I was moved on to Germany as a squadron second-in-command. But the damage was already done. I was becoming restless for an exciting time and moving to yet another seemingly administrative position was not the answer.

We did lots of training in our capacity as 1 British Corps' amphibious bridging capability. But I didn't get to drive the boats or build the bridges, merely coordinate them. Out of the exercise season I organised and planned the adventure training for the squadron but I didn't get to go on it myself. It was much more important that the squadron had a leg on the ground back at base in Hameln. That leg was me.

The Junior Division Staff College course, which followed very quickly after arriving in Hameln, crystallised my thoughts. On the one hand it was becoming very clear that in order to get on in the Army one had to do the right things. Attend Staff College. Make your first pension date. Complete an officer commanding tour, preferably in Germany because the perceived wisdom at the time indicated that the real threat would come from the Soviet Union. A couple more staff jobs prior to commanding a regiment. Two more staff jobs to notch up another pension date and before you knew it you would all be brigadiers pushing for general!

On the other hand there were three guest speakers throughout the six-month-long course who held my attention from the moment they started and helped me to see slightly beyond the norm that was being carefully laid out for us. One was General Sir Peter de la Billière who simply, effectively, eloquently and to the surprise of many, from a sitting position in the middle of the auditorium a million miles from the stage, recounted his military life story, spent principally with the SAS.

Another was Charles Watt, an Intelligence Corps officer, very jovial, very round, enormously clever and yet very down-to-earth. He was advertised as a specialist from Ashford dealing with all aspects of the Warsaw Pact. He made us look at the West's military capability from the Soviet point of view. It was a mixture of pure treason and lecture-theatre badger baiting. He disagreed that the Soviet equipment was inferior. He disagreed that learning tactics by rote was necessarily a handicap. He argued strongly that superiority of numbers alone might carry the day. He introduced the Soviet concept of reinforcing success and abandoning failure. Finally, he talked of the culture of the Soviet way of life, the history and geography that shaped the people into what they were now. He implied that it was by no means certain that we would win an encounter with the Warsaw Pact. One of the course asked him a question in broken Russian that he returned fluently. Having struggled through O-level Russian myself and then dabbled with it again for three years at university as a subsidiary subject, I was desperately impressed. He was astute enough to translate the reply quickly for the benefit of the rest of the audience, for it was quite clear that the questioner was already out of his depth.

Finally, a most intriguing familiarisation talk by an officer from 14 Intelligence Company, Northern Ireland. He spoke of such daring-do on the streets of Belfast that we would have probably all signed up on the dot had it not been well known that Northern Ireland was not the place for us Staff College hopefuls. It distracted from the planned schedule of one's career pattern. He called it Special Duties and explained that it was basically an intelligence-gathering function conducted undercover. This was more like it.

The intriguing thing about all three was that they spoke passionately, without notes and, unlike the normal lecturers, didn't ask us stupid questions precisely one minute after they had finished speaking. These were take it or leave it addresses. Get involved if you want but we can do without you if you aren't interested. Above all else they were real, they weren't about training, they weren't about what might be, they were about what was happening now and all three of them were on top of their subjects.

Once again they made me start thinking and I remembered my conversation about Brixmis with Chippy Wood back in Hameln. I knew that this was what I wanted to do but I still didn't have a bloody clue as to what this Brixmis organisation actually did. However, it was clear that several strands of my previous education and experience seemed entirely appropriate: my brief dalliance with intelligence at Ashford, my knowledge of both Russian and German languages, plus the fact that I had actually lived in Berlin for three years and understood the Berlin Wall only too well. It all convinced me that Brixmis was going to be my calling.

On return from the staff course I resolved to pursue the Brixmis option further. There were no Defence Council Instructions on the subject, which were the normal way of discovering forces-wide policies and schemes, covering everything from training course volunteers to the latest boarding-school allowance rates. If they did need volunteers then they certainly weren't advertising very hard. I had to ask.

'You do realise that it is overt spying, nothing more nothing less,' my Commanding Officer explained, adding, as if to present me with a moral dilemma, 'you will probably be asked to lie for your country.' It sounded very intriguing, although I couldn't work out the conundrum of overt spying. It seemed like a contradiction in terms. The images were running riot in my mind and I was resolved, or more accurately hooked, to find out more. I formally requested to apply for a place and an interview was duly arranged in West Berlin, where they were based.

For anyone driving to West Berlin for the first time in the days when the Wall was up and West and East Germanies were divided by the Iron Curtain it was a very intimidating journey. It was as close as you could get to living a spy thriller without the danger. The Berlin corridor was the single vehicular access route to West Berlin for British military personnel. It was manned at both ends by East German authorities whom the British rigorously refused to acknowledge and Soviet border guards who rigorously scrutinised ID cards, travel documents and vehicles for the slightest excuse to restrict journeys. The guard posts were strung out almost a kilometre deep at each end. The West German border crossing into East Germany was constantly patrolled by armed guards and dogs on loose wire runs. It was stuffed with lookout towers, searchlights, concrete chicanery to prevent speeding and the odd person taking photographs from behind one-way mirrors.

At the other end the crossing into West Berlin was equally daunting. The road linking the two was a concrete motorway with no central reservation, no lights and precious few signs and thus could double for an emergency runway. I knew that much from my time with the Harriers. Speeding was prohibited by the Royal Military Police (RMP), who were responsible for behaviour during the passage. You were not allowed to deviate from the motorway or indeed stop on the route at all, unless in an emergency. In the event of a breakdown you had to await the presence of the 'sweep', an RMP vehicle which regularly patrolled the corridor looking for any waifs and strays. You were clocked in and clocked out by the RMP and that was how they could tell if you were speeding or if you had broken down.

There was very little traffic on the motorway. The odd Trabant or Wartburg popped and pootled along. Because of the self-imposed speed restrictions they would overtake us belching out 2-stroke exhaust and looking ridiculous in the outside lane. There was nothing but wood or open fields on either side which, when it was dark, was punctuated only occasionally by the lights of a small village.

On reaching the Berlin end, the change was distinct and glaring. There were electric lights, road signs and thousands of BMWs and Mercedes all travelling as fast as they could. West Berlin was a bustling, industrious and prosperous city. The contrast was immediate and stark. Having lived in Berlin with my parents I had made this journey several times. It was only on this occasion that I was beginning to ask why was it like this. How had this all come about? The trip from darkness into light, from despair into hope, from the have-nots to the haves was so vividly exemplified by a trip down the Berlin corridor. It was only a simpleton who could not begin to question how and why this arrangement had been devised. A walk along the Berlin Wall served to confound your wildest explanation. It was a mystery and an anachronism. In one's strangest dreams you couldn't have come up with a method such as the Berlin Wall for dividing one city into two, splitting communities and families down the middle of their own houses. More bizarre still, a visit to Checkpoint Charlie and its museum revealed that German was still

Sachsenhausen concentration camp. A chilling and intensely moving place – silent and deathly. This pit is where hundreds of prisoners were hung.

killing German for trying to cross this man-made border from one Germany to another Germany. It was obscene and inexplicable. Passing through the final checkpoint and into the safety of West Berlin, I exhaled deeply.

I was due to meet the Chief of Mission the next morning. It was a curious title. The only chief I was familiar with was the chief clerk of my own squadron who was responsible for the day-to-day administration of the unit. However, this chief was the head of Brixmis, the unit I was trying to join. He was a brigadier and as such was a pretty rare species to a young captain. This particular brigadier was also a former director of the SAS, by the name of John Foley.

I made my own way to the Olympic Stadium Headquarters, having ascertained from someone in the officers' mess where Brixmis was located. It was strange that no one had come to meet me or, indeed, left me any details on my arrival. I was escorted by a security guard to the top floor and left outside a large iron-grilled gate behind which stretched a long corridor, bending round to the left and out of sight. I must have waited there for a good minute before I noticed the buzzer on the gate. I felt completely stupid and hoped that no one had been watching me from a CCTV and seen that I had just failed my first initiative test. The buzzer prompted a head to come out from one of the doors along the corridor on the other side of the grille. It was a lieutenant-colonel who introduced himself as the SO1 Ops. He took me down the curved corridor to a door marked 'Chief of Mission', told me to knock and go in.

I walked into a large office with a desk at one end, a side table on one wall, two easy chairs and nothing else. On each of the walls there were drawn curtains as if ready for some ceremonial unveiling of a dedication plaque.

'Come in, sit down,' a voice said. It certainly came from within the office but I couldn't pinpoint it . The curtains didn't seem to be concealing anybody.

'Won't be long,' the voice continued. I could hear clanging sounds as though there ought to have been a plumber in the room fixing the pipes. I wandered if this was another test.

'Finished.'

From behind the desk a tall slim man emerged with a spanner in one hand and a broad smile on his face. It was an instantly disarming pose that put me completely at ease. Here was a brigadier of SAS fame emerging from behind his desk having fixed his own radiator. A 20-minute-long innocuous discussion followed, made remarkable only by the fact that we did not discuss Brixmis, me or any potential connection thereto.

I left the Chief's office and went back to the SO1. I was informed that they knew a little bit about me already. They were aware of my Russian and German language ability. They thought that I was possibly suitable material for the unit but that there were no vacancies and that there were unlikely to be for at least two years, whereupon they would call me back for further interviews if I was still interested. With that I was escorted out of the office and directed back to the officers' mess. The whole thing had taken just under two hours and I was on my way back to Hameln. It seemed quite absurd. I knew nothing more about the unit than when I had arrived and my chances of getting anywhere near it were more remote than ever.

Many months later I was summoned back to the commanding officer, having dispelled all thoughts of an exciting posting, to be told that one of the Brixmis officers had been returned to his regiment. I was not told why. I was to pack immediately and join the Russian language course at Beaconsfield (Buckinghamshire) where I was now twelve months late!

I discovered much later, when researching the official history of the Mission, that 1987 was a most difficult time for Brixmis. On 30 May that year the West German, Matthias Rust, flew his light aircraft from Finland straight through Moscow's air defence system, known as the 'ring of steel', and into Red Square. The resulting shake-up in security measures was extensive and certainly felt by tour crews in the DDR. July had seen the latest vicious attack on a British Mission crew for some years, when Flight Lieutenant Dave Browne and Flight Sergeant Andy Peacock were assaulted outside their vehicle while carrying out an air OP for electronic countermeasure helicopters. The driver locked inside the vehicle was forcibly removed and dealt with similarly. All the tour equipment was stolen and Chief SERB[35], Colonel Pereverzev, was quoted as saying: 'A poacher must expect to have his equipment confiscated when caught.' Fair comment

---

[35] SERB: Soviet External Relations Bureau. The link between GSFG and the Missions. Staffed by GRU, they would, in the most charming and amiable way, pump us for information. Their role was liaison and as such their officers invariably spoke German, French and English as a matter of course.

but not in line with the spirit of the Robertson-Malinin agreement. The whole episode was sinisterly led by two civilian clothed thugs, thought to be GRU. There were no 'get out of jail free' cards then. Rudolf Hess had finally died in allied custody in August. The Mission, I was to discover, was closely involved with his imprisonment. In September that year Master Sergeant Charles Barry from the US Mission and, interestingly, a former British citizen until joining the US military, was shot and wounded in the arm while leaving an air tour OP in Walsleben, near Neuruppin The crew were ambushed by a group of Soviet air force officers and helpers who, in their enthusiasm to detain the tour, fired AK-74 automatic weapons at the vehicle. Seven rounds hit G-wagon number 29 and one round hit Master Sergeant Barry in the upper arm. He was awarded the Purple Heart in December of that year.

The language course was sheer hell. Given that I was twelve months behind the rest of the course, I couldn't afford a single day off. I had extra lessons and extra vocabulary each night just so that I could make the required interpreter grade by the end of the six months. It was the worst time in my army career and Beaconsfield was about as far from the real army as you could get. The only bright points on the course were the infrequent forays up to London with the naval submariners to try and eradicate everything I had stuffed into my memory hitherto. I passed the interpreter's exam but I only just made it. My German was still much better and more natural. It was difficult for me not to be formal in Russian as I was still trying to get the colloquialisms into my head. The course at Beaconsfield had been a nightmare trying to regain the ground that the other guys had on me by virtue of a full extra year's study. I was determined to make the best of the Ashford course given that I was starting it with everyone else.

The Special Duties intelligence course was indeed a godsend but it was merely an introduction to the work of Brixmis. It simply wasn't possible to replicate the exigencies of the real job because they were too varied. At one end of the spectrum they were looking for language ability in both Russian and German to undertake liaison roles from the ambassador's cocktail party to delicate exchanges across the Glienicke Bridge. At the other end they required a degree of 'roughy-toughy' soldiering, sufficient to cope with both the mental and physical demands that touring required: whether it was three nights out in -20°C watching a railway line, repeated three or four times with only a couple of days in between, or ducking and diving across a training area with a Spetsnaz unit on your tail, intent on ripping you out of the vehicle. You had to be able to cope with all the pressures as well as meet the basic requirements to complete the job. The skill of the drivers, the recognition skills of the NCOs and the collective experiences of the crew had to gel together to achieve set objectives, and more, if possible.

There was also a need by all ranks to show enormous understanding of the bigger political picture they were wrapped up in. What happened on the world stage affected how we were treated in East Germany. If the Soviets were pissed off then we carried the can. We were an easy target for retaliation. Brixmis was a very small but strategically significant cog in the wheel of the Cold War. It had unique access to all aspects of the Warsaw Pact in the DDR. It was an opportunity which had to be maximised while maintaining cordial and businesslike relationships. It was a game, but the game had very high stakes and very high rewards.

Brixmis was responsible for some of the most striking intelligence gains in the Cold War period and yet also responsible for brokering diplomatic relations, promoting confidence, trust and liaison at the highest level of military relations between Nato and the Warsaw Pact. How was it possible to train these people or select the right calibre in the first place? As I was to find out later, when it was my turn to meet and train potential new recruits, the final criteria really boiled down to whether or not we were trusted by the other members of the Mission and whether or not we could cope with the extreme demands, constant alertness, high standards of professionalism and painstaking attention to detail that a Brixmis tour required.

There was an unwritten probationary period before which a new tourer did not go out on his own without someone of experience. The rank was irrelevant. Learning how to operate behind the front lines had no better finishing school than on the job itself. The Ashford course allowed you to survive the probationary period. The real tricks of the trade, the operational techniques, the extra equipment and the clandestine tasks not mentioned on the course but routinely requested from all the customer agencies were taught while you were out there and handed down from generation to generation of tourers. It was the time done, experience gained and incidents lived through that marked you out as a survivor in the Mission. We seemed to get the right players for the game in the end.

CHAPTER THREE

Tommy

There was a short break after the Ashford course before having to report to Berlin. My trip up the corridor in 1989 was very different to the one I had undertaken eighteen months before in 1987 when I first applied to the Mission. I was much more aware of the surveillance techniques used at the crossing points, their likely location and who would be operating them. I was conscious of the rank, unit and distinguishing medals of the Soviet sentry that checked my Berlin Travel Document (BTD) and identity card. I could name every Soviet vehicle that I saw in the compounds tucked away from the glare of the floodlighting and I scoured the route for signs of military activity. Somewhere out there five Soviet armies and two East German armies were garrisoned directly opposite the British, French and American sectors of West Germany. I was going to be watching them.

August 1987 coincided with the death of Rudolf Hess. Hess had been appointed deputy führer to Adolf Hitler in 1933, designated successor in 1939, taken prisoner in Scotland in 1941 and sentenced to life imprisonment at the Nuremberg trials in 1946. He was incarcerated in Spandau prison, Berlin, where all the allies, particularly the Soviets, could keep an eye on him while sharing in his administration and guard duties. Given that Spandau was in the British occupied zone, the British Military Government had the job of supplying interpreters to liaise, on behalf of the doctor and prison governor, with the Soviet authorities when it was the Soviet turn to mount guard, as well as conduct interpreting duties between the Soviets and Hess himself.

In 1982, Mr Sanders, the civilian interpreter for the British Military Government, retired. Thinking that Hess would not live much longer, it befell Brixmis to provide temporary interpreting cover. As time wore on and there was little sign that Hess was either going to die or be released, the commitment to him and the rituals surrounding his imprisonment became greater and more involved. Brixmis created a dedicated section of interpreters responsible for the duties. Meetings between Soviet and Brixmis personnel were regular and conveniently placed for the backdoor exchange of information that might otherwise have necessitated more formal arrangements. As Hess became more frail he would regularly visit the British Military Hospital (BMH) just outside the Olympic Stadium, always accompanied by members of the interpreting staff, now formally known as the Spandau[36] section.

---

[36] Spandau: so called because of its early involvement with interpreting duties in Spandau prison for Rudolph Hess. Later called Training, Coordination and Support. The section

Hess died in the BMH on 17 August, two days before I visited Brixmis for my first interview. That Brixmis and Hess were connected was then unknown to me. Captain Bill Hogg, who was in charge of Spandau at the time, formally took responsibility for the body from the BMH. Given the sensitivity of the cadaver to the Soviets, he needed to have supporting paperwork before removing the body. In the absence of anything else a simple Army Form 1033 (normally used for the routine exchange of stores and equipment) was ignominiously issued by Brixmis to the BMH signifying responsibility for the body as follows:

> Prisoner No. 7
> Body Complete – 1
> Coffin Complete – 1

Hess was taken away from the BMH and cremated. There was no shrine to his past and therefore no focal point for the future. Spandau prison was razed to the ground and buried in the middle of Gatow airfield, several feet underground. A new Naafi complex was built on the site and in the tradition of Berlin black humour became known as 'Hesscos'. The final story of Hess has still to be told; rumour has it that he was poisoned. Knowingly or unknowingly, helped or self-inflicted, it remains a mystery, possibly known only to those directing his incarceration. Rumour also has it that not all his personal possessions were completely destroyed. Speculation suggests that while many of his personal effects carried with him on his plane to Scotland in 1940 were recovered and destroyed, some of his most private and intimate possessions remain under very closely guarded lock and key.

Like the connection to Hess, the extent of Spandau section's operation was not finally revealed to me until my third tour. Its role in the Mission, conveniently disguised by its trips to Spandau jail, went far beyond simple interpreting duties. Soon after Hess died the section was renamed with the deliberately bland title of Training, Coordination and Support. It concealed the fact, as much from our own manning vultures as from the Soviets, that we suddenly appeared to have three dedicated interpreters without a job. Certainly the Soviets might have wondered what this posse of very experienced linguists, all of them Intelligence Corps, might do now. But they were not 'on-pass'[37], so in effect not really of numerical concern to SERB. It was assumed that SERB knew they were Intelligence Corps, but it wasn't something we advertised. Like all the Intelligence Corps and SAS staff with the Mission, they wore different cap badges for the duration of their posting so as not to cause offence or reveal who was doing what in the Mission. In the same vein, some of the NCOs were temporarily commissioned in the field in order to take out tours when tour commitment was high, thereby ensuring that the officer quota of tour passes was permanently filled.

---

in Brixmis responsible for all intelligence material gathered requiring specialist Russian interpretation and analysis.

[37] On-pass: only thirty-one tourers were allowed into the DDR at any one time. They were issued with Soviet passes and this became known as 'on-pass'.

Not surprisingly, Training, Coordination and Support remained known in the Mission as Spandau. Nor was it a surprise to find out that Hess was not their only commitment. They had been industrious in several other areas. Like tour officers who spent part of their time justifying their official title as Liaison Officers by engaging on meetings and interpreting duties with SERB but for the most part toured East Germany, Spandau's three Intelligence Corps personnel had been hard at work using their outstanding linguistic abilities to set up a whole new avenue of intelligence product. Clearly, they had used the routine contact with their Soviet equivalents to glean low-level information but their real benefit had been completely unconnected with these official duties. Spandau had set up and initiated the Mission in Operation Tomahawk, or a Tommy, as it became known in the trade.

'We'll drive past and just take a look at it, Boss. Take a note of what's happening, who's there, see if anything's changed. You know the form. Try not to look too interested in it. Don't be seen looking at it by anything that passes us. We don't want to attract any attention. We're just driving past. Mac, no stopping, just take it nice and slow, straight past.'

Graham Geary, my instructor only a few months ago, was now my Tour NCO. Nothing much had changed. He was still very much a fount of touring knowledge and far more experienced in its techniques and skills than I was. The difference was that having deemed me suitable for the Mission, it was his intention that I should now meet the very highest standards that the Mission operated by and if possible take them on and improve them for the next generation of tourer. He was utterly unselfish and in the great tradition of the relationship between NCO and Officer in the British Army, he made me look good.

Graham had the task of introducing me to the niceties of Operation Tomahawk. It hadn't even been mentioned at Ashford. It was only my third tour and this was my first Tommy. I was beginning to realise that there was a lot that I hadn't learned or been shown on the course. The course was merely an instruction in the basics, as well as a chance for the instructors to observe you to see if you might be able to survive out on the ground. The full mysteries of touring would not be revealed until in-theatre. There were certain operational details, Tomahawk being one of them, that were not passed on to potential tourers for fear of releasing information to someone who didn't complete the course. Furthermore, the course was tri-national, with both French and American participants. Both had their own additional objectives over and above routine touring. Operation Tomahawk was not a tri-mission task and results were not always disseminated to them. Operation Tomahawk was an exceptionally successful and closely guarded secret and yet it was a stunningly obvious undertaking. The operation itself was as revolting and horrible as it was rewarding.

'OK, Mönchenholzhausen is on your left-hand side. The entrance exit is coming up now. It's one way in, one way out. Seen?'

'Seen.'

'It's not fenced. See the barracks on the skyline and the training area between it and the barracks?'

'Seen.'

'There's a track on the far side from the barracks down to it. See it?'

'Seen.'

'OK. Swing round to your 7 o'clock. See the hedge line about one 'klick'[38] on the far side?'

'Seen.'

'Come down to the first gap in the hedge from the skyline.'

'Seen.'

'That's the vehicle lay-up point. It's about 600 metres away from the far edge.'

The detailed target reconnaissance, conducted on the move, was punctuated by Graham's check questioning and my confirmation. The vehicle slowed as if by magic while Bud MacKenzie, the driver, accommodated for my lack of observation. The question and answer session didn't proceed until Graham was sure that I could see all the things he was indicating.

This was already my second tour with Graham. He was my designated chaperone. The other tour had been with Ian Cameron-Mowatt, a Royal Signals officer and senior army tour officer on the Mission. Any new tactics, techniques, equipment and ideas concerned with the ground tours would be run past Ian before they went further to Ops. Andy Farmer, the senior air tour officer, took on the equivalent role for the air tours.

On the first two tours Graham and Ian had merely shown me the ropes and put into practice, with slight modification, some of the tricks and procedures learnt at Ashford. It was quite normal to be getting such expert attention so early on. John Wallis, the other new tour officer who was on both courses with me at Beaconsfield and Ashford, was getting the same treatment.

My first two tours had been quite eventful. The first had seen us uncover a completely new vehicle-mounted satellite dish at Wismar and an unidentified aerial complex in use with the Spetsnaz brigade at Mirow. The second was my introduction to the Black Banana and a return to Wismar to obtain more detailed imagery of the radar already designated by Nato as 'Sky Board Bravo'. The Black Banana was a long-range directional microphone about 5 ft long that allowed us to record for the first time the rate of fire of the still relatively new 2S6 self-propelled, anti-aircraft gun from a range of 4 kilometres, deep inside PRA.

We had now finished the breaking-in process. We were moving on to the extracurricula activities. It was immediately obvious that this was a different type of target: altogether more important, more disastrous if compromised and therefore more meticulously executed. Graham had conducted my first tour with enormous humour and style. At times I thought he almost welcomed a reaction from the Sovs to liven up his day. But he had learnt not to provoke them, rather to carry out the reconnaissance tasks without creating a single ripple in the pond. That way it was possible to achieve so much more.

It wasn't always possible to avoid trouble. Graham and many tourers like him down the years received their share of close scrutiny from the Sovs. However, this target was conducted more formally and more seriously. The implications arising from getting it wrong had been made very clear in the briefing and he wasn't going to let anyone cock it up, whoever they were. We'd gone through it all back in the Mission with Ops. It sounded pretty straightforward. The only difference

---

[38] 'klick': slang for kilometre.

was that we had collected a special brief from Spandau and I had been issued with some kit that looked remarkably as though it had come from the DDR itself.

'The Sovs use that track. OK, the target's not very big . . .'

'What! How the hell are you supposed to cover all that?' I interrupted.

Graham turned to face me in the back, a big grin all over his face.

'We're going to be there for at least three hours, Boss, more if we strike lucky. And Boss, this is small!'

I sat back and thought about this one. Our target for tonight's night work was a dump . . . literally. A Soviet rubbish dump.

Operation Tomahawk, previously known as Tamarisk (the name changed at the whim of Spandau, usually because someone outside the 'need-to-know' circle was briefed about it and we didn't trust them to keep their mouth shut) was a very well-kept secret. Operation Tomahawk, a Tommy or just plain 'doing a dump', was the systematic exploitation of Soviet and East German waste disposal tips. The logic was simple, the execution horrendous.

The East German infrastructure was not comparable to that of the West. In large towns and cities the disposal of rubbish was crudely organised. There were designated areas to tip waste but it was primitive by comparison with Western standards. The dumps, sometimes fenced off from the public for safety but usually not, were normally tended during the day by a site-guard placed on the exit and entrance and possibly worked by a bulldozer and operator. In rural areas they were not even that well organised. They were usually abandoned by the official contractors come nightfall. I don't recall coming across one that was ever lit up at night other than by their proximity to local towns or installations. There was a route in for tipping lorries and this was usually their way out. Some started off life as big holes in the ground with vague guarantees to fill them later: most were not. Most simply started as convenient spots to fly tip and grew from there. The Soviets were no exception to this carefree disposal of waste, quite often simply dumping their rubbish outside the back door of their barracks. Only around large cities did there seem to be some sort of municipal plan for the disposal of waste.

Either way they ended up the same: huge piles of rubbish, badly maintained, a stinking, rotten eyesore that attracted all manner of carrion, and us. They were regularly scavenged at night by the local population for any second-hand goods that might still be useful. Where there were no workers on them by day then it was quite normal to see locals scavenging them in the open. They were infested with rats and all manner of small rodents. Packs of wild dogs would routinely visit them. Above all else the smell was probably the most noticeable and striking phenomenon. It was indescribable.

Four years previously I had the unfortunate task of recovering two dead bodies as part of a Royal Engineer diving operation in Belize. They had been missing for nearly three months in the humidity and heat of the Belizean jungle. We eventually found them in a waterfall rock pool, trapped underwater. The bodies were distended and bloated by their long exposure to the water. Upon recovery from the water their stench filled the valley. The smell of rotting flesh is a powerful and repellent odour that you can remember years later. Two of the divers who had struggled with the bodies from the waterfall edge to a flat area on the cliff were instantly sick as they placed them down. Smelling the air as we passed this rubbish tip flashed me back to the jungle and the recovery of those two bodies.

I recounted the story to Graham and Mac. Graham, obviously keen to go one better, switched to story-telling mode. He recounted how, during the course of his last Brixmis posting, some eight years earlier, the Mission had learnt that Soviet soldiers with chemical warfare injuries among other horrific wounds from the war in Afghanistan were being evacuated back to East Germany for treatment. Brixmis was tasked to recover evidence for further medical examination. It was presumed that they were being recovered to the DDR in order to receive the best possible treatment the Warsaw Pact could offer. More cynically, it was considered that they were being returned to the DDR in order to keep them out of the Soviet Union, thus avoiding a possible political outcry.

By 1981 the Soviet-Afghanistan war had been going on for two years and was attracting much public criticism from the 'Babushkas' at home, let alone the rest of the world. This internal criticism from such a respected quarter as the matriarchal grandmother, the head of every Soviet family, was a relatively new phenomenon. It proved difficult to ignore or extinguish. The last thing the authorities wanted was to compound the difficulties with the evidence.

There followed some of the most harrowing work ever undertaken by the Mission. A spate of Tommies was ordered, centred on the most advanced hospitals in East Germany. Hauls from their refuse dumps included used syringes, bloodstained surgical dressings and human remains. The latter, usually limbs or intestinal remains with shrapnel still embedded and wounds still evident, were recovered and returned to the Mission. The dumps were frequently signposted with 'plague' warnings, enough to keep off the most curious and hard-up East German. It was disgusting work by any standard and of course it was carried out after dark, usually between 2 and 4 a.m.

Graham had been on the Mission at the time and was part of one of the teams that undertook the task. It was a gruesome haul and together with information gleaned by MI6 in Afghanistan it proved what we had suspected, that first the Soviets were using chemical weapons against the Mujahidin and second, that they had probably inadvertently used it on their own troops. Tomahawk provided some exceptionally stunning finds on these targeted dumps and the reasons were very simple. The first revolved around the general sanitary and social conditions of life in a Soviet military installation. The second was linked to the troop rotation pattern of GSFG generally.

The average Soviet soldier was not supplied with disposable toilet paper in his rations, as British or American soldiers are, and furthermore, the Soviet army in East Germany, being an army of occupation, was unlikely to have it available in their barracks, let alone on exercise. As far as they were concerned they were on operations, whether they were in barracks or out on the training ground, and as such the luxuries that Western soldiers were supplied with through their respective Naafis or local shops were simply not available to them. The most abundant supply of paper for carrying out the most basic of ablutions was that officially supplied as part of their work of occupation: military documentation. This would include signals paper, notebooks, letters from home, Pravda, Izvestia,

The recovery of unexploded ordnance was sometimes no more sophisticated than this!

private notebooks and all manner of officially supplied training books and technical manuals. The list was endless and we exploited it to the full.

The annual troop rotation programme that GSFG practised every winter through to spring necessitated a percentage of troops to be returned to the Soviet Union for duties elsewhere and be replaced by a fresh round of new recruits in East Germany. These movements were of interest to the Missions in their own right. We would be able to deduce where the new intake was coming from and where the old troops were going to and thus provide an insight into the bigger picture of the Soviet Orbat and how they organised themselves. One of the consequences of such a large move, involving many thousands of troops in one go, was that everything an individual soldier had acquired in his two-year stay was abandoned prior to leaving. It simply couldn't all go on the plane home.

Undoubtedly there were appropriate security procedures to follow with the disposal of classified documentation at rotation time. But laziness and the desire for a shortcut can take their unsuspecting toll on the most vigilant of armies, as even the fully professional armed forces of the United Kingdom have found out. People do not follow the rules and the more people there are the more times the rules are broken. It was an important means of gathering intelligence. In fact the information gained was so complete, its authenticity so indisputable that it progressed the intelligence puzzle in startling leaps and bounds.

Like all material recovered from these dumps, it was initially sorted back in Brixmis for onward transmission to the appropriate agency in the UK. Written material was retained by Spandau for initial assessment and photographic record by Special.[39] Reports were written by Weapons[40] or Spandau as appropriate.

The only regret throughout all the years of the Tomahawk operation was the realisation that for all the good stuff we collected there must have been significantly more that we could not retrieve. It was quite often covered up by subsequent tipping, perished by the effects of weather, particularly rain, which turned everything to papier mâché, or bulldozed over during an infrequent tidy-up.

There were certain operational reasons that prevented us from carrying out a Tommy. Occasionally the dump was being scavenged by Soviet soldiers themselves. It was not an uncommon occurrence given their own poor social conditions. Alternatively a recent fall of snow that would reveal tracks back to an obviously parked vehicle would postpone it. Or if there was the slightest suspicion that the target had been compromised in any way during a final recce then we would never appear for the actual task. There was little possibility, given all these extenuating circumstances, that the intelligence we might gain from a Tommy could have been deliberately planted or shown to us. How could you possibly ensure that the proverbial needle in one haystack of many haystacks would be picked up at the right time and by the right people? Some of the target dumps covered several acres. There were thousands of them scattered throughout the DDR and the timing of our collection was completely random. There was little chance that we would recover planted information. The enormity of an operation to ensure that would have been staggering and so the integrity and value of the intelligence gathered was of exceptional quality.

In his previous posting at Brixmis, Graham had also been involved with one of the most significant finds in Mission history, a find guaranteed to prolong the operation for as long as it could be maintained. On a Soviet tip outside the back gate of one of the Neustrelitz installations, recently used by the outgoing tank troops returning to the Soviet Union, he helped to discover documents pertaining to the composition of armour for the currently in-service T-64 and successor T-80 tanks.

This discovery was of enormous technical intelligence significance. It showed that the perceived levels of titanium and vanadium used to strengthen their alloy composite armour had been vastly undervalued. Therefore, the calculated protection levels that had been derived for these Soviet main battle tanks had been significantly underrated. In short, it became apparent that it was unlikely we could penetrate their armour with existing anti-tank weapons, such as the 84-mm Karl Gustav, and certainly not the throw-away 66-mm Light Anti-Tank weapon. The ramifications of this single piece of intelligence were staggering. Not only did

---

[39] Special: the section in Brixmis responsible for all photographic development, enlargement, reproduction and official PR work. A twenty-four-hour job towards the end of Mission life. It was called Special in order to avoid any inference of photographic intelligence gathering.

[40] Weapons: the Brixmis section responsible for all technical intelligence targeting, gathering and analysis. The fount of all knowledge recognition wise, and the section most likely to wet itself when a scoop was captured.

they have more tanks than us but they were now shown to be immune to the entire range of our hand-held anti-tank armoury. The only thing that could possibly defeat them was our own tank armament and that, too, was questionable.

The decision to build more tanks or invest heavily in new anti-tank missiles was singularly and significantly influenced by this find. The 'long rod penetrator' or Armour Piercing Fin Stabilised Discarding Sabot programme was born, rapidly introduced into service ahead of time and undertaken regardless of budget. These new missiles were designed to deliver more penetration energy at the point of impact in order to overcome this newly evaluated armour protection level. The value of the Mission's intelligence-gathering function was established beyond doubt and Operation Tomahawk, coded Secret, was expanded. Tomahawk remained a closely guarded secret to the very end of Mission life. The parameters were known by a few and its conduct was undertaken by a handful. Even within the Mission, it was not disclosed to everyone who worked there.

We proceeded to the next checkpoint on our recce which was designated as first RV[41] should anything go wrong. This was a more obvious landmark, a crossroads, another kilometre away from the lay-up point, again for the benefit of the driver. Only the tour officer and NCO would actually walk onto the target. As always, the driver stayed with the vehicle. Normally we would expect to return to the lay-up point for the vehicle but if, for whatever reason, the driver had to leave then the first RV was where we would meet up with him again. It was important for all members of the crew to be familiar with this point on the ground should the need arise.

I often thought how much more difficult it was for the driver on these operations. He was on his own, in the dark, miles from anywhere, the target of every Sov in the country, trying to hold his nerve for two, three or four hours while the other two were away from the vehicle. The driver was always given very specific instructions as to 'actions-on' in the event of him being compromised. In all cases if he could get away then he was to do so.

Although the vehicle could be up to a kilometre away from the dump, if it was spotted and recognised it may not have been too difficult a leap of the imagination in some bare-arsed places to work out a connection between our presence and the dump. Additionally, it was rare that a driver would be out on his own. That would have been difficult to explain if caught and would have prompted a more thorough search for the two other crew members out on the ground. While touring was normally done in crews of three, it was reasonably often that we travelled in pairs for more mundane or smaller tasks, such as check mapping, visiting industrial sites or check-measuring civilian bridge lengths against satellite imagery measurements.

Only in 1988 an incident involving Corporal Douggie Murray as a very new tour driver had resulted in him becoming separated from his crew, forcing him to drive round for a whole day on his own before being able to pick up his separated colleagues. He had been pursued throughout, avoiding capture and several attempts at ramming that had resulted in a punctured tyre, while the two

---

[41] RV: rendezvous.

out on the ground had holed up until they could return to the prearranged RV safely. It was a remarkable achievement.

If the vehicle could leave the lay-up quietly, pre-empting a possible compromise, then so much the better. The driver would then go to the RV, visiting it every twenty minutes or so. The RV was prominently sighted for obvious reasons. The two out on the ground had no map or compass in case they were accidentally dropped or ripped out of a pocket on the target and thus compromise the whole operation if found by someone else. Therefore, they had to be able to get to the vehicle with the minimum of navigation difficulty. It had to be done in the dark, without lights and rapidly, to prevent crews suffering exposure during some of the harsher winter nights.

If the first RV was itself compromised then depending upon the circumstances we usually nominated a second. The vehicle could then yo-yo between the two, waiting to be flagged down. In the event of the vehicle being compromised suddenly and the driver unable to take evasive action then he would be instructed to make a public departure with lights on. If he couldn't get away, then he would accidentally sound the horn or put on four-way flashers, depending upon his distance away from the target, in order to alert the remaining crew members who might still be on the dump.

The chance of being detained on or near a dump was not treated lightly but it was simply not an option. The potential loss of the intelligence gained from this operation was too great. To my knowledge there was never such a detention. If there was any doubt at all then the target was abandoned in favour of another go at a later opportunity. Some of the most valuable intelligence was still coming off these sites right up to the last day the Mission was in existence, thanks to the maintenance of the operation's integrity.

When the last remnants of Brixmis left Berlin in 1991, nearly two years after the Wall came down, the systematic rifling of Soviet dumps was continued by the BND.[42] That year one of their operatives was shot and wounded while scavenging one of these dumps. However, I have no doubt that it is still a valuable intelligence source used in different ways by most intelligence gathering organisations from the Foreign Office to the media.

In the early years Tomahawk operations were only carried out by the SAS representatives on the Mission. Later, as touring techniques and crews became more sophisticated and capable, it was undertaken by all tour officers and NCOs considered suited for the task by Ops. It was not usually carried out by part-time tourers, unless the product or the tasking was pertinent to their responsibilities and thus vital that they should understand the difficulties involved. It was certainly not conducted by the Chief or Deputy Chief of Mission other than by way of introduction so that he might get a feel for it. It was only introduced to new tourers by an experienced hand, usually a senior tour NCO or tour officer, when it was felt appropriate that he should become initiated in such events.

---

[42] BND: Bundesnachtrichtendienst. Federal Intelligence Service. West Germany's foreign intelligence agency, loosely equivalent to British MI6. Took over some of the Mission's roles in the early 1990s.

The G-wagon's cross-country capability was unsurpassed by any other vehicle the Mission ever used.

It presented the usual source protection dilemma. The intelligence product was so valuable that more was always requested. Statistically, doing more would inevitably result in a compromise some time or other. I undertook a Tommy almost every tour after my first ten or so tours, occasionally two a night and certainly on every night there would be a planned target if current activity hadn't taken priority.

We selected a second RV on the other side of the dump. It was a large tree all alone on the main road which we reckoned would be skylined and visible from the dump itself. It gave no cover to the car but we could lie low in the ditch if necessary until it passed for a pick-up. Having circled the target in daylight we sat and watched it for an hour or so, well concealed and well away from civilisation.

'Here we go,' said Graham. I looked in the direction he was pointing to under the dashboard. It was up towards the installation. An old ZIL-131 came out of the camp and made its way down the track. Its normal troop-carrying body had been removed and replaced with a tip-up skip-like contraption. It looked like a botch job. Its front bonnet and grille were painted light blue, designating it a quartermaster's service vehicle. It meandered down the path into the corner of the dump nearest the barracks and proceeded to extend the perimeter of the tipping area by another couple of cubic metres of rubbish.

'Mmm. Fresh today. That's our start point I reckon, Boss.'

He was rubbing his hands with delight. This was bizarre. That pile alone was the size of a dustcart's worth. This was not going to be easy.

We disappeared off to complete the schedule of other targets that was part of my introduction to this area. Some three or four hours later we were on a rail watch. Nothing of interest was passing, certainly nothing of interest to us. Rail watches lasted three hours minimum. Over the years it had been established that military equipment trains ran at such intervals. This was determined by the length of time it took to load a train from the ramp on to the flatbeds rather than the vagaries of the East German train timetable. In theory we could have arrived just after a train had passed, hence for complete security of mind you watched for just over three hours. If a kit train did come past then you waited another three hours for the next one. And so it went on until one didn't turn up within the three-hour rule.

This standard operating procedure (SOP), as part of current activity, overruled doing a dump because the dump would still be there when all the trains had gone. It could play havoc with the tour schedule, extending you beyond the three days that you normally spent out and reducing your time to the next tour. Worse, it meant postponement of the Tommy until 4 a.m. and that was knackering.

Sleep became more and more necessary as a three- or four-day tour progressed. Events on the ground prohibited it. The cumulative effect over a pass period of four or five months generated enormous tiredness and stress. That was partly why we toured with three in a vehicle rather than two, as was usual for the Americans and French. They had fewer tour passes accredited to them and so were at a disadvantage from the start. But they tried to put out as many tours as us by using only two man crews. Given that the driver never left the vehicle, it would take a superman to complete in three days what a three man crew could do in the same time.

Fortunately, or perhaps unfortunately, this particular rail watch produced nothing. My mind was wandering back to the rubbish tip. I'd seen it all in the file before the tour but in reality these dumps were more enormous, repulsive and dangerous places than they seemed on paper. I was having severe misgivings about it, both from the point of view of security and, rather selfishly, from the point of view of my own health. There was little opportunity to get away if caught out on the ground or on foot. Bullets are quicker than feet and vehicles but at least the G-wagon offered a degree of protection. God knows what was out on these dumps that you might catch. Used needles were commonplace, whether they were from the installation medical centre or used by the soldiers themselves in an effort to occupy their spare time. Discarded bits of rusty metal tore through clothing and punctured the skin. Rotting vegetables and kitchen waste oozed like a slurry around your wrists as you delved for an elusive bit of paper that caught your eye. Then there were the animal dangers. We'd seen dogs on our run past and the target file back in Berlin warned that dogs quite often roamed this particular dump at night. We had no guaranteed procedures to deal with dogs, wild or of the guard variety. Various gadgets including ultrasound beams were being looked at but never brought to trial. The best method was usually to convey submission and withdraw gracefully. Finally, the file mentioned that it was not uncommon for local East German civilians to scavenge this particular dump at dark. So what would we do if we ran into them, have a chat about the resident chef's health and safety programme? To be truthful I had not really been concentrating that whole afternoon or evening. And we were doing a small one. You could have put Wembley stadium into it.

It was about 1 a.m. when we came off the nearby rail watch and ran the escape route in reverse. Vehicle lights had gone off the moment we left the main road and joined the minor road running west and straight towards the dump. We stopped on the roadside well before the lay-up point. The windows were cranked and we listened for nearly ten minutes. It seemed like an eternity. Nothing. It was quiet, eerily quiet, so quiet I was suspicious. However, the smell was real enough. Almost 2 kilometres away it was discernible. Mac paused to put his PNGs on.

With good night vision it was possible to drive unaided in most conditions. In this case it was not so much to see the road but what else was around. If it had been an installation or a ramp then we would probably have not used PNG, preferring to maintain night vision and observe what was lit up for us. In this particular case it was more important not to get bogged in or run into a ditch and thus be forced to undertake a noisy winching manoeuvre so close to a sensitive target. Moreover, it was important to know if we were being watched, and PNG gave us that edge. We stopped again, just beyond the first RV.

As usual, what we had seen by daylight looked significantly different at night. The crossroads were deserted and barely recognisable now that the cover on all sides hid it from view. Graham pointed out the spot where he and I should meet up if anything happened to us out on the dump, if we were separated ourselves and the vehicle was no longer at the lay-up point. He instructed Mac to be facing east if he felt safe to wait here or approach it going east if he didn't feel safe to stop. He was to wait no longer than two or three minutes before moving on and return every twenty minutes. If he felt that this RV was unsafe then he was to revert to the second and drive past the tree, also at twenty-minute intervals.

Beyond that there were no instructions. There was no room for it going wrong and there was no plan for a detention. You could easily run out of answers to 'what if' scenarios. The calibre of personnel on this unit could deal with the 'what ifs' as and when they arose. Every waking minute of the tour involved a constant readjustment, appraisal and reaction to what was going on outside the vehicle. It was just that the stakes were slightly higher here. Operation Tomahawk necessitated two of the crew outside the vehicle and anything up to 1 kilometre away from it, without radio contact between each other, let alone back to the vehicle, and quite often right under the noses of sentries outside the back gate of their own barracks. There was no need to overcomplicate an already difficult task with a whole extra string of 'what ifs'. There came a time when you just had to get on with it. It was simply a question of keeping one's nerve and following the drills precisely in order to avoid anything going wrong at all. The one thing we did have in our favour, as with any target, was that we knew we were there. Anyone else who did spot us or bump into us would not be expecting an encounter with a Mission crew and would probably be more scared of meeting us than we were of them.

The vehicle crawled into the lay-up point at no more than walking pace. The dim glow from the barracks was clearly visible. It was an orange hue that looked like the distant light of bonfires. The smoke from a tall chimney rising out of the gloom was illuminated by the artificial light coming from below. This was probably the central boiler and heating unit for the barracks. The unmistakable lignite smell mingled with the rotting mush from the dump. We had stopped three times on the route in to listen and observe. The engine was switched off. Both Graham and I were using PNGs now to check the lie of the land and make sure nothing else was out there. We waited and just listened. Although it was late August it was bitterly cold. It was not uncommon in this part of Europe for a frost to follow a warm summer's day. The wind was going to make it even colder. It was almost 2 a.m.

I was so tired I was no longer as worried as I had been earlier in the afternoon. This was still only my third tour in the space of fifteen days and my eighth day in the DDR. I was simply keen to get on with it and if the truth be known, to get it finished. My first tour started on Saturday 5 August. It was now Sunday 15 August. I had not experienced this pace since Sandhurst, five years ago. But Sandhurst was only training. There was a safety net if things went wrong. Even the Ashford course, hectic and full in its own right, couldn't reproduce the tiredness and discomfort of three days and two nights of ceaseless activity with barely four hours' kip in each twenty-four-hour period and that routine repeated more than six times a month. It didn't stop back in Berlin. Standby duties and interpreter duties could shatter the night's sleep quite regularly. During the day tour reports had to be compiled and tour briefs prepared for the next tour. The only guaranteed full night's sleep was probably the night your tour finished. The course could not replicate the sapping effect that this combination of mental and physical exhaustion had upon the body. The constant watch, the constant listening, the constant anticipation and the constant decision making based upon the endless need to keep thinking ahead was all-consuming.

In time I would get used to the lifestyle. After my first six months or so I became so keyed up with either planning, debriefing or being on tour that it became difficult for me to sleep beyond four or five hours a night anyway. I would be so keen to get on with the job or so intensely wrapped up in an operation that I couldn't wait to get on with it. What seemed to pass for a normal life had all been eradicated by now; shopping, socialising and free time became unimportant, days of the week had no meaning, weekends and holidays were a waste of time in comparison to Mission life. Occasionally I had to force myself to keep a pace that would not completely drain me. But right now, on my third tour and first Tommy, I realised that I was going to be a liability if I didn't get a grip.

'OK. Let's get ready.' Graham was content that the coast was clear. I was very much in his hands. Experience and competence led here, not rank. I reached into the back and got the Tomahawk kit out of the rear-side wall stowage nets. It consisted of an East German sack, stolen from previous excursions, that would for all the world look like it had originated from the dump if dropped in an emergency, a pair of slip-on, rubber overboots, smooth-soled to prevent footprints and a pair of rubber overgloves that would prevent skin puncture by anything sharp or unsanitary. The only thing we went in were the clothes to keep us warm and the outer garments for deception. All badges of rank, Brixmis flashes and anything remotely incriminating were removed. All outer garments had Velcro patches on the sleeves so that we could remove our Union Jack insignia before leaving the vehicle rather than it being ripped off by a tree branch or fence near the dump. No coins, jewellery, keys or loose items of any description were taken out of the vehicle.

We also left our GSFG passes of accreditation which would ultimately entitle us to some semblance of diplomatic immunity. Above all else they would definitely give the game away. Somehow leaving them behind symbolised crossing the line between what was defensible and what was not. It marked out to what lengths you were prepared to go in order to gather your information. Literally sifting around in someone else's shit was a revolting but undeniably fruitful task; it was degrading and thoroughly unpleasant the first few times around but gradually you got used to it, even perversely keen on it. The rewards were so great.

Security for these dumps was everything. It wasn't that we would not deny the operation if caught. We would, of course, although being caught on a rubbish dump with a sackload of rubbish would be a difficult one to get out of. What we were minimising was the risk of the Mission being associated with the operation by accidentally dropping something that could tie us into it. It wasn't that the operation was any more dangerous than a normal target, (although this one at Mönchenholzhausen was just inside PRA and therefore doubly contentious) where reactions to our presence might range from being merely chased away to being rammed or shot at. It was simply that this operation could not be blown. It was too important.

To all intents and purposes we looked like any other East German civilian scavenging a rubbish tip at 2 a.m! It was certainly not uncommon to meet the odd East German as you rounded one of the many huge rubbish mounds. These places were so big that occasionally, however thorough the recce, it could not be helped. It was normal to avoid anyone else on the dump, avoid any obvious visual contact, as much as you could have in that light, and continue with what you were doing. Neither party was interested in what the other was doing on a Soviet rubbish dump. It was not a place for chit-chat. If it was considered too difficult to work with civilians present then the two of us would slip slowly away and leave it for another day.

The weather often played its part. Many more dumps were attacked in winter than in summer partly because the cover of darkness was better and partly because the desire by the locals to visit them in the middle of the cold winter nights was less pressing. When it was cold, and it could be even in the height of summer, then we would put on a Canadian parka for warmth as well as several layers of clothing underneath. Often we would put 'Noddy' suits[43] on beneath our outer garments to really insulate us from the low temperatures. To the outside world we still had the appearance of dishevelled tramps. It was figured that you probably couldn't drop anything that you were wearing, apart from maybe gloves or hats. The hat was usually some innocuous woollen affair, again often purchased in East Germany. If the gloves had to be taken off to separate pages of a letter or a book then they were placed inside pockets rather than on the floor. When you slowly moved around the dump it was very difficult without a light to find the last location where you might have put something down. In short, nothing was taken to the dump that was attributable to any of the missions or that couldn't be left there in an emergency.

---

[43] NBC: Nuclear, Biological and Chemical. NBC protective suits are referred to as 'Noddy' suits.

Whenever we came across Soviet accidents, then we would always help out where we could. We may have 'stuffed' them otherwise, but one day it might be our vehicle in an accident and us needing help.

Getting out of the vehicle was the noisiest part. Opening the doors was loud, shutting them was painful. We firstly clicked them into the catch and then leaned on them to push them to. Everything was a whisper. Graham gave Mac his last instructions: 'Stay awake and keep watch! We'll return through your 3 o'clock.' And then to me, 'Let's go.'

We walked down towards the dump and on to the freshly tipped heap that we had spotted earlier that day. There was no talk until we were a good hundred metres from the vehicle. Once we were happily out of sight of the G-wagon we walked openly as though we were meant to be there, looking for all the world as though we were making for the dump and for a bit of thieving from it. There was a time for skulking through the undergrowth and this was not it. Swag sacks draped over our shoulders and just a hint of caution in the step, we looked as though we were locals coming to rifle the tip. What did anyone care if we were? It was one of many open, bold-as-brass deceptions that we employed. There's nothing that attracts interest so quickly as suspicious and furtive action. Being too cunning drew suspicion more surely than simply blending in with what was normal.

We talked quietly. Graham was constantly pointing out little features on the ground to remember. All the time we were watching and listening for any sign of life. There were many. What was important was distinguishing what was threatening from what was not. In the dark, when your eyes are not so clever, your hearing becomes more acute, compensating for the temporary loss of another sense. The screech of a night owl could pierce the silence and scare the living daylights out of you. Owls and other night animals punctuated the black stillness from miles away. Wild pigs in the forest fed by night, their rustling, snuffling nose digging fittingly emulating our own occupation. The noises from the nearby barracks were easily interpreted. Metal hangar doors would bang open and shut in the wind. The first round of soldiers that ever get up in a barracks, the chefs, would sometimes be rousing just as we were leaving. Sentries on duty all night could be heard changing shift. Their slightest conversations could be heard for several hundred metres. A cigarette being lit could be seen perhaps 500 metres away. The faint, imperceptible and curiously fresh smell of tobacco might drift over the wall and be detected from 200 metres away as we neared the barracks on our approach route. But all the time the pervading stench of the dump loomed closer and closer until nothing but the foul air it exuded encompassed everything.

Graham pointed out the position of the sentries still barely visible to us. Their movement in the light of their raised boxes perched precariously at the top of the walls at the corners of the installation cast shadows that we could interpret. They were moving to keep warm. It would be very unlikely that they could see us with the naked eye and it was highly unlikely they had II equipment down to that level to help them. Nevertheless, we were careful to approach unsighted to them and we were careful to remain so while on the target. And if they could see us then it was very unlikely they would bother us or indeed recognise us for who we were.

We scavenged avidly. We were only 5 or 10 metres apart. Searching for the right stuff was a slow, shuffling process. It was fingertip stuff until we spotted something that required excavation. We would sweep meticulously metre by metre rather than dart about, gradually turning the rubbish like a gardener double-digging a bed for the first time. Every so often we would stop and listen to ensure that we were safe. Graham would bring over the odd manual or letter for a quick translation from me before consigning it to his sack or back to the tip. It was a bizarre sight as we sifted among the detritus that is human waste: everything from cardboard boxes soggy with rotting vegetables to old uniforms from which we routinely removed any identifying insignia and badges. There were old fridges and bed springs, all manner of metalwork. It was not unknown for live rounds and unexploded ordnance to be recovered from these sites. The variety of rubbish was unimaginable.

Two things in particular made the practical job of retrieval more difficult. Quite often, ash deposited at random on the dump from the lignite fires that powered the barracks would still be smouldering. This would either burn up the paper that we were going for or give you a nasty burn if you went in too deep. Where it was dry and the wind caught it there would be perpetual clouds of dust to walk through. It stuck in the throat, on our clothes and got in the eyes. Worse than the ash was the effect of rain. Not only did it make the task more difficult, turning paper into slime, but it also combined with the ash to form a sort of glue that held everything in place.

The written word was our principal target but not exclusively. Anything that remotely looked like signals equipment was always high priority. Not a terribly sexy catch, but extremely important in the intelligence war. If you know and understand how your opponent's communication systems work then you have the opportunity to disrupt it. Imagine if all the telephones in the country were to suddenly go down. It would be a powerful weapon. Better still, if you could know what it was made of and how it was constructed then it would be a useful indicator as to how you might go about destroying it. The intelligence war conducted in the electromagnetic spectrum is a field in its own right and will in time, I am sure, replace the need for anyone to go out on the ground to collect information. Many operations conducted against the Soviet communications capability throughout the latter stages of the Cold War tested their ability to respond under extreme duress. Some of the information for those techniques was derived from the work of Tomahawk.

Anything that looked like vehicle equipment was also fair game. Track pins or armour attachments were high priority. You could tell the type of tank, its weight and size from a track pin. Furthermore, with scientific analysis, the source of the metal, its likely stress, strength and fatigue levels could all determine its capability. The jigsaw of intelligence work was made from incredibly small pieces which, when compared with another piece from somewhere else, such as a source report from the Khargovsk tank plant or the discovery of a piece of equipment for sale at an Asian trade fair, suddenly made the picture nearer completion. The added value of our finds was that they were so incontrovertible.

Almost three hours later and true to his word Graham indicated that we had finished our search. We made our way back to the vehicle with two sacks full of swag. I was cold, I stank and my mouth was very dry. Wind had been whipping over the tip, spraying dust into my eyes. It was not a pleasant experience. Back at the vehicle, I detected that even Graham had had enough. The route back was conducted in the same manner as the route in. We always went back the same way. The locals would have done, so we did too. Rule two applied!

Reaching the vehicle was joy itself. The sacks were handed into Mac, who lowered his PNG as we approached. The sacks went in as first priority. Now was not the time to relax. If we were going to be jumped here, then better without the evidence actually on us. Mac put the sacks into plastic bags and returned them to the back of the vehicle. Graham took the PNG and maintained a watch. I started to clean up as much as possible. The overboots and gloves were put into a spare sack ready for the next Tommy. They were usually caked in all manner of muck, so the boots came off first and the gloves peeled over the hands like a surgeon. They would be washed down back in Berlin or left in the sack in the vehicle to dry out if there was a second Tommy the next night. It wasn't a perfect system but the hygienic consequences were lost in the slightly macho environment we worked in and the knowledge that the results brought in were exceptional.

Neither of us got in until Mac was ready. As we re-entered the vehicle a sense of relief came over us and the tension dropped noticeably. At least we could not be caught on the dump. Every stage of the recovery was a little more plausible to explain away if bumped, a little safer from unsolicited attention. We drove quietly away from the lay-up and off to the Z-platz. Resisting the urge to fall asleep after a long period outside in the cold followed by the change in temperature on returning to the relative warmth of the vehicle was very difficult indeed. But the Z-platz had to be navigated to and then checked out for safety. There was never a time to ease up.

I completed many Tommies after that. Each one was conducted in similar fashion. They were not pleasant, but they were rewarding. After a while the reward, in terms of their product, created a relish and zeal for them that I have found difficult to explain! Some I had to abandon because they were too busy. That is to say there were too many locals on them, more a reflection on their social conditions than anything else. Some were no more than 20 or so metres from the back gates of their adjacent Soviet installations and were conducted right under the noses of sleepy Soviet guards. Some were abandoned in mid-operation as Soviet sentries and soldiers themselves wandered on to them to undertake a little scavenging of their own.

On one particular dump, immediately outside the back wall of a barracks in Gardelegen and the home of 21 MRD, I was showing the ropes to Ian Comerford, the Intelligence Corps NCO from Research and newly posted into Brixmis. We were walking round the first mound to where we had observed a likely area that had been tipped over the back wall when we ran into three Soviet soldiers coming the other way. We nearly knocked them over. God knows where they had come from. A sort of Charlie Chaplin sketch ensued as I motioned to Mike to stand our ground. There was no hesitation on their part. They turned and ran away. We waited until they disappeared and then ran like hell back to the vehicle. It served to remind me that we usually had the element of surprise on our side even if everything else wasn't going well.

The next year I was to find my own little gold mine of information on one of the many dumps that littered the Jüterbog training area. It was almost a year before the outbreak of the Gulf War and therefore particularly relevant when the time came. It was the first exposé of the Soviet possession of fuel-air explosives. It was a technical manual describing their use. Although it did not specifically mention that they were present in East Germany, it clearly indicated that this was part of the Soviet arsenal. Fuel-air explosives were essentially weapons that could be exploded off the ground, creating enormous volumes of heat and over-pressure, covering vast areas of territory. They would be particularly useful in open ground and thus their connection to Iraq and the open spaces of the desert (Iraq being fully equipped by the Soviet Union) was available before the Gulf War started. Like many finds throughout the Mission's history, it would allow prognosis of their capability before they might be discovered for real in war.

CHAPTER FOUR

To Catch a Train

The remainder of my third tour with Graham and Mac was spent observing an artillery concentration at Crawinkel. The deployment of guns, including the full range of self-propelled artillery pieces, 2-S1, 2-S3, 2-S5 and 2-S7, took place deep into PRA and was therefore off limits without special approval. The 2-S5, an army-level piece and the 2-S7, the front-level piece, were key targets.

We found some high ground, sat right out in the open and simply observed them from our remote OP, a distance of about 3 kilometres. Graham used his sniper's scope, affectionately known as a 'swiftie', and I used my bins. We were just able to pull side-numbers with the swiftie, but at this range imagery was restricted to video coverage, not that they showed any inclination to move once dug in on their battery positions. Even the 1,000-mm lens with doubler[44] and the film pushed as far as it could go were not sufficient to obtain the detailed technical imagery required on these targets.

Although we were always on the lookout for minor modifications to equipment, either known or unknown, these self-propelled pieces had been well documented already. This was merely an opportunity to see how they operated on deployment, the kind of protection and camouflage they adopted and the general drills of their crews.

Three days later, after completing my first Tommy at Mönchenholzhausen, I was back out on tour with Jim Edgerton and Paul Bunce, 'razzing' up 27 GMRD and the Halle railway system that nearly ended with us spread across the front of an extremely irate BTR-60 PB. Two days after that, the usual three-day break curtailed because of our extension in Halle, I finally visited the infamous Letzlinger Heide (LHTA) and Jüterbog training areas, playground to the real enemy, 3 Shock Army. 3 Shock Army was what the Americans might call 'front and centre' troops. As their name rather euphemistically described, they would be the first troops to smash through the Inner German Border (IGB), steaming full ahead for the Channel ports as and when the time came. They were of considerable interest to us because they were ranged immediately opposite 1 British Corps, with the British Army of the Rhine (BAOR), immediately behind, their second-echelon target.

In conjunction with GSFG's assets, 3 Shock Army had under its command three tank divisions, three motor rifle divisions, a tactical air army, an artillery division

---

[44] Doubler: a device placed between lens and camera body that effectively doubled its focal length, i.e. 1,000 mm lens became 2,000 mm.

and a guards air assault brigade for good measure. Its right-hand northern boundary in its push towards the Channel was the River Elbe up to Hamburg; its left-hand southern boundary the Harz mountains. It was a formidable force to be ranged against the three armoured divisions of 1 British Corps. If 3 Shock Army was not sufficient, immediately behind it, less than 100 miles away, were the second-echelon armies based in Poland, and behind them countless Soviet military districts all the way back to the Urals.

The tour started off quietly enough. A small comms deployment passed through Fishbeck junction, a regular watering hole for tour crews transiting westwards to the LHTA hoping to catch sight of potential prey dabbling at the water's edge. We called and photographed the column without incident. The vehicle crews waved back to us. They probably thought they were stealing a march on us. Their only view was of two guys in the front of the G-wagon, nonchalantly drinking coffee, apparently disinterested in the presence of so many Soviet comms vehicles. Like so many that had gone before them, they couldn't divine the simple façade that we had put on for them. In the back my camera was singing away while Martin Brain was chatting to the tape recorder resting on his lap and Graham Heaman was checking the backs of the vehicles for troops, any other weapon systems and the tell-tale sign of reggies. All the time the two in the front intermittently waved and held up a coffee cup to conceal the fact that they were talking away for the benefit of the tape.

We toured the LHTA and the Jüterbog but again it was very quiet. As the natural course of the three-day tour ended we began the trek back to Potsdam and the Mission House. On the way back we observed a UK registered car completely off the normal transit route between Helmstedt and West Berlin. It was our obligation on behalf of the Foreign Office to discreetly photograph such vehicles, noting the passengers and number-plate for their further investigation. It didn't sit well with us, spying on our own nationals and it was rather reluctantly that we occasionally had to undertake the duty. However, I was consoled by the fact that less than thirty years ago the traitor George Blake, operating out of the MI6 station in Berlin, only a few doors along the corridor from the then Brixmis office, was routinely passing our operational plans and tour schedules to his sponsors and thereby regularly damaging the operational effectiveness of the Mission for more than three years. A British vehicle so far off the beaten track in an east European state not recognised by the authorities, whose passport stamp would prevent you from obtaining work in any government, defence or public role back in the UK, was a rare sight. It had to be followed up. We would take care to ascertain first that it was not a serving soldier or dependant who had genuinely come off the Berlin corridor and simply needed redirecting.

Coming off the corridor was easily done. There was only one turn on the route and that was at Magdeburg where the corridor deviated from one autobahn to another. It was badly lit at night and easily missed by day if you weren't concentrating. Military personnel were so well briefed and also slightly paranoid about missing the turn that it very rarely happened. Unfortunately, missing the turn could result in a vehicle ending up in Leipzig. In the late 1960s a group of cavalry officers transiting a team of polo ponies to West Berlin got themselves completely lost on the Berlin ring road and ended up at Stettin on the Polish

A classic 'bridge-over' shot enabling the tour to get hull-down perspective and thus capture more detail than normally possible from ground level.

border where they were stopped and questioned by East German, Polish and Soviet border guards as their horses grazed along the banks of the Oder Neisse rivers. Needless to say Brixmis was requested to deal with the incident! We never heard what, if anything, came from our sightings of errant UK civilians. For the most part I'm sure they were simply adventurous holidaymakers or cranks who thought there was something to offer behind the Iron Curtain.

We were less than 50 miles from Potsdam when the bleeping started. Concealed in the roof of the glove compartment was a bleeper device about the size of a large Mars bar. Martin pulled it out and quickly turned it off, dismantling it in the process. Then on my fifth tour, I had no practical experience of what would happen next. I knew it was Operation Talon Snatch, the code name for extending a tour as a result of the Soviet imposition of a Temporarily Restricted Area (TRA). Exactly what the drills were I had only briefly mugged-up on in Brixmis SOPs. The Mission did not have two-way communications between its tours out on the ground and its headquarters back in Berlin. There were several reasons, most of them simply logistical. At the distances we operated, up to 300 kilometres away or more, the only practical means of radio communication would have been long wave. This would have required a massive antenna and correspondingly bulky radio equipment fitted for the vehicle to carry, in addition to all the other survival and surveillance equipment essential to operate with. Furthermore, given the nature of our work, all transmissions would have had to be encoded and decoded for security, taking up valuable time as well as leaving scope for erroneous encryption. Most importantly, there was an operational trap to avoid that possession of a communications ability might have jeopardised. If tours were able to communicate with Brixmis headquarters then we were also theoretically contactable by the Sovs through SERB. This alone was considered too inflexible for our methods, having serious repercussions upon our ability to move freely. If for some reason they didn't want tours in a particularly sensitive area then they could simply have us called by radio and have us return to Berlin. It was much better to abandon communications, let the tours have their head and thus avoid any possibility of being directed by the very people we were trying to observe.

Once out on the ground tours were on their own and their actions and decisions were final. They could not be interfered with. Even as late as 1989 mobile telephone networks were still to be demonstrated practically and satellite links, first seen on active service during the Falklands conflict of 1982, were still too few and far between to resource Brixmis. While the means of communication that an army of the 1990s takes for granted was absent in the late 1980s, it meant that the planning, briefing and coordination of tours had to be meticulous. Ops, at worst, had to know where we were likely to be and at best had to be able to second guess our actions when the shit hit the fan.

The degree of coordination and teamwork had to be of an exceptionally high standard, not just between Ops and the tourers but between Ops and Slops[45], who controlled the air tours, the tourers themselves and between all the three missions. This resulted in an extraordinary self-perpetuating work ethic. No detail was too small, no problem too difficult that someone somewhere in the Mission hadn't come across before and could solve. There was always time to help someone out with a particular target, route in or OP. Information was swapped readily and all the time. The Mission was a living operation, everyone kept informed and able to adapt to a changing environment, no questions asked. It was no exaggeration to say that when people's lives depended on that extra little bit of knowledge then no expense or personal effort was spared to ensure that it was available. The atmosphere generated by this constant demand for the very best standards coupled with rigorous attention to detail created a virtuous circle of improvement, better results and more effective intelligence gathering that increased with each generation of tourer that came to the Mission.

The bleeper was a one-time, one-way communication system. The only guarantee that Ops could be sure that we had heard it was by turning it off. Martin dismantled it completely to ensure that it was off. Inside the battery casing was a coded grid reference which we were to make for in order to effect an RV with the standby tour. They in turn would be similarly briefed back in Berlin as to where to meet us. Apart from refuelling, in anticipation of an extension of the tour, we made for the RV by the most direct and inconspicuous route.

RVs were carefully conducted affairs. The RV itself was usually a geographical feature such as a track crossing or a small bridge over a stream. The snatched

---

[45] Slops: Squadron Leader Operations. Responsible for the direction of air tours and the overall touring programme in conjunction with Ops, on a tri-mission basis.

crew and the standby crew would both 'de-nark'[46] before approaching the RV and would only arrive at the specified minute past the hour designated by the code inside the bleeper. If either vehicle wasn't there then the other would leave the scene and return precisely an hour later. It was imperative that neither vehicle was observed and that the meeting was hassle free. The stakes were high, not simply because the intelligence gained might be extremely significant but also because the Sovs would know that a tour had not returned and would be keen to track it down.

A TRA generally signified Soviet intent to carry out an imminent and usually very large movement of equipment in a specific area. It might also feature items of equipment never seen before, but more importantly it might also presage something much more significant than simply an army or divisional exercise within territorial borders. Brixmis and the two other Missions really came into their own at these times. If the balloon was about to go up either on the IGB or, as previously, during uprisings in Poland and Czechoslovakia, then there were Nato troops already out on the ground and behind the front lines, able to report on what was happening.

The transition to war would not be neatly timetabled. The various checks and markers that constituted the hostile indicators board would not be ticked off one by one to confirm all the stages had been reached that officially declared us at war. It would be messy, confused, full of bluff, dissemblement and smoke screens. The first warning the West would get would be when it actually happened. Accompanied by a clever electronic warfare plan and a carefully chosen time, the transition to war would occur quite suddenly. Satellite imagery doesn't work through cloud and Sigint can be all too easily deceived. In reality it may very well have caught us on the hop. How many Army and RAF personnel were really in BAOR on any Christmas Eve or *compos mentis* by New Year's day? What was very difficult to deceive was the guy out on the ground seeing it for himself. Brixmis performed that function and Talon Snatch was one facet of it.

Fortunately, in the late 1980s, as a result of the Conference on Security and Cooperation in Europe (CSCE) agreements, visiting inspection teams were able to pick and choose exercises above a certain scale which by virtue of their size had to be notified to CSCE. An exercise that necessitated imposition of a TRA would be a likely candidate for one of these inspections. I wondered what it must have been like in the 1960s and 1970s when such safety nets had not even been thought of. This system of checks and balances went a long way to easing tension post-Afghanistan. But for all the MBFR, INF, CSCE and SALT talks, treaties and inspections, they were not infallible. Inspection and verification teams could easily be diverted from the core of any large-scale exercise activity. As time went by these teams were themselves staffed by ex-Brixmis hands who were not so easily put off by the charm and trickery of the hosting Soviet officers.

The standby crew brought out extra food, six hot Thermos flasks and all manner of other things they thought we might need for an extended tour. They also brought out our revised target area relating directly to the imposition of the

46 De-nark: get rid of nark surveillance.

How close can you get? Some very close photography of soldiers undertaking live firing, this time with the automatic grenade launcher, AGS-17.

TRA with precise areas for us to concentrate on. The standby crew left the RV first to draw away any narks and allow us a chance to plan tactics and routes and leave quietly. If there had been narks the standby crew's reappearance within a few minutes would have alerted us to take precautions. The standby tour would then spend two or three days out on the ground to conceal that it was anything other than a normal tour.

The logic behind TRAs was simple. In order to avoid their larger exercises being observed by the Missions, the Soviets would command huge areas of the DDR to be temporarily out of bounds to Mission activity. In order to do that they would have to provide us with an overlay so that we could warn forthcoming tours and brief them accordingly before they left. Because we didn't have comms in the vehicles, those tours already out on the ground when a TRA was imposed couldn't possibly know about the imposition. By implication they were exempt from the ban and therefore pardonable if subsequently caught in the TRA. Operation Talon Snatch was conceived with that in mind. The lack of comms was overcome by a prearranged plan that revolved around a single phone call to a bleeper that would respond almost anywhere in the DDR. 'Snatched crews', the one thought at the time to be in the optimum position relative to the TRA and Potsdam, would be clandestinely briefed by the standby crew at the RV. The Sovs knew we did it but they didn't know how we effected it. Infrequently, because a TRA was an internationally notifiable event and therefore too big a deal to fool around with, they would impose a TRA by way of distraction from other activity they wanted to carry out somewhere else in the DDR. A nil report from a Talon Snatch operation in one area was a likely indicator that something had happened somewhere else. Rule one applied. Sometimes we covered that clandestine activity too and sometimes we missed it!

The RV was selected for its remoteness, usually on the perimeter of the local Potsdam area. The RV we had been given was a barely perceptible cross tracks in the middle of acres of farmland. As always there was good cover that prevented anyone seeing us and yet allowed us to see a long way for any suspicious tails. It was nearly dusk when we met. We were told where the TRA had been imposed and for what reason. If we were lucky and Sigint from 'the Hill'[47] had been passed to Ops then our briefing might be supplemented with further detail of exactly who and what we should be looking for.

On this occasion four areas had been imposed in the far west of the DDR, linking the Jüterbog with the LHTA PRAs, where we had just come from: 3 Shock Army was the target formation. We briefed the standby crew on the comms unit we had observed nearly three days earlier, passed over the film to them, together with hastily scribbled notes that Martin had made en route, and conjectured that they were probably part of the advance party for 3 Shock Army. We were beginning to put two and two together. The standby crew would take the film back to the Mission House in Potsdam for delivery to Berlin. The Mission house driver would find a lame excuse to make an unscheduled visit back to Berlin, thereby getting the film back for processing as quickly as possible. The film would be developed and the information gleaned passed to an inspection team, if one was called, and other agencies who needed confirmation of the deployment. The intelligence cycle would be turning swiftly as a result of that sighting alone. The combination and type of vehicles photographed would give a clue as to the level and scope of the exercise. The types of antenna would indicate which waveband they would be using and therefore what distances they would be covering. Distances would rule in and rule out which headquarters they would be reporting back to. This would allow eavesdropping facilities back in Berlin to turn and tune their antennas more effectively. Inspection teams would decide whether or not it was worth a costly trip to inspect. They only had a certain number of visiting rights to exercise in one year and they didn't need to waste them. Satellite imagery would be redirected on to the likely exercise area. The satellite operators would in turn be calling for the latest weather forecast to see if it was worth complex changes from existing tracks on to new tasks. Slops would check for antennae linking ground to air missions and re-task Mission tours to adjacent airfields to look for any increased or abnormal activity. The knock-on effects were never ending and links to other activity elsewhere were inevitably made. The intelligence gathering cycle has a dynamic

---

[47] Hill, The (aka Golf Ball): the source of Sigint in this part of the world. A huge golf ball shaped listening post mounted high on the Teufelsberg, dominating the plains of East and West Germany. Information from the Hill was used to task Brixmis tours.

of its own. It has no start and stop point, it is a circular conveyor belt, a continuous loop that takes information on board, digests it, throws it off as appropriate and always asks for more. It doesn't stop.

We returned to the LHTA, this time more carefully and cautiously than normal. We performed de-narking drills frequently. If we were seen now then it was open season for the Sovs to catch us, whatever we were doing. We stayed off main roads and made the 100-kilometre trip back cross-country, cutting as many of the known tac-routes in the area as possible in order to maximise the chance of sighting any movement.

Some 112 rolls of film later and as August became September we were still out in the middle of it all. Towards the end of the fourth day we were watching a ramp being unloaded when several units arrived in the wood we were sitting in and began to deploy all around us. We were well concealed in some very thick scrub and although not wanting to leave the kit we were observing being unloaded we gradually became more and more anxious that the rapidly expanding encampment around us would eventually stumble across us. All through that night we became increasingly nervous as voices and vehicle movement could be heard only a few metres away. We sat tight, senses taut for the first sign of compromise that would prompt us to leave. It was the first of several occurrences in the Mission where I was truly petrified and thought that I had got myself in further than I was capable of handling. We were completely surrounded, the only way out was straight through the wood towards the ramp and away. But while it was still reasonably light we couldn't launch ourselves straight towards the Sovs on the ramp without getting caught, at worst, and merely chased at best. Talon Snatch required crews to stay undetected as long as possible. A certain extra degree of risk was expected, commensurate with the imposition of TRA. There were many more deployment areas to check out while the TRA was imposed. They could last for weeks or just a few days. We had no way of knowing and we had to cover as much of it as we could in order to find what it was they didn't want us to see. We stood our ground and hoped that the dark and close cover would be kind to us. For the moment they either simply couldn't see us or they thought we were another vehicle from an adjacent unit. Either way, it was not until the early hours, when the deployment had settled down, that we made a calm and controlled run for it.

The second incident happened only a few kilometres away from the deployment. We could smell burning and very quickly noticed flames leaping all over the back of the vehicle around the spare fuel tanks which had been filled earlier that day. The reflection in the wing mirrors of the flames against the dark sky was particularly bright. I watched helplessly as Graham brought the vehicle to a stop as quickly as possible. Martin and I leapt out and fought the fire with extinguishers while Graham stayed inside, ensuring that the vehicle remained occupied. We had pulled bundles of scrub along with us in our bid to get out forward from our OP position, which had caught round the axle and slowly but surely ignited. Inevitably, we only saw the funny side of it, thinking it a much luckier escape than being ripped out of the vehicle back in our OP.

We continued the quest for more kit. Our final incident on that tour saw us almost on the IGB skirting the LHTA, waiting for kit to go into it. We had come across a tac-route that had been recently trafficked, judging by the track prints, and waited in a makeshift OP throughout the day, leaving intermittently to check other likely routes in the area. When returning we checked that no further tracks had been added and that we had not missed anything in our absence. By now we felt pretty confident that most of the deployment had already taken place. We had run part of the IGB to check that nothing untoward was happening there and we were now contemplating returning to Berlin, given that it was very unlikely we would see anything leave the LHTA for the next couple of weeks while they exercised. If our earlier information had been processed by now then other agencies would be able to determine whether or not they wanted to call an inspection and have the Letzlinger Heide opened up to them. Someone else could watch them dig in for two weeks.

As we pulled out from the OP and made for the track away, almost out of nowhere to our rear 7 o'clock position, the barrel of a T-80 poked its way through the trees facing down the tac-route that we had been observing. A low rumble turned into a roar as it went past us. We were astonished at how quietly it moved and how it had taken us by surprise. We tried to roll slowly back into the OP, without attracting attention. It wasn't going to work. We were only 20 metres from their track and the trees between us were sparse. It was still quite early in the morning, the light wasn't good and a heavy mist hung in the trees. The sun was rising in the distance, the tanks would pass between us and the shafts of light coming through the trees. That was in our favour.

I decided that we should stay still like an animal that doesn't move in the presence of its hunter. We had spotted them first and that gave us the upper hand. A column of sixteen T-80s proceeded up the tac-route to our left, each one emitting the familiar whine of the turbine as they passed by. Almost elephant-like, slowly plodding one behind the other, sniffing the air as their barrels swung left and right, they dutifully followed the one in front. We were so conspicuous, having moved from our bolt-hole just at the wrong moment. Once again, we held our breath as one by one their commanders, heads out of the turrets, concentrating on the way ahead, failed to look round far enough. We had an escape route but we didn't want to use it unless forced. I'd gone over that with Graham. It nearly worked. I had the video mounted on the pole already and simply turned it on them. Martin started calling and I supplemented the video with 'stills'. They were frighteningly close and the detail to be gained was too good to miss. It wasn't until the last one, playing tail-end Charlie and, looking around behind him, performed the tell-tale double take. 'Charlie' had clearly spotted us and knew exactly who we were.

The reaction was instantaneous. He put one hand up to his throat mike and simultaneously the barrel slewed round to point at us. Given that they were on exercise and that the LHTA contained a live firing range, I suddenly felt like the proverbial rabbit caught in the headlights. Now it was time to move and Graham needed no second warning.

We shot out of the trees and made for open ground. The T-80 followed hot on our tail straight through the wood, simply flattening any trees in its path to get to us. It was farmland, sticky going for us, easy pickings for the T-80. At the far end of the field a more substantial track leading back through the wood towards the nearby autobahn gave us the edge. We flew through the wood, the track

This photograph was taken in hasty retreat by Stephen Harrison. Several seconds later the armed soldier on the right (wearing sunglasses), fired eleven rounds at the G-wagon to hasten their departure.

now converging with the road. It twisted and turned, the trees coming perilously close to the G-wagon, the T-80 still behind us. We could see the cars on the road, some we were overtaking. I wondered if they noticed the chase to their right at all. Graham picked his moment carefully. The vehicle swung hard left off the track, avoided the few remaining saplings at the edge of the wood and careered onto the autobahn slow lane. We startled several vehicles driving past, including a British family who must have wondered what the hell was going on. The T-80 stopped inside the wood line thinking better of trying to tackle us in the open.

We drove back to Berlin having managed to stay undetected for six days and having recorded the move of some elements of 3 Shock Army into their Emergency Deployment Areas (EDAs) facing 1 British Corps. It was my first experience of Operation Talon Snatch, another activity not disclosed on the course. We had several narrow escapes but had the distinct and significant privilege of observing our immediate Eastern Bloc opponents in full flight. The TRA, confirmed by our sightings, had been imposed to cover the army-level exercise of 3 Shock Army. On the basis of our first report at Fishbeck junction, inspection teams had been launched to watch them further.

Three days later I was out again, this time sitting on the Halle–Jena, Halle–Weimar railway confluence, observing both the railway junction and the adjacent tac-route in the town of Naumberg. I was touring with Nick Hamer and once again Graham Heaman was the driver. Nick was a flight-lieutenant and ex-flying-school instructor. He must have been in his forties but was as sprightly and agile as a twenty-one-year-old with an immensely positive attitude to go with it. Graham was one of the mission's more experienced drivers. He'd just proved that to me. He had recently extended his posting with Brixmis into a fourth year. He knew the country like the back of his hand and was an invaluable aid to any map reading. Nick was equally senior, now coming to the end of nearly three years with the Mission, and he had invaluable expertise on the air tour side as well as with the secret Chipmunk operation, Oberon.

Berlin had two RAF Chipmunk trainers, ostensibly to maintain flying hours and flying pay for RAF pilots posted to desk jobs in the various headquarters. The Chipmunk had a flying height of 500 feet and a radius of 20 miles from its airfield at RAF Gatow. Conveniently, this took it over Potsdam, the most concentrated Soviet military area in East Germany. The top-down view of equipment laid out in the open or of engine decks raised for repairs added an enormous amount of detailed technical intelligence that no other source could offer. Its timely patrols under the guise of flying training could also alert the local tours to concentrate on certain areas before they left the Mission. Like all other tours, it was routinely monitored, chased and even shot at. Nick was having a breather from doing all that by coming on a ground tour with me.

We had completed two fairly intense days touring with a rail watch the night before. The touring day started at sunrise, which at that time of year was still around 6 a.m. Prior to that we would leave the Z-platz where we had camped the night, the tour officer and NCO outside the vehicle in bed rolls wrapped inside one-man Gore-tex tents, the driver remaining inside the vehicle. We would shave and conduct ablutions on the move to save time, making for an OP that might catch any early morning deployment. In the OP the driver would boil up water sufficient

Exceptionally close detail of the surface-to-air missile system SA-3, revealed serial numbers, designators, launching instructions and other intricate technical details.

for the day's brew stops and take the opportunity for a stretch at the back of the vehicle. It was the only chance he had to leave the vehicle. All his ablutions would take place there and then, ready for another twenty-four hours in the driver's seat.

Our last port of call had been the Haufeld training area, a well-known SAM site guarding the approaches to Halle from the south-west. We'd watched it carefully, updating the target files with new panoramas, checking for any alterations or additions to known routes in and out and looking for any evidence of deployment, in particular the abuse of signals paper or other such documentation in the 'shit-pits' that we could recover for Spandau. It was now about 2 a.m. and we were on our second night or third morning of a planned three day tour. It was approaching that time of the twenty-four-hour cycle when bodily responses are telling you to wind up for the night. Reactions are not good, you feel dirty, itchy and you can smell your own body odour, having been unable to change for the duration of the tour. Everything is an effort, you feel pretty low but you know that you have to be sharp and alert. Above all else the cold is gnawing away at you as you desperately try to fight it off.

It was still early September. I had yet to experience the winter nights of January and February in eastern Europe. You keep still to avoid losing body heat but you get cramp if you don't move a little in the confined space. The joints begin to ache from the permanently seated position that you are forced to adopt day in, day out. The metal lump of the G-wagon acts as a cold sink, radiating heat out and attracting more cold in as the night wears on. You can't turn the vehicle engine on because that would give your position away and prevent you from hearing warning noises that will stimulate you into activity. All the layers of clothing you've been issued, plus some more you weren't, are already on. Only the eyes and the ears are exposed to the cold air, together with the fingers that will work the cameras.

We were parked up, in the gap in the 'Y' formed by the railway lines just before they merged together. We had crossed the northernmost line further back in order to ease our way into some scrub about 40 or 50 metres from the junction and less than 10 metres from the lines on either side of us. The whole junction was built on a raised embankment watched from the southern side of the line from a control box built slightly down the embankment on stilts that raised it above the level of the track.

The control box doubled as living accommodation and was thus permanently manned by its single woman occupant. This job was her life. The junction itself was lit up by a single light on top of a pole. Whether it was because they couldn't afford any more lights or they were security conscious, I don't know. It was not the sort of street light that you would choose to park your car under in Britain but it was sufficient for our purposes. The funnel of light was between us and the track and directed back towards it, an ideal arrangement for the Modulux. But for the control box it would have been a perfect OP.

East German railway officials were either for us or against us. There were few half measures. In some cases we had gone so far as to bribe[48] them for information on significant military or industrial railway movements. In my time at the Mission, Major John Walker, the senior Intelligence Corps officer, was working a guy from Dessau, whom he would meet up with while out on tour in order to glean likely routes and timings of military rail shipments. His payment was in kind, usually food or whisky. He wouldn't take money and his motive was pure hatred for the Soviets and their imposed regime. There were probably many others like him, infuriated by the regime but too frightened to do anything about it.

Unfortunately, there were many more who took the opposite view, willingly doing state jobs for the extra privileges it conferred upon them and keen to report on us into the bargain for even more brownie points. All that concerned us was information and the chance to see how good it was. It was usually reliable and saved us considerable time by obviating the need on that particular part of the network to watch the line twenty-four hours a day, seven days a week.

It was well known that the woman running this particular signals junction was not friendly. If spotted by her, it was guaranteed that the Stasi would be round to hinder or chase us away. It wasn't that we were afraid of them or what they could do if provoked. It was much more the fact that we could not do our job so easily with them around.

The Soviets were constantly on the lookout for the opportunity to prove that we were spies. They knew we were but they needed evidence. It would give them great pleasure to produce a photograph of a tour crew taking a photograph of

---

[48] In the original book, the phrase 'recruit and run' was used for 'bribe'. But, it was understandably (mis)interpreted by the *Sunday Times* (amongst others) to infer a regular agent-running arrangement. The author has no personal knowledge to attribute this activity to a regular agent-running operation.

some installation or piece of equipment. This could later be used against that particular tour officer or as tit-for-tat with some Soxmis infringement.

Ironically, I had been present at SERB only a few days before with the new Chief of Mission, Brigadier Ian Freer, to discuss such an incident. As duty interpreter for the week I would be called upon at any time of day to liaise with SERB, assuming I was not out on tour. The incident had actually concerned Nick Hamer himself. He had been photographed removing a Mission Restriction sign, a normal trophy for a tourer about to leave the Mission. Colonel Polozov, Deputy Chief SERB, was having great delight in exposing this flagrant abuse of Soviet authority to the new Mission Chief with hard photographic evidence. The Chief was very relaxed about it, pointing out that Nick Hamer was coming to the end of his posting and was simply collecting a souvenir to take home, that Mission Restriction signs were contrary to the spirit of the Robertson-Malinin Agreement and that we did not impose any such restrictions on Soxmis in West Germany. A spiral of tit-for-tat exchanges ensued, designed more to test the new Chief's metal and gauge how he might react in the future, than to berate Nick for his misdemeanour.

The meeting concluded in good humour, with the customary several glasses of vodka, when the real point of it emerged in a frank exchange on the relative strengths and weaknesses of the Warsaw Pact and Nato. Direct questioning was a common tool of the KGB and GRU. There was nothing like a straight question to elicit an honest answer from a Brit. Well, honestly put anyway! All of this would be reported back on both sides as Humint[49] for further analysis and discussion. Polozov was a known GRU officer. Everything he said was measured, coded and designed to trigger some sort of reaction. He was well aware that his conversations would be memorised and passed on, as we were well aware that the same would be true of our remarks. As we left in the staff car back to West Berlin we would go over what was discussed, I would summarise the meeting and send it on to BAOR. It was yet another contribution to the intelligence gathering puzzle.

I did not enjoy the interpreter's role nor rate the value placed upon this form of liaison as a means of gathering untainted intelligence. Characterised by double speak, bluff and double bluff, conducted by professional spies who skirted round the truth, at the end of the day you didn't know what to believe. Consequently, most of it was ignored by the tourers in favour of what you could believe with your own eyes and ears. I was much happier touring and finding out for myself what was going on in the DDR. Because I did everything I could to get out of the interpreter's duties I was flung more deeply into the touring role, which I relished. By the same token because I felt that I was not taking my fair share of the liaison side of the house, I would work harder and harder on each tour, staying up later, visiting just one more installation, just driving that extra bit further and allowing the crew a little less time for breaks. Sometimes it paid off.

Graham had manoeuvred the vehicle quietly and smoothly into the predetermined OP. There was still no movement in the signals control box although the light was on when we arrived. It had gone off just after midnight. Fanatical she may have been but she had to sleep sometime. All the lights in the

---

[49] Humint: Human intelligence, e.g. agents and informers.

Our liaison role covered many facets. Here General (later Field Marshal and Lord) Sir Peter Inge toasts with General Snetkov, Commander Western Group of Forces, inside the Mission House. The two Commander's-in-Chief are assisted by interpreters Major John Walker (Int. Corps) and Colonel Robert Polozov (GRU) from the Mission and SERB respectively.

G-wagon were off. The route into the OP had been memorised and our external lights cut as we pulled off the road about a kilometre back up the line. The engine was cut as we arrived and the process of watching and listening, together with getting colder and colder, commenced. Nick held the tape recorder in one hand and brew in the other, his window cranked open. He was in the NCO's seat because, although much more experienced and senior than me, this was a ground tour. Had we being doing an air tour of the airfields then the roles would have been reversed. As tour officer it was standard practice for me to make the majority of brews simply because I had sufficient space in the back to do it.

As the night wore on the number of brews increased. It relieved the boredom, kept us awake and warmed the blood in the small hours. The constant state of alert was sapping and took a lot of getting used to. Anything over a week's gap between tours rested you too much, took you off the boil and it became a hard slog to get back into the swing of things. It was very easy to drift off to sleep but you had to force yourself to stay awake. When it was possible, a short walk outside the vehicle would clear some air but in close and difficult OPs like this it simply wasn't advisable. Every second delayed in getting back into the vehicle was a second given to the narks or Sovs to get you. Graham was beginning to nod and we'd completed three hours so I decided to call it a night and move to the Z-platz for some safe shut-eye before starting again the next day. I was not terribly concerned for the tour NCO or myself when it came to getting sleep, but the driver was a different matter. Allowing him to fall asleep at the wheel was inexcusable negligence on my part.

If we left now then, to the best of our knowledge, this OP would be preserved for another day. I dismantled the Modulux from the camera. The bolt-on phosphorescent tube, about 18 inches long, amplified the available ambient light. Using 800 ASA film 'pushed' to 6,400 ASA we were able to take highly detailed photographs in very poor light indeed. It didn't work out in the 'sticks' where there was virtually no ambient light at all. Then we would have to use the twin spotlights filtered to let through only IR or a hand-held highly powerful beam normally used by search and rescue crews. To the naked eye these IR lights were invisible but with the Modulux attachment it was clear as day, except that the day it created had a very strong green tinge and acuity dropped off the further from the centre of the lens the subject matter. The tube weighed about 4 kilograms, was fragile if abused, a little unwieldy because of its length but bloody good kit if used correctly. The IR spots were a double-edged weapon. Soviet tanks, among other vehicles, were known to have II devices themselves. The IR spots, invisible to the naked eye could be easily detected with II equipment. Then they became the proverbial candle to a bunch of moths in the wrong circumstances.

'OK, let's get ready to go.'

In a routine withdrawal from an OP it was inevitably the tour officer who called the time to break cover. Kit had to be put away before the vehicle moved, the tour officer usually having most out. There would be at least one camera on his lap, the video would be mounted on a rigid pole in between the two seats in front of him and he would need a couple of seconds to plan the route out and on to the next location.

'Everybody ready? OK. Let's go.'

Graham backed out of the scrub.

I was ready to resume navigating just as soon as we got clear of this OP. Nick would follow on his map.

We routinely navigated on 1:50,000 OS maps. The DDR was roughly the size of Ireland and funnily enough roughly the same shape. It took 264 1:50,000 OS maps to cover it, joined together in nine strips covering nine separate bands of the country. There were no markings on them other than changes to the going, petrol stations, tac-routes and any information that the Sovs would very likely know anyway. The only slightly dubious information on them were useful OP positions. But there were thousands of them for every eventuality, built up over the years by scores of tourers. The wisdom was that if such information fell into the hands of the Sovs, and it already had as various crews over the years were ambushed and relieved of their equipment by force, then in order to cover every combination of possible OP they would have to use all their available resources in the DDR to watch them round the clock.

In these early days at the Mission I regularly wondered why they didn't catch us more often. It was simply a question of time, resources and money. The enormity of the task would have driven them further into financial ruin than they already were. They simply did not have the resources to sustain an operation of that scale.

We were the proverbial needles in a haystack. On average there were three tours operating from each mission at any one time. Trying to find nine vehicles that bore an uncanny resemblance to Soviet vehicles in a country the size of Ireland, and about as remote, was a tall order. That these vehicles were manned by skilled and professional armed forces personnel trained specifically in advanced navigation, escape and evasion, hot pursuit, surveillance and counter-surveillance techniques, and fitted with a range of vastly superior equipment, made their job very difficult indeed. Selective targeting had to be their best *modus operandi* and that could be achieved only if we gave them the opportunity. Regrettably, they did achieve it every now and again. The consequences were occasionally extreme.

We reversed back the 300 metres parallel to the southernmost track to a point where it was safe to cross the line and away. Graham turned the vehicle round and cranked the window to listen for the sound of any train before crossing. I switched on one of my rear map-reading lights. It was mounted on a flexible arm with a switch at the business end. I had another on the other side for sorting out camera equipment if I needed it. The tour NCO had one coming out of the front glove compartment for his map. They were directional and easily masked but they didn't go on until we had cleared any potential danger area and then only when necessary to avoid losing night vision.

'Shit! There's a train coming from behind us, Boss.' Graham had heard it.

The map light went off instantly.

'Back off the track.'

Graham reversed the vehicle away from the track but we could only get about 5 metres away before we would have crossed the other line and dropped down the other side of the embankment.

'Bollocks!'

My Modulux was already packed for the trip out. We were facing away from the only available light source and too close to the track to get shots with the 85-mm lens and the IR spots. We were also balls-up on the embankment with no cover whatsoever and no idea which side of us the train was going to go and worst of all probably facing towards it. The angle was wrong for Nick to get a chance to call it at all. At least if it was going away from him he would have had a longer glimpse to recognise the kit.

'Spin us round, Graham, and put full beam on when the engine passes. We'll be covered from the signals box by the train.'

Graham quickly but carefully executed another three-point turn between the lines to face the vehicle back again towards the control box. The distinctive inverted triangle of lights on the front of the train could be seen down the line. At least we had chosen the right track to face. If only we had waited just another minute we would still have been in the OP and perfectly placed to photograph as well as call the kit. I cancelled this self-chastisement with the counter-argument that if we had left a minute earlier we would never have known that a train was coming at all. I once mentioned to Graham Geary, by now my touring mentor and buddy, that the art of touring seemed like so much luck and very little science. As usual he had an answer for everything and why not, he'd almost completed six years with the Mission and was a living legend among the touring fraternity, if not half the intelligence community. He said that you made your own luck. It was how you exploited it that mattered.

Watching them, watching us, watching them . . .

The train was upon us about three seconds later. It thundered past about 6 or 7 metres away, physically rocking the vehicle as it went. The beam went on and the longest kit train I had ever seen shot past completely untarped. It went on and on for a full sixty or seventy flatbed loads. There were BTR 70, SS-21, T-80 with reactive armour plating and a host of KAMAZ Silver Box Signals vehicles whose precise definition we would not fully determine without supporting imagery. At least Nick was shouting them into the tape above the roar of the flatbeds as they passed. I was sitting quite still, unable to do a thing about it. We were too close to the line and the train too fast in this light for the unaided camera. The photographs would have been too blurred to make any sense and we were prevented from moving by the fall of the embankment.

'Copper Log, Boss!' Graham shouted as he identified one of the tens of plain box vehicles whipping past us as the highly sought-after Copper Log variant of the Silver Box series of vehicles. Copper Log was an army-level command and control vehicle, a computerised air defence system coordinating ground-based air defence targeting and communications. As such, any and all information pertaining to it was a high priority, particularly radio and computer fits inside the vehicle, all aerials protruding from it and especially any other vehicles associated with it.

'Chase it, Boss?' Graham enquired as the familiar click-whirr of the camera motor drive was conspicuous by its absence. Nick was still shouting above the noise of the train to make himself heard by the tape. We had no imagery and no excuse.

'I think so, Graham.'

'Oh shit,' came the response from the other front seat. Nick was quite happy doing acrobatics with the camera at 200 feet in the Chipmunk. He was less happy flying across country in the G-wagon.

As the last flatbed went past Graham tiptoed the vehicle over the line and then slammed his foot down, virtually launching us off the bank in the process. We traversed the slope of the embankment so as not to nosedive in at the bottom, joining the concrete slab access road that jinked and turned to avoid overhanging gas pipes alongside the railway line. We motored alongside and parallel to the by now single track that had more gradually and leisurely crept down off the embankment and back onto the level than we did.

The G-wagon was flying and Graham was in his element. I shouted to Nick to find the next likely road-rail crossing point for this line while I navigated Graham as close to the line as possible. The concrete track soon gave out. We were back onto the tarmac and bare cobble patches that were typical of the run-down, built-up areas of East Germany. We were skirting the environs of Halle. We slowed marginally before joining each new road. Every jink and turn lost us momentum, while the train was travelling at a constant 50 m.p.h. in a straight line.

I remembered my lessons. It was not normal operational procedure to travel fast. First, if there was no need, then you were simply quickening time to an accident. Second, travelling too quickly more often than not meant that you would miss something, a glimpse or a reflection of something in the distance that might lead you to more activity. Even if chased it was sometimes advantageous to slow the pursuit down. However, every situation was different and left entirely to the discretion of the crew on the ground. In this particular case we absolutely had to catch the train to gain the imagery I had failed to get first time. Moreover, it had a priority target on board. We had to catch it at the right spot to be able to photograph it. This usually meant at a road-rail crossing or in a station, both of which usually afforded some degree of ambient or artificial light. We would need to fly!

'600 metres, T junction turn right.' I couldn't see to confirm it. I was navigating by the map alone and trusting that the map replicated what it said on the ground.

Nick automatically reset the trip-meter as we passed each check-marker and I called the distances to the next one. The vehicle braked at the last possible moment and lurched violently into the new road at the designated turning. The engine whined as it raced off, the familiar clunk and shudder as the automatic transmission notched up another gear change. These vehicles had a top speed of over 100 m.p.h. and phenomenal acceleration from standing for their weight. Because of their weight, maintaining momentum was critical.

'We're back parallel to the track, about 600 metres to our right. Can you spot a good crossing, Nick?'

'267 838, about three klicks further west.'

I looked down at the map.

'OK. Got it. We'll try that.'

We were on a straight road now, the red rear safety lights of the train distinctly visible across open countryside. We were gaining on it but we had to get ahead of it. We passed through a small village at about 65 m.p.h. There was no one about at this time, thank God. I thought of the odd drunk who might just stagger out into the road. Fortunately, it was just too early for the first farmers to be getting up for work.

The vehicle accelerated out of the village and the road veered away from the line. The automatic transmission whined as Graham thrashed the revs out of it.

'50 metres right off this onto a track. Trip. I'm going to try a shortcut to it, Nick.'

Graham swung the vehicle right as the track appeared but didn't drop any speed. The vehicle bounced down what was no more than a farm track, throwing me about in the back. I was barely watching the road ahead, trying instead to keep my eye on progress across the map to the possible OP.

'200 metres, back out onto the road, bear right.'

This road would take us directly back to the railway line. I had spotted a straight run on the other side of the line leading directly towards the crossing point. We were closing on the train fast. As we approached the crossing point the barriers were down but fortunately they were only half barriers. We barely missed the back end of the last flatbed as we dodged round the half barriers, not waiting for them to open. A news item of several months ago flashed through my mind about commuters in Britain dodging this type of half barrier on their way to work. At least I was getting paid for it. Graham had his foot down hard. The line was now only 50 metres to the left of us as we started to overhaul the train. The road was a cobble-tarmac mix but wonderfully straight. The light at the chosen crossing came into sight. It was a single light but on the other side of the road and therefore shining towards us. It also had the red flashing warning lights either side of the line. They would flare out the Modulux if we didn't position the vehicle accurately. We had to get back across to the other side to get useful imagery, otherwise the train would block it out as it passed in between us and the lamp.

'400 metres, turn sharp left and get across the other side, 45 degrees facing back down the line.'

Now we were taking a risk. I was asking Graham to cross back over the line, this time in front of the train carrying God knows how many tons of equipment. The driver probably wouldn't even notice if we became stuck on the crossing, let alone be able to do anything about it. I was also assuming it was another half barrier.

The flashing red warning lights came on as we screeched left and approached the line. It was a half barrier. I fought with the G-force created by the turn to connect the Modulux to the 85-mm lens. The G-wagon slewed around the barrier, spun through 180 degrees on the far side and wobbled like jelly coming to rest. There was no time to tee-up the vehicle. There was no need, Graham had placed it perfectly first time. All lights went out and three or four seconds later the train sped past.

'Gotcha, gotcha, gotcha,' I mumbled to myself as each flatbed and each bit of kit on it was perfectly framed and perfectly lit. Nick had the opportunity to call the train a second time while changing film for me. I changed reels three times as we notched up over eighty vehicles on the one train. Copper Log appeared and that alone, together with the other vehicles on the train that could now be permanently associated with it, would have been worth the risk, chasing the train. We noted the direction and thus likely destination for further tasking. We had another brew and waited a further three hours before turning in for the night. Another rail OP had been established and a route for a train chase proven should the need arise again.

CHAPTER FIVE

Scoop

'Trip. 150 metres take the left fork. 600 metres to target. Doors and windows.'

'Can't see any more of them, Boss. Looks clear for a while.'

'Ways out, Stan, will be the right fork when we come to it or a one-eighty back down this track.'

'Roger that, Boss.'

'Through the trees or J-turn it?'

'Through the trees, Boss, no problem.'

'Tape starts. 18 September '89,' Paul interjected. 'Storkow NVA Engineer Training Area. 11.27 hours. Grid reference VT 280 911.'

'Trip. OK. 100 metres, track hits the main fire-break, turn right up the break and we'll be nose on to the target. 350 metres to target. Still no sign of our friends behind us and nothing up front.'

'Roger, Boss. Track's fine. No problems for the vehicle.'

'Nothing seen my side. All clear so far.'

'Trip. OK, about 200 metres should see us break the wood line. We'll nudge beyond it to the rise and take a peak at what's playing on the lake and the hard.'

'Roger, Boss.'

It was eleven days since my first Talon Snatch and train run tours. I had conducted two three-day local tours of Potsdam between then and now. The three of us were talking, almost at once but not interrupting each other. We were partly confirming for the benefit of the others that we were performing our own individual parts of the job as well as confirming that we were all working on the same plan.

'Wood line in view. Shit!'

'What the hell is that?'

'Check on.'

As we made the right-hand turn and started on the gentle rise along the fire-break to the edge of the wood, all three of us caught sight of it, causing us to question in triplicate.

'Paul, take the map please. Stan, pull over nice and slowly. I'm on cameras for one second.'

Stan pulled our vehicle off the forest fire-break and nudged slowly into the little cover afforded to us behind the trunk of a single pine tree. It was a gentle manoeuvre, the driver imparting just enough extra energy to climb the small earth berm and roll to a rest. We had been travelling at no more than 4 or 5 m.p.h. for the last 300 metres in order to keep the noise to an absolute minimum.

These vast East German pine forests muffled and distorted sounds. Normally there was very little to hear anyway and the slightest noise against the background of virtually no noise at all became easy to pick up. The muffling effect made the direction of noise difficult to determine. A buck calling to its mates or a wild pig grunting in the dirt would roll around the forest, overwhelming the ear's sense of direction. It was a double-edged weapon that we could both exploit and fall foul of.

This was no wild animal in front of us but it was an enormous beast. Our 3-ton Mercedes Geländewagen stuck out sheepishly either side of the tree, almost embarrassed at the position it had allowed itself to adopt for a surveillance operation. Paul looked briefly down at the map on his lap. He'd been following it anyway and could take over the navigation straight away. He placed the pointer of the distance scale on our precise location on the map. I checked shutter speed against aperture on the F3 and eased the 180-mm out of its bag to a more readily accessible position.

'Switch off, Stan.'

Stan cut the engine. Paul cranked the window down a couple of inches. Thank God they were wind-ups. Subconsciously I found myself reflecting upon the consequences of electric windows. How slow it would be to raise them compared to the furious turning by hand that necessity had accustomed us to. How unnatural the high-pitched whine of an electric motor would be in this ancient and peaceful forest. How far away might it be heard? It wasn't worth thinking about.

The binoculars went up to my eyes. Being stationary even for the briefest moment increased our vulnerability. Turning the engine off redressed the balance considerably by allowing us to hear any unwelcome movement, probably before we would see it, in this close cover. Every time we switched off I thought of the reliability of being able to restart the vehicle in an emergency and the result if we could not. I was doing it again. It was a paranoia among several others that I would repeat a thousand times more.

I realised that I wasn't concentrating, slightly knocked off the job in hand by the unexpected. I forced myself to dispatch the thought and focus on the object ahead. Stan started scanning forward and right. Paul commenced a similar scanning process forward and left. I concentrated on the monster to our front with the bins. I knew that both of them would be flicking over the wing mirrors in order to maintain a lookout behind. Such was their training that I did not have to remind them. I observed the scene that had stopped us but I still did not connect it with the morning's difficult passage into this normally quiet East German engineer training ground. We still had a further 150 metres to go to our target proper.

About 120 metres away, between us and the lake that we could not yet see, skylighted by virtue of being pulled up at the entrance to one of the many fire-breaks running through the wood, coincidentally the one we had selected to make our approach on, was an absolute monster of a vehicle carrying what appeared to be four large canisters on its back. We paused for a good ten seconds before anyone spoke. The suddenness of its appearance had taken us by surprise. The density of the forest had masked it from view until we turned the corner and repelled any noise of it away from the wood and into the open area it was facing on to. Both East German and Soviet soldiers were scattered around it in various states of dress. It was difficult to tell straight away that both were present. Most were stripped to their vests, which didn't help. A couple of them had the distinctive NVA side caps and yet others had the dark brown rather than drab olive tunics that defined them as Soviet rather than East German. I continued to stare at the vehicle.

'They look like flotation devices, perhaps they're rolled off in some sort of bridging operation.' Talk was at a whisper. Although they were some way off there was no need to alert them. It sounded good, plausible even. Paul lifted his binoculars and I routinely lowered mine in order to maintain all-round observation while his scope of vision became limited to the target.

'Boss, I haven't got a clue. You could be right.'

I passed my bins forward to Stan and switched lookout to his side of the vehicle, while Paul resumed arcs on his side. So close to a target and in such close country only one pair of bins went up at a time.

There was no response to my theory. Stan shrugged his shoulders and passed the bins back.

'Not a fucking clue, Boss.'

This was encouraging on the one hand because I would have got short shrift if I had said something stupid. On the other hand it was clearly not a shared theory!

I looked again. It wasn't a great view of the vehicle. At least half of it was stuck behind the trees. I surmised four canisters by symmetry from the two I could see. We had stumbled upon something unexpected. Stumbled not in the geographic sense because we knew exactly where we were to the nearest 10 metres, the chief instructor at the Special Duties Intelligence Course Ashford had seen to that – 'you will know where you are to within 10 metres at all times of the day and night' – but rather in the sense that this was not what we were expecting to see in this location. Each of us had spent about three to five hours a day on the course and half an hour to an hour every morning subsequently in Berlin devoted to Warsaw Pact vehicle and aircraft recognition. Between the three of us we must have known several hundred Soviet and East German equipment types, not to mention their respective variants. Two days earlier we had gone through the target files together, updated ourselves on the likely equipment, troops and training that we should encounter on the ground at this target. Finally, before leaving, I had checked with Ops, Slops and Weapons for any final updates on particular items of equipment that we should keep an eye out for.

This vehicle was unknown to any of us and with my recent amphibious engineering background and now finding myself on an East German amphibious engineer training site, I was beginning to put two and two together to make five.

'Not a fucking clue, Boss,' Stan confirmed again a few seconds later.

It had taken about 3 hours to manoeuvre through this vast coniferous forest towards a predetermined OP about 100 metres from the edge of a 10-acre lake. The target was an East German NVA engineer training ground. The lake and its adjacent hard provided the training ground for this East German Military Division's amphibious engineers, while the forest itself concealed several East German and Soviet units, including a chemical weapons research establishment and a railway ramp for loading and unloading military equipment trains. They were the next two targets on the itinerary.

One of the very first shots of 2S-6, revealing it as a new anti-aircraft weapons platform incorporating radar, missiles and guns. Its rate of fire was later analysed using the 'Black Banana' long-range microphone during live firing exercises on the Baltic coast.

Both Paul and I had Royal Engineer backgrounds. Paul Seager had come from the survey branch and was the Mission's current map specialist. It probably explained the superficial reason as to why we had picked up this particular set of targets. The real reason was that although this was my eighth tour it was the first tour out on my own. That is to say I was no longer being chaperoned by an experienced tour officer or NCO.

As such these should have been easy targets and an opportunity for me to command a tour for myself, without too much undue pressure from the opposition. Stan Matthews was a corporal driver in the RAF. He had been selected from the RAF's motor transport wing, passed his Special Duties training just like the rest of us and then further trained in the more pertinent driving skills that he would require for this job. Stan was decisive, brutally frank and exceptionally funny. He could tell the most humorous Mission stories for hours on end. How he remembered them all, I don't know. Ordinarily, because of his RAF background, he would normally have been driving on an air tour rather than a ground tour but drivers' schedules were often more haphazard than the NCOs' or officers', and their skills equally applicable to both types of operation. The NCOs and officers tended to specialise in either ground or air targets, covering both only as required. We all covered naval targets. On reflection, it must have been painful for Stan not to be sitting at the end of an active runway calling the planes completing bumps and circuits instead of firkling through this endless sea of pine trees without seeing a single plane or an expanse of blue sky. However, although the junior of the three, he was the most experienced on board.

This was probably only Paul's fourth tour. He'd been at the Mission much longer than me but his duties in charge of Geo[50] kept him back in Berlin running the mapping section and therefore restricted him to the part-time tour roster. He knew how to map read though, that was for sure. He was already the Berlin orienteering champion several years running. I had every confidence that he could get us around when necessary. But Stan had been in the Mission for three years now, with at least a hundred tours under his belt. Experience, common-sense and good decision-making were not the preserve of rank in this game. I would readily defer to Stan's judgement without hesitation during the course of these three days on my first solo. Furthermore, he was in control of the vehicle and thus affording us the best means of escape when the shit hit the fan. I had not toured with him before but he had a fearsome reputation for handling the vehicle when it counted and in that department I trusted him with my life completely. If he didn't know what the monster was either, then perversely, I was more relieved.

The plan of attack for the target location was well and truly out of the window. Furthermore, there were now several things not quite right. First, we had a vehicle that we did not recognise. Second, the reason we had taken so long to get into this normally quiet training area was due to the inordinately large number of NVA sentries scattered around the area, unbeknown to them successfully diverting us away again and again from our prime target. Why they were there I still couldn't yet connect with the apparition before us, other than to think it was a bit of overkill for an amphibious pontoon carrier. Finally, around the vehicle itself, was this apparent mix of Soviet and East German troops working together, itself a rather uncommon sight in what was normally a low-level training area. They hated each other and avoided working together as much as possible. They did it only because they had to, because the common enemy drew them together more than their mutual historical hatred pushed them apart. Sure, during full-scale Field Training Exercises (FTXs) or in support of operations against other satellite states they worked together reasonably closely, but not on a bog-standard engineer training ground.

It was very quiet inside the cocoon of the G-wagon. Outside, the wood muffled most sounds coming from the detachment of soldiers digging and fussing around the vehicle to our front. There was a small generator up there, helpfully masking any noise we might have made in our approach. Tension in the vehicle was rising steadily, controlled only by the need for certain drills to be performed. It was a mix of sheer adrenalin and fear. The adrenalin arose from the excitement of being so close to the enemy and yet remaining undiscovered, the fear from the thought of being discovered. It was a common feeling. It wasn't panic, it was an intense excitement. Suspense. Release from this mounting sensation would only come on leaving the scene or being spotted. The former wasn't possible until

---

[50] Geo: short for Geographic Section, responsible for all mapping requirements within the Mission.

the job had been done. The latter would prompt a more frenzied series of drills. More often than not a tour would go through these emotions on every target. Each member of the crew had to contain the welling anxiety in his own way. Getting on with the job itself was the best method.

The vehicle was a near-silent hive of activity. We had paused for only thirty seconds at most. In that time, while all-round observation was maintained to avoid being unnecessarily jumped, I had fine-tuned the cameras and film. My eyes diverted only briefly from scanning the scene to my front in order to coordinate my fingers on to these minute adjustments to the cameras. A camera case, inside a wooden box permanently mounted on the right-hand side of my chair and doubling as a makeshift table top, housed three Nikon F3 cameras with lenses already fixed, 85-mm, 180-mm and 1,000-mm. All three had film loaded, 100 ASA for the small lenses and 400 ASA for the 1,000-mm. They were continuously brought out of the box and adjusted for the changing light and prevailing conditions. F-stop balanced shutter speed, balanced depth of focus and balanced likely targets every waking minute of the tour, day or night. Contrary to popular belief we were otherwise unarmed. These were my personal weapons and I had to know how to use them.

There was nothing worse a tour officer could do than cock up the imagery. Imagery was the sole responsibility of the tour officer. Recognition was the preserve of the NCO and the vehicle was left to the driver. Without supporting imagery the value of any observation was degraded. Furthermore, it would give rise to the most severe earache from my peers back in the Mission.

Paul was still scanning all round as well as continuing to talk into his tape recorder held between his legs. He was now describing what he could see and what was going on. A 1:50,000 OS strip map was on his lap, index finger on our exact location now and his mind, if not his little finger, probably on our selected exit point from this target area as well as noting mentally the entry point for the next target, which would not now be so easy.

Stan was constantly moving his head to cover all arcs. It was a conscious regime that most tourers practised unceasingly while in the DDR as well as subconsciously back in Berlin, despite being in the relative safety of the accommodation blocks, married quarters or Naafi. You just did not stop looking around, scanning for someone or something to appear a couple of metres behind you out of a bush or a couple of kilometres in front of you on the horizon. After a year of this work both one's reactions and senses noticeably changed. The constant roving eye, down left and right roads as you passed through a crossroads or down a railway line as you crossed a level crossing, was disconcerting to friends and relations when you were in the relative safety of West Berlin or worse still when back in the UK. The ability to hear the slightest noise at further than average distances or being able to distinguish strange and unusual noise from the background clutter was enhanced. All the time we were looking and listening for clues that would lead us to or warn us away from the enemy. The inability to sleep for more than five or six hours a night and be easily disturbed when you were was a state that necessity perfected. Finally, an uncanny knack of sensing something was about to happen, almost a sixth sense that could not be simply explained other than perhaps by experience and intuition, was developed. It was an awareness, not simply that one's presence might provoke a reaction, but being able to predict when it would happen and where it was going to come from. Being able to react accordingly and only at the last moment necessary enabled tourers to stay one step ahead of the game. Controlling all of these emotions gave you a better chance of getting the job done.

I dialled plus one stop on the Nikon F3 exposure compensator for the 85-mm lens and held it in my right hand. The vehicle was partly highlighted on the brow of the hill and in the entrance to the fire-break. The 1,000-mm lens was out of the question given the close range. The 180-mm on the third F3 I placed on my lap, manipulated it with my left hand to remove the lens and placed it back in its protective box. The naked F3 stayed in my lap ready for any swap. It was decision time. I both loved and hated these moments. The proverbial calm before the storm. I felt as though all three of us in the vehicle and the scene we observed outside were in suspended animation. It could have gone on forever. It was like a lion that has stalked its prey and just before it launches into the final attack it pauses, tense and taut, waiting for the right moment to explode and commit itself.

We had to get a photograph of this vehicle but as yet I had no idea of its designation or its significance. The techies would tell me that later. It was simply a question of how close we could get and therefore how much better the detail would be in the final imagery. The tour officer sat in a single seat centrally located in the back of the vehicle, the camera equipment and video in the compartment to my right, six brew flasks filled with boiling water stowed in a fixed container on my left.

I was now perched on the edge of the seat, leaning forward into the front where Paul, the tour NCO, sat on the right and Stan in the left-hand driver's seat. This was rapidly becoming an opportunity target and one that we might have to run past. Ordinarily we would observe and photograph a target, whether it be barracks, equipment, training or people, and withdraw without being seen at all. No one would ever know we had been there. This derived two key benefits. First, it made the target as safe as we could possibly hope for, prior to the visit of a subsequent tour, whether it was me, someone else from Brixmis or someone from our sister missions in the American and French sectors when it was their turn to work the area. Second, it would preserve the integrity of the intelligence. What they didn't know we knew was quite a powerful weapon. It would also probably mean that we would not get caught or detained or, more seriously that we would not be shot at, rammed or chased. The vast majority of touring was conducted unobserved. Intelligence was gathered, returned, analysed and distributed without fuss and without anyone knowing. However, there came a time when it was considered more important in the balance to ensure that intelligence was acquired than to worry about the consequences. It was a calculated risk, the decision being very much the preserve of the tour commander, the guy on the ground. It was a decision based upon his judgement of the relevant importance of the target versus the potential danger of the situation he was putting his crew in. Risk versus gain. It was usually a snap decision.

There was no disgrace back at the ranch for having taken the decision to withdraw gracefully. Since the deliberate shooting of Major Nick Nicholson in April 1985 and the deliberate killing by ramming of Adjutant Chef Mariotti in March 1984, Brixmis operated very much along the lines that there was nothing out there worth dying for and certainly nothing that a tour officer should risk his crew's lives for.

There was also a spoken or unspoken consensus for the final target run within the vehicle, based upon the cumulative experience of the people in it. A run past necessitated deliberately exposing the vehicle and crew to the target in order to obtain satisfactory imagery. It was never a preferred option, the reaction was so unpredictable. It was a foolish tour officer that didn't listen to the wealth of experience available to him. The risks of being caught and the consequences of that were weighed up against the chance that the target was of high intelligence value and that it might never be seen again. The two fundamental guiding principles were first, that the crew on the ground was always right and second, that there was nothing out there to get killed for.

We were in that position now. We could not make the target we had come for because this great leviathan of a vehicle was in our way and yet this vehicle had now superseded our original target as the new objective of interest. I could not get a useful shot from this position.

'We'll run the vehicle.'

Each of us moved even further forward onto the front of their seats, our senses were working overtime for the second or third occasion in the last twenty-four hours. It was uncanny how one's eyesight became so acute, one's hearing so sensitive and how generally one developed an awareness of things about to happen in anticipation of them actually occurring. Everyone constantly discussed possible moves, possible reactions, routes in, routes out, actions on, what might happen and what we would do about it. Everywhere we went we spotted ways out, routes back and actions on if we were bumped. Most of the time it was a nugatory practice but those of us who had been caught knew that it was never wasted. All of this was done to avoid being seen, thereby avoiding being caught and therefore getting the job done. Running a target was a balls-up approach, showing yourself to the opposition, doing the dirty on them and getting away as fast as possible.

'They've seen us, Boss.'

One of the dozen or so soldiers working around our target vehicle had been looking in our direction as we were watching him. He had taken a break from some heavy trench digging. His mates were digging scrapes for the wheels, either for protection to the tyres or to prevent the vehicle rolling backwards on recoil after firing. He arched his back and started looking around quite innocently, his gaze coming to rest on us. He wasn't looking for us and he clearly did not recognise what he saw. He probably thought it was another UAZ 469 on the training area, the standard small army vehicle for both East German and Soviet troops, if he was thinking anything at all. Funnily enough, we were all looking at something we didn't recognise. The difference was that we knew it and he didn't.

Slowly the penny must have dropped and realisation crept across his face. If that was not enough to give him away he turned round to his colleagues far too suddenly and sharply for Stan's liking. That prompted his warning. We were masters of body language at anything from 3 to 300 metres. For a split second the top half of his body bent back the other way and although we did not hear what he said, his call coincided with Stan turning on the engine and Paul cranking the window back up. He was obviously shouting to someone near him. His right arm came up pointing in our direction and everyone stopped around him, their gazes following his arm and coming to rest on us. He'd blown it. He shouldn't have done anything quite so dramatic. My first action was to remind myself that at this stage we had not yet observed any weapons. We still had the upper hand. There was no panic inside the vehicle. Decision time had come a little earlier than I would have liked, that was all! This whole encounter had lasted no more than three maybe four minutes at most since we first spotted them. It would take them a few more seconds yet to react. We were still in control.

'Thank you, Stan. Square across the fire-break, right hand down. Get me a shot out of the left window. Route out back down the fire-break. Happy?'

'No problem, Boss.' The reply was gently mocking. There was no other way out and we all knew it. Going back the same way we came in was never very clever, particularly given the number of armed sentries that had been deployed in this wood. However, going forward was past the target vehicle and through the soldiers who were by now turning towards us. That was easily judged to be beyond the sensible. We'd worked out all the possible routes for our original target but this had rather changed things. Stan's tone was also clearly confident. He was the bloody driver and as such getting caught would have been a severe blow to his pride, not to mention cause for stick among his fellow drivers back in Berlin.

My right hand pulled the curtain across the right rear widow, momentarily swapping cameras to the other hand and back again in the movement. I lifted the camera up above the bottom of the window for the first time and swivelled to look out of the left side. The curtain now behind my back prevented light coming in behind me and therefore anyone seeing in to observe first, that I had a camera and second, what I was doing with it. It was strictly forbidden for Missions to take photographs of Warsaw Pact equipment, soldiers and barracks. Come to think of it was forbidden for anyone to take such photographs! But they knew we did it.

'Shit. There's someone behind us.'

Paul had spotted something in the rear-view mirror. The air turned blue as Stan confirmed the sighting. Things happened more quickly than normal but still calmly. There was no need to say go. Stan sat more upright in the seat, shifted his foot from brake to accelerator and floored it. He was concentrating hard now as the fortunes of this particular tour swung once again under his control. All our vehicles were automatic transmission. This allowed for ease and comfort during long driving spells and speed of response in an emergency. The G-wagon accelerated forward onto the wide forest track, the same fire-break that housed the target to our front and now a pursuing East German soldier. This was no time for finesse but there was every need for controlled aggressive speed. The force thrust me deep into the back of my seat, arms instinctively raised, holding the camera in my right hand and the empty body in my left, both of them up and out of harm's way.

I caught sight of an NVA officer moving rapidly on foot towards the back of us about 20 metres away. I presumed it was an officer, without having to check for rank, because he was completely done up at the front of his tunic, wearing a forage cap and generally looking quite smart. Clearly, he had not been sweating away like the other guys up by the vehicle. He had obviously spotted us by chance on returning down the fire-break from wherever he had been. His intention was also clear from his actions.

Stan spun the vehicle violently to the right and stopped. We were facing down a small track, perpendicular to the fire-break. This new track was unseen to us before. I doubted whether it was on the target map at all. It certainly wouldn't be on Paul's strip map. We were about 30 metres further forward and nearer the target. Stan had made up his mind about the new track. This was his intended way out and he was positioned accordingly, waiting for the word to go again. He knew that I had to get the imagery and that he had to make the time and a stable platform available to me. Paul was desperately trying to identify this new track on the target map to see if it was a goer. I had already decided to take it whether it did or it didn't. The fire-break was now blocked front and back. This new track would put us in a better position than we were in right now and might throw up more opportunities later. It was quite a simple choice. More importantly, at this moment I had to perform with the camera.

'It's yours, Boss.' Stan reminded me nonchalantly.

Stan had delivered us to the best position that afforded the closest camera shot, the best chance for Paul to describe the scene, while preserving the opportunity to get the hell out. It wasn't that getting caught would be embarrassing or that it might also come with an unspecified quantity of Soviet or NVA manhandling, or both in this case, but that not getting away might involve the vital loss of photographic evidence and that would mean that the mission had failed, no intelligence would have been gathered at all and frankly we would not have been doing our job. All we could have done was talk about it.

Skylined at the end of the firebreak, less than 100 metres away, was this huge four-barrelled beast of a vehicle about three times the size of a British Army 4-ton truck. We had a very clear view of its left rear three quarters but nothing else. We were still 30 metres from our nearest pursuer, the officer to our rear. The working party surrounding the vehicle had downed tools and were making their way towards us and it did not look as though it was going to be an orderly march past. I remembered the armed sentries posted around the perimeter that we still had to negotiate in order to get out.

I took two shots with the 85-mm lens that I had set up before being spotted. Way too few. I knew I was going to suffer back at the ranch. The only consolation was that an 85-mm shot was more likely to be in focus at this range and therefore more easily blown up later in Special. It was the best practice to take safe shots first before trying for close-ups. The 85-mm didn't fill the frame. A 180-mm shot was likely to capture more detail but would be slightly more difficult to focus under these conditions. It was always a compromise. Everything we attempted on tour had to be weighed up for pros and cons, whether it be the ideal brew stop or in which order to run a series of targets. It was a painfully constant decision-making process. Every waking minute and then often in my sleep. Would it be better doing it this way or that. Every option had knock-on consequences and each one of those had to be planned and weighed up, too. After three days this continual round of 'do we do this' or 'do we that' and 'for what reason' was mentally very tiring.

I needed more detail of the vehicle. Two further choices naturally followed. Pull out the 180-mm lens from the camera box and reconnect the 180-mm lens to the lensless F3 in my lap or simply change lenses and readjust for speed and aperture.

Both would take the same time. We had now paused for about three, maybe four seconds. The decision was instinctive, the other F3 was set for the 180-mm lens already. I ripped the 180-mm lens out of the box and attached it, dropping the 85-mm into my lap. Juggling bodies and lenses was a constant process. The picture outside changed all the time, whether it was the light or the distance or the depth of focus required. Furthermore, I reasoned that it would be better to have two cameras on the go in case we got out of this spot and there was something else waiting round the corner. The picture filled the frame perfectly. While the camera was up to my eye I was no longer in control of the tour. It was momentarily relinquished to the next person who made a decision. I sacrificed everything including the chance of being detained, manhandled, rammed or shot at, in order to take that photograph. Being stopped and forced to relinquish the film would have been highly embarrassing.

I heard Paul shout, 'Go, go go!'

Simultaneously, I heard the motor drive whirr forward one frame only. Time seemed frozen in that instant and instead of being petrified, the view down the lens seemed to wipe out everything else going on around me. I was thrilled and excited to have captured the instant on film. It would be another three days before I would know if it was worth it.

Stan launched the vehicle down the track. My camera came down. I had taken a total of three shots. Not nearly enough. The scene around me became very real once again. The whole episode from being spotted to committing and leaving must have been no more than twenty seconds. There was no second-guessing the decision to move. Paul raised his palm to our palpitating German officer, by now only 5 metres from the right-hand side of the vehicle, as if to say 'sorry we're in the wrong place, we're going'. All he had to do was put his hand on the front of the vehicle and we would have been in a different game. We were not in the business of deliberately running down East German officers, even if we didn't recognise the authority of their state. Some of the working party were now giving chase down the track behind us, others cutting through the wood to meet us side on. There were no other vehicles in sight or sound. Please don't let there be motor bikes, I thought.

'Shit!' It was Stan who saw him first, Paul and I were watching the pursuers.

About 150 metres ahead of us, one of the armed sentries was sitting just off the track, his back against a tree facing away from us. He had been oblivious to the commotion behind him. He stood up square across the track, still facing away from us. He must have been asleep. The noise having roused him, his natural reaction was to look down the track in the more likely direction of approach. Maybe he, too, was disorientated by the origin of noise in the forest. He was probably expecting a senior officer to visit and whichever army you were in that, more than anything else, was likely to throw a soldier off balance from what he was supposed to be doing.

Turning towards us but unable to take in and react quickly enough to the vision of a G-wagon hurtling towards him, pursued by a dozen or so of his colleagues, he stood motionless. He couldn't miss us now as we were picking up speed towards him. It was clear from his face that he was having difficulty trying to understand the situation. This vehicle had emerged from behind him, from the centre of his own training area. It was drab olive green and not too unlike a UAZ-469 at a glance. Its number-plate was obscured so that didn't help. Was it one of his? Had he missed seeing a senior officer's car come in? And yet it was being chased. Were they trying to stop us because we'd forgotten something? Thank God they had not issued radios to the sentries. He was one poor confused soldier. But couldn't he hear the others shouting at him?

I glanced back at the pursuing bunch through the left window. The rear windows of our vehicles were painted out to block any view in at the enormous amount and range of equipment that might be carried for any particular tour. I had to crane my neck round, my cheek up against the glass. The pursuing bunch were in a mixed state of dress. It was a warm September day and as Paul had remarked for the tape they had clearly been digging in or finishing off a prepared vehicle scrape so it was not surprising that they should be stripped to the waist. I still couldn't work out if they were just NVA or a mix of NVA and Sov troops. If there were Russians here and they were shouting at him then no wonder he was confused because he was clearly East German. This had probably been the most interesting three or four seconds of his week. He didn't take aim. His AK-74 stayed down. Too late, we were almost on top of him. It was almost his last three or four seconds.

'Shit, he's not going to move,' Paul cautioned.

'It's Bugs Bunny time then,' retorted Stan.

The sentry was so stunned he stood his ground, unable to react to what was going on. Stan span the wheel and the vehicle veered right, slamming into and over the berm of the track thrown up by years of endless vehicle manoeuvres down the same route. Stan had read my mind and did not give the sentry the opportunity to think any longer about it. We could only have been about 10 metres from him, the loose earth and thick top dressing of fallen pine needles must have sprayed him with the ferocity of the turn. The vehicle slewed violently. We had almost come back round through 180 degrees, the loose forest floor like a skid pan. Stan forced the G-wagon back the other way and perpendicular to the track. The accelerator stayed to the floor. The vehicle would have to catch up the engine. Stan was really working the G-wagon now. The power steering and the soft forest floor allowed him to use the palm of his hand flat on the steering wheel rather than gripping it conventionally. The back end swung left and right as it was forced back into a straight line. The regularity of planting and the thorough maintenance of the forest meant that the trees were arranged in straight lines whichever way you looked. There was enough space between the trees to manoeuvre the vehicle.

We threaded our way round the trees, moving at right angles away from the track and away from the training area we'd come to visit and never got to see. The course away was deliberately erratic. Left for two trees, right for one, straight on for three. There was no pattern. There was not meant to be. The needle was touching 40 m.p.h. on the straight, braking hard to turn and back up to speed. We simply had to put as much distance and as much cover between us and the pursuers as well as to confuse the poor guy further if he did decide to take aim.

I picked up the 1:25,000 target map of the training area, dropping the second camera into my lap and took up the navigation out of the forest. When it was quiet again I would remove both films, number and bag them. It was best practice to separate films according to the target rather than have two separate targets in one roll of film. Film was easily the cheapest part of the operation. We didn't have to worry unduly about how much it all cost.

We rejoined a different fire-break heading roughly away from the target. A UAZ-469 was coming the other way, again the driver rather surprised to see another vehicle coming towards him. There was probably a well defined circuit, entry in one way and exit out another. He was another proverbial rabbit in the headlights. Stan swept round him without slowing, keeping a line of trees between us before rejoining the track. A minor inconvenience.

I resumed control of the tour. Decision making had passed round the vehicle at least twice in the last minute. There was no need to tell these guys what to do. With eight tours under my belt this was not a new experience to me and certainly not to Stan. It was probably a complete stunner for Paul. As a part-time tourer this was probably his first brush with the Sovs and NVA at such close quarters. He was probably more excited than I was. This was undoubtedly his first chase. He should have been wetting himself but not as much as he would have been had we been caught. Detentions and incidents had eluded me so far. I knew it would happen one day but I was determined to put it off for as long as possible.

Stan executed a final series of slalom turns and we resumed normal cruising speed of about 20 m.p.h. back to the track and out of the target area. The forest came to an end and we emerged back out on to what passed for a main road in the DDR: it had tarmac on it. There was exhaling and deep breathing all round. I think I held my breath for the next two minutes just waiting for something else to happen as I navigated us out of the darkness of the forest and back into the light. Tension gave way to elation as we knew that we were now out of danger. It had not been the preferred, unobserved exit but speed, aggression and surprise had certainly got us out.

A trabbie passed us with four or five people on board. We waved to them, beaming broad smiles, muttering 'you don't know what we've just done'. If they'd been narks they wouldn't have looked at us or waved back as this lot did. We pulled out onto the road and kept moving until the road offered a better field of view of our surroundings and we were a good 2 kilometres away from the forest. We travelled in silence, no doubt each of us thinking about the encounter.

'There's a good place to stop up ahead. We'll brew up there.'

It was a crossroads where two main roads intersected with a tac-route back to the training area.

Ideally, we would find a brew stop overlooking a railway line, which crossed a main road, which coincided with a tac-route, which was manned by reggies. Heaven indeed! But they were few and far between. Anyway, Stan looked as though he needed a cigarette and bloody well deserved one in my book. He'd handled the vehicle well and spotted ways out for himself without being told. In situations like that it was preferable to let a driver have his head, give him general directions and run with it rather than deal in specifics and get the vehicle trapped from the back seat. I didn't know exactly how many tours he had done but this one was performed as meticulously as ever. I found out for myself why he enjoyed such a fearsome reputation over the course of the next few tours I would undertake with him. This one, although passing off uneventfully for the remainder, was yet to reveal how memorable it was going to be.

We visited the chemical research establishment several hours later, photographed a line of trees outside it and collected some of the foliage. Even for September, autumn had apparently come too early for these trees. The foliage was clearly disfigured by something. We bagged some leaf samples and slung them in the back for later dispatch to Porton Down, the UK's Nuclear, Biological and Chemical Defence Research Establishment. I heard nothing more about them. Either someone diverted them back at Brixmis to save me any embarrassment as a wandering leaf collector or they simply proved what we already knew, that they had been affected by the waste product belching from the chimney of what was an already established chemical research unit.

Some targets we were asked to visit were even more bizarre. We quite often checked out industrial complexes, photographing burn-off flame at chemical establishments or gas and oil refineries. At Greifswald we monitored the integrity of construction of the DDR's nuclear power station, taking water samples from the surrounding rivers, streams and as far out into the Baltic Sea as we could get. Occasionally we would break into underground storage bunkers in the middle of nowhere to photograph what were clearly nuclear fall-out shelters. The range of extracurricular targets beyond the military was extensive. From surveying the size and scale of lignite mining on the Polish East German border, the types of aerial on the roof of a tax office in Rügen to red herring grid references that turned out to be ploughed fields or thick woodland, the scope of out targets was as varied as the agencies requesting use of the extraordinary access that we had.

We also visited the ramp at Storkow, part of the original itinerary prior to our encounter, much later that afternoon, but I recall that there was nothing to be seen on it other than the beginnings of another beautiful East German sunset. Two further days saw us move from Storkow NVA Training Area to Cottbus and the Soviet parachute brigade's training ground. We passed through Gollmitz and Koebbeln where we discovered an unidentified (U/I) NVA installation, quite unintentionally provoking a very determined chase from two cars, one military and one civilian, that took us around the local roads. We tied them up in loose ground having seduced them off-road and returned to finish our study of the installation before leaving. It never ceased to amaze me that even after forty-odd years of this work there were still many installations that we had simply not encountered before.

Finally, we ended up in the infamous Luebben triangle, so called because the three major transit roads running round the outskirts of the town of Luebben intersected to form a small triangle in which the town itself resided. It was a major military thoroughfare for columns traversing the country from east to west or north to south and as such was a favourite haunt for mission vehicles. There were so many different ways of observing and recording the convoy movement that it was rather meat and drink to us. We could either do it fully in cover or completely out in the open eating ice cream on the side of the road. In cover the passing vehicles were completely oblivious to our activities. Out in the open the passing vehicles and their commanders would need a very good reason to stop and detain us in the middle of such a public place. They couldn't see the cameras and video and quite often we'd be parked up among local civilian vehicles in the town's main car park. It must have been very frustrating for them. The terrain was in our favour. There was little chance of getting boxed in and there was plenty of room for manoeuvre. They were open roads and we had every right to be sitting there. It was quiet but we waited and watched for a good three hours before moving for home.

There were certain procedures to go through before the tour was finally finished. All tours went through the Potsdam Mission House. It was like a safe house behind enemy lines except that everyone knew it was there, particularly those agencies watching us. They owned it and staffed it, after all. Despite the difficulty of the house being bugged, which we simply accepted and worked round, information was swapped between incoming and outgoing tours when they happened to cross. In particular, information was swapped with the Local Tour, virtually a standing patrol concentrating on Potsdam and its environs alone, where by no coincidence at all some 20 per cent of all GSFG troops were stationed. Potsdam bordered West Berlin to the east on the other side of the Havel lake. The units in Potsdam were stationed there simply to take West Berlin (Warsaw Pact title: Operation Centre) when necessary.

Many long walks were taken down on the lawn towards the lake at the back of the house and away from prying eyes and microphones. Even then we talked quietly and in veiled speech that would not have meant very much to anyone else. If it was difficult to talk outside because, as was only recently discovered, there were long-range microphones and lenses trained on the garden from the top of the Armeemuseum and Marmorpalais on the far side of the Heiliger See, which the Potsdam Mission House property backed onto. We would then have to exchange information by writing it down out of the watchful eye of the house staff, certain members of whom were alleged to be in the pay of the Stasi, and anyone else who seemed to visit under all sorts of delivery pretences. We usually conferred on the respective mood of the troops we had encountered, difficulties with roads, any encounters with narks or other agencies and whether or not we felt we had razzed up an area too much to make it more difficult for the next tour visiting. The Mission House was fully bugged. We simply assumed everything could be overheard and responded accordingly. Quite often we used it to our own ends, not for disinformation purposes but for getting much needed repairs and supplies on time by simply broadcasting discontent to the chandeliers and other light fittings.

The Mission House was also a place to calm down before returning to West Berlin. Crews would have a quick wash and brush up, vehicles would be lightly cleaned to remove excessive mud and debris, not because we wanted to be presentable but to avoid unnecessary attention on the bridge. If there was any damage to the vehicles then we would try and square it up before leaving if we hadn't been able to do it out on the ground. Generally we would try to create the appearance of having had three or four days of fairly sedate travelling around the East German countryside. They knew we hadn't but we weren't going to give them any excuse to hold us at the bridge in order to find out. For local tours, those specifically targeted to cover Potsdam with its high concentration of Soviet and NVA targets, the Mission House provided the most glorious full fried breakfast on earth.

After three days with other targets and priorities to cover, we had forgotten our brief encounter with the 'U/I engineer amphibious' vehicle, as we had decided to call it. We left the Mission House, waved to the East German sentry on duty in the box opposite the Mission House on the other side of the road, and made for the bridge. If you looked carefully in the wing mirror just before turning out of view you could sometimes see the sentry pick up the telephone to report our departure in his eagerness to please. We always waved to these guys. They were only doing their job. Ostensibly they were there for our protection ever since the Mission House had been threatened and stormed in July 1958 as an organised response to British actions in the Gulf at the time. We complained about the lack of security for an accredited organisation and they seized the opportunity to guard us – ceaselessly – day and night – without fail for the next thirty-one years! The sentry had already clocked us on arrival, but he was much more discreet in showing it, given that we got out only 10 metres from his box.

It was a more complex procedure on the Glienicke Bridge, or the airlock as it used to be referred to, replicating the passage from one environment into another without taking anything from either through. Apart from, of course, the little gems of information concealed about the vehicles. There was never an incident on the bridge. Maybe they would refuse entry to someone for some curious reason, but this was usually a genuine administrative error on someone's part and was quickly and courteously sorted, in most cases.

There was never any violence, retaliation or manhandling on the bridge. We may have stirred up a whole Soviet divisional route march 200 miles away, exacting an aggressive response from several of the units, but on the bridge it was all sweetness and light. There were several reasons for this. First, the bridge was in SERB's backyard. SERB was the organisation responsible for direct liaison between us and the Commander-in-Chief Group of Soviet Forces Germany (they didn't care to differentiate between East and West Germanies) who was based in Zossen Wünsdorf and to whom we were directly accredited. Brixmis was his liaison organisation back to the Commander-in Chief British Army of the Rhine. SERB did not want difficulties on the bridge that could otherwise be sorted out by discussion at meetings or by telephone that we undertook with them on an almost daily basis. Second, the nearer we got back to Berlin the less isolated and more public the environment became in which to conduct operations for both parties. The Glienicke Bridge, although forbidden territory to all but a handful of people, and its transit certainly restricted to a few, was a very well-known landmark, both politically and diplomatically. It did not need extra attention.

The final port of call before the Mission proper was the United States Military Liaison Mission (USMLM) headquarters or 'Spam House' as it was called by us and the French Mission. Here the key points of the tour were summarised in a two- or three-page statement known as a 'tour highlight'.[51] It would be collated with all the other Mission reports arriving that day and that distillation put in the

---

[51] Highlight: the key points of a tour. Reported to the US Mission immediately on return for collation with other intelligence sources.

The G-wagon could not always cope with every condition. This one required the assistance of the Soviets. Although grateful for the help, the tour crew would be extremely wary throughout.

melting pot with all other sources of intelligence, principally Sigint, Elint[52] and satellite imagery to give a daily summary of the state of readiness of the Soviet machine in East Germany. We were literally an early warning device, an indicator of hostility, to see if they were coming.

There was still one more visit to make before being released from the tour. We had to check back in to our own Mission to ensure that they knew we had returned safely. We also had to off-load all the equipment we had taken out and deliver the film and any other items that we might have collected. It was quite normal for a tour to extend its three-day schedule because of current activity. A twenty-four hour extension of tour drew little attention. A forty-eight hour extension put the tour on a watching brief and would necessitate revising some of the other tour schedules in Ops' plans. At that point it would be normal for an overdue tour crew to phone in to the Mission House and just say something innocuous like they were having a very nice time and intended to continue the visit.

It was not possible to call West Berlin from East Germany without going through an operator. That would have attracted immediate attention. All phone lines into the Mission House in Potsdam were routinely tapped, so messages were relayed in veiled speech that conveyed only general intent rather than any specifics. There were code words for certain observations too important not to be followed up, as well as code words and phrases for certain situations that required explanation.

---

[52] Elint: electronic intelligence e.g. bugging.

Usually the mere fact that a crew had phoned and identified themselves was sufficient to avoid crashing out the standby crew or paying a visit to SERB to enlist their help in establishing whether a crew was genuinely missing or being held against their will.

Our office in Berlin was on the top floor of the Olympic Stadium headquarters. Access was via a small and inconspicuous back door. All the gear we used or any items that we had recovered on tour had to be lugged up the three flights. It was a tiring climb after three or four days out on the road. There was a lift but that was used for stuff that could not be physically manhandled to the top. Entry to the top floor was controlled by the duty NCO via a CCTV camera positioned outside the back door with a monitor in his bunk. Occasionally, the odd strange character came through the door to meet up with MI6, who were located on the floor below, blandly disguised under the title of the Protocol Department.

To all intents and purposes this back door was an insignificant tradesman's entrance to the main Berlin Garrison Headquarters that simply had a single security camera outside it. Once inside the building, access to the tourers' section was through a steel grilled door with combination code. The Operations end of the building was strictly off limits to non-military personnel with the single exception of Bill Emery, who ran Electric Light. On the whole there was little toing and froing between offices without a purpose.

At either end of the corridor beyond the grille a red flashing light with a siren used to go off to denote an uncleared visitor to the area, usually a plumber or electrician to repair something or other. He or she would be attended at all times and watched like a hawk. An electronics sweep would be done as a matter of routine after any major repair work. The Ops room had its own flashing light outside and no one entered there if it was going. I was convinced that they sometimes put it on to get some work done in the incessant, almost twenty-four-hour operation to control all the crews out on the ground. If you were unfortunate to come back off tour after a code change on the steel grille then you had to walk the whole length of the top floor to the duty NCO's bunk to get the new code and back again.

Along the entire inner wall of the corridor, some 80 or 90 metres in length, was the 'wall map'. The wall map was the single key working document for all tour crews. The entire DDR was mapped out in 1:50,000 with every barrier, OP, rail-crossing light, danger area, installation, EDA, barracks, Tommy, likely going, bunker, electric fence, sentry post and so on that could possibly make tour planning more meticulous. It was the bible and final authority for what was out in the DDR.

I shared an office with two other Army tourers and three RAF tourers. All the noticeboards had curtains drawn in case visitors were chaperoned in when there was no one there. Cleaners never came up this end of the corridor. In theory we did it ourselves! There were never any bullshit inspections, inventory checks or quartermasters fussing whether the lights were on or off. I checked my desk. It was already loaded up with the target files and brief for the next tour, which I would have to plan the next morning. I was going out again in three days with John Buchan and Graham Heaman.

I delivered my film to Special who had already been called in from their accommodation to meet us. They would have the film processed and on desks by the morning. They worked very unsociable hours and were constantly under pressure to develop film from incoming tours and reproduce copies of interesting shots from previous tours for dispatch to the various branches of Tech Int Army, the Foreign Office or wherever they were most appropriately directed. Theirs invariably was a twenty-four-hour operation. It was rare not to find someone in there at all times of the day or night. In the busier summer months their staff was sometimes augmented to cope with the load. None of the tourers had any sympathy as we quite often worked day and night for three or more forty-eight-hour periods in a row with snatched periods of rest and sometimes none at all. They were working in the warm and without the hassle.

It was gone midnight before I got into the mess. Even that had a combination lock in these days of terrorist activity in Northern Ireland. To cap it all my room was in an annexe to the main building which itself had a separate code. I had at least three to remember just to get home. The room in the mess had a phone installed by virtue of my job. I could theoretically be summoned at a moment's notice. If I was in the standby crew for emergencies then I would also wear a bleeper which could reach me anywhere in West Berlin. The phone rang at 7 a.m. It was Ian Passingham, the Ops Officer. He wanted me over before normal start time to debrief early. On arrival, this time through the front door of the Olympic Stadium, beyond the two impressive golden eagles set on high pinnacles, because I was clean, shaven and in proper uniform, I was met by Paul and Stan, who had received similar calls.

'What have you done, Boss?' Stan joked.

Ordinarily the Tour Officer debriefed alone with the Ops Officer. Slops listened in case there was an air interest and also because they shared the same small office: he had to listen! Adrian Pryce, the Weapons Officer, was the first to stop us in the corridor. In attendance was WOI Corcoran, Assistant Weapons Officer, whose hobby, let alone his job, was equipment recognition. He could determine a vehicle type from the wheel nuts alone while standing on his head looking through a frosted window from at least 2 kilometres. His recognition skills were better than average if not legendary. We were motioned into his office adjoining the Ops room.

A series of open questions followed. The tack was obvious because he was having difficulty retaining an air of indifference.

'The vehicle you saw in Storkow. Can you describe it for me?'

I described it.

'Was it wheeled or tracked?'

'It was wheeled, definitely. Two pairs on the rear axle and probably three axles.'

'How many canisters did it have?'

'Four.'

'Do you think it would have floated?' I spotted the trick question a mile off. As the Weapons Officer his knowledge of equipment and its capability was second to none. He was trying to understand what it wasn't before defining what it was.

'No.'

Then followed a series of negative questioning.

'You didn't see any Soviet soldiers there?'

'I think it was a mix of Soviet and NVA but I wouldn't swear to it.'

'You weren't challenged?'

'Not till we left, but we had some difficulty getting in past several armed sentries. They didn't see us until we left.'

After a few more rounds of this banter Adrian relaxed, sat back and uncovered a line drawing from some obscure Nato reference paper and placed it on top of the mound of paperwork, photographs and journals that were already covering his desk.

'Does this look like your vehicle?'

Stan and Paul crowded round. The match was instantaneous to all three of us. Although it was a side-on sketch of a vehicle and we had only had about a twenty-second view of its rear three quarters, the similarity was obvious.

'Where's the imagery?' I asked, sure that he had probably already seen it. If he was asking, then maybe I had screwed up the photographs.

'You only took three shots and two of them are blurred.' There was a reprimanding tone now.

I wasn't sure what to say next. I was still the junior tour officer and therefore eminently teachable.

'But they'll do,' he added, smiling now. 'And this one is really quite good.' He couldn't disguise his excitement. It was the single 180-mm shot that filled the frame.

'It's an SA-10B Gecko Transporter Erector Launcher,' adding for good measure, 'they don't have them in East Germany . . . until now.'

A little smile crept across my face. A scoop.[53]

Ian Passingham walked in and, as if he'd been listening to the conversation, simply added, 'and you're going back tonight with Brian and Heaman to find them again. There should have been at least four of them. We're not completely sure who they belong to, GSFG Army Group or East German Air Force. We also need better detail and if possible mensuration.'[54]

We never did find them. We found the location and the evidence of tracks. We photographed and measured them by way of collateral forensic evidence but otherwise the area was dead. They couldn't be seen in any of the barracks in the vicinity. To my knowledge satellite imagery revealed nothing. I went back for a third time, this time with John Buchan and Graham Heaman again, a few days later. We were really pushing our luck, but there was no sight of them.

It was a further year to the day before I sighted them again in a road move to Rügen Island for ferrying back to Russia during the withdrawals. They were returning to Russia through Poland along with other high-value, high-technology equipment. They were not seen at all in the intervening period. Some weeks after the initial sighting the single photograph was shown at the Allied Technical Weapons Intelligence Conference (ALTWIC) and given the title of the sexiest

---

[53] Scoop: the first sighting, backed up by imagery, of a new piece of equipment or the obtaining of tangible information pertaining to the new equipment.

[54] Mensuration: the science of accurately measuring life-size dimensions from a photograph using a known dimension in the photograph.

The Glienicke Bridge crossing point, summer and winter.

intelligence photograph of the year. Another couple of weeks passed and the Mission received a signal from the Pentagon congratulating us on our efforts, adding that the photograph had been put on the President's desk and, as a result of this single find, all offensive air operations for Nato in Western Europe were to undergo a thorough review in the light of the new threat now demonstrably present in the DDR. It was a staggering discovery, once again justifying the value of our behind-the-lines operation. Interestingly, the system is about to resurface outside Russia. It has been bought by the Republic of Cyprus for air defence duties against mainland Turkey and in that permanently bubbling flashpoint will no doubt cause considerable anxiety in the region when it is finally introduced in 1998. At least as member states of Nato they will both have access to the details for the system!

1. Part of a battalion's worth of T-80 are preparing to fire on a live firing range. This photograph was taken at first light from about 30m, without being seen by any of the crews.

2. This is simply a great photograph of a HIND-E. It looks 'mean' and is one of the most versatile, able and potent weapons platforms. This quality of photograph is hard enough to reproduce at an air show let alone at a range of 1 km, in bad light, with a 2,000mm lens and never really sure when and where the next aggressive response might occur.

3. This was the sort of response we were constantly trying to avoid. This signals soldier was disturbed by something and came out of his box-body to investigate. His intention is pretty clear.

4. The Opal Senator had an impressive turn of speed and good cross-country ability. This was the vehicle chosen to get a job done quickly.

5. The DDR was blessed with some curious village names that provided us with amusing light relief.

BRIXMIS
MAR 1990
B. F. P. O. 45

WPNS OFFICE		
GSO 2 (W)		
WPNS NCO		27/3
CIRCULATE		
FILE	3E	
REMARKS		

Copied to:
chief,
appropriate tourers.

6. Tour officers were encouraged to take plenty of photographs to maintain skills. This couple were photographed with a 2,000mm lens from a range of nearly 1km. The MOD signal refers to the technical intelligence value of the 2A-65 imagery. The two were put together for our own amusement.

7. One of the drivers sorting out the early morning brew and flasks for the rest of the day.

8. As part of the liaison function, we often arranged formal meetings with Soviet Kommandants. Here the SO1 – Colonel Robin Greenham, the author, and SSgt John Buchan (out of shot) meet with the Kommandant of Leipzig (rear left of table), his interpreter, and someone (?) in a suit, in the Kommandant's office, after a very pleasant lunch at the Hotel Astoria. It was 24 November 1989, so intriguing to observe a very tetchy exchange between the Kommandant and 'mere' hotel staff that, two weeks previously, would have been unconscionable; the writing was clearly on the wall that things were going to be different.

9. Voted the 'sexiest' intelligence DIS photograph of the year – SA-10B – a surface-to-air missile system not thought to be deployed as far forward as the DDR. This photograph changed NATO air strategy in central Europe. The system was subsequently sold into the Republic of Cyprus for defence against mainland Turkey.

10. A Brixmis RAF Tour Warrant Officer 'watching them'.

11. The Glienicke 'Bridge of Spies' photographed from the air by the Chipmunk. The bridge was lightly trafficked by diplomats and 'diplomats'. The two buildings at its right hand end are the Soviet (top) and East German (bottom) control points. Mission tours only acknowledged and transited through the Soviet control point.

12. OBERON imagery reveals the detailed breech mechanism of the tracked artillery piece – 2-S5.

13. A typical and rather obvious 'nark' vehicle with 3 or 4 MfS (Stasi) surveillance officers inside pointing to the camera.

14. By 1990, the Mission's tasks had come to include the observation of Soviet equipment withdrawals. This task was still undertaken 'clandestinely' if only to test that advertised withdrawals actually did leave the DDR and not just return the next day or week. Paradoxically, at the same time, new equipment still entered the DDR. At the time – unsurprisingly with hindsight and given the enormity of the geo-political change – confusing and contradictory 'signals' abounded.

15. Two near complete BTR-60 equipped battalions on parade with ancillary equipment displayed.

16. Operation OBERON – surveillance and imagery from the Chipmunk – classified at 'Secret' or 'Top Secret', provided several clear advantages over regular ground surveillance: it could catch military activity unawares; it often 'described' entire unit formations in one picture (as in the next photograph); or, as in this photograph of the internal workings of a PAT HAND SA-4 radar system, it could provide detailed technical intelligence right into the 'guts' of key target equipment.

17. The G-wagon's cross-country capability was unsurpassed by any other vehicle the Mission ever used.

18. Except on this occasion, clearly!

19. A typical target showing a selection of air-defence radar – BAR LOCK and FLAT FACE variants – surrounding an air-defence site.

20. Low-light surveillance imagery using the Modulux image-intensifier turns night into day. It was easily sufficient to distinguish vehicle type and identification number. In this case a then sought-after BTR-70, side number 108.

21. While it was difficult to cross the border between East and West Germany, it was possible to cross the Polish or (then) Czechoslovakian borders, on foot, fleetingly, and out of curiosity rather than directed, in certain remote places near Stettin (Szczecin) or Zittau respectively.

22. Mission Restriction Signs were simply ignored, or, to demonstrate the spirit of Christmas and the Mission's 365-day role, removed in order to present to a leaving Mission member or even – tongue-in-cheek – to a departing SERB Officer.

23. Soviet naval capability was also targeted; usually centred on the port facilities of Rügen Island in the Baltic Sea.

24. This is either an extremely 'brave' photographer, or one who has not quite recognised the situation.

25. Bunkers of all varieties were a key target for Mission tours. An elaborate underground network, including communication systems, linking forward to rear and flank to flank, was known and shown to exist.

26. West Berlin and East German police try to control the crowds crossing the Glienicke Bridge, the 'Bridge of Spies', on 11 November 1989.

27. General Snetkov – Commander-in-Chief, Group of Soviet Forces Germany – at the last Soviet War Memorial parade in West Berlin just days before the Wall came down. He looks as though he knows what is about to happen. Although, throughout the next few months, it became clear that he had no inkling; his prime concern was to become the welfare and safety of his troops.

28. Mission Restriction Signs (MRS) were posted to keep Missions out; they mostly signposted the way! Tour crews carried 'passes' issued by SERB, and routinely wore Brixmis flashes to distinguish them from other soldiers operating in East Germany. Interestingly the author's pass pictured here was signed as 'guaranteed' until 31 December 1994!

29. In 1989, East German Head of State Erich Honnecker's view – 'The Wall will remain for another 100 years' – clashes dramatically with reality.

30. Just another 'prick' on the Wall. Two days previously anyone attempting this sort of stunt would have simply been used for target practice.

CHAPTER SIX

Just Another Prick on the Wall

At dawn on Friday 10 November 1989, two months after the Mission's first encounter with SA-10B, I was awaking to the second day of a tour with Brian and Al Tipping way down in the south-west DDR around Erfurt, Weimar and the Zella-Mehlis anti-aircraft radar sites. The preceding twenty-four hours had been deathly quiet, with very little activity out on the road and very little activity in barracks. By all observations the Sovs had been tucked up in bed all day.

Quiet days were never wasted. It had been a good opportunity for updating files and familiarising ourselves with new target sites; their going, escape routes, likely OPs and so on. We had visited the Mönchenholzhausen Tommy the previous night for the first night's task. It was a becoming a regular visit for me. It passed off without incident, just as it should have done.

We transited direct to Rudolstadt to investigate a little-known OP overlooking an 8 GTA tank barracks in Rudolstadt itself. Rudolstadt was situated at the bottom of a very narrow steep-sided valley running north to south. We were perched high up on the west side of the town giving us good views into the barracks and down the main road towards the town centre. There was a little track going off to local allotments that gave us a route in and out whenever we needed to use it. The OP was covered from view of the barracks by a thin screen of ash saplings alongside us. It was the net curtain routine. We could see through it but they couldn't see us. Any locals coming along the track would have thought we were just having a cup of coffee somewhere out of the way, sheltered from the wind. They wouldn't have thought that we were watching anything.

My window was fully down, the 1,000-mm resting on it. I was slowly picking off the vehicles in the compound one by one, getting side-numbers and VRNs to check against Electric Light's database. Everything was peaceful. We were getting the intelligence without hassle, without causing a fuss and without being seen. It was clearly going to be a quiet tour. I hadn't had many, but they were welcome in their own way. It gave us the chance to talk to the locals more than normal, try and understand their fears and concerns and quite genuinely gain their confidence. If we could elicit information regarding barracks, equipment types and so on, then we would. More often than not they would be quite willing to tell us anyway.

If we wanted information from a local we would ask them directly rather than try and trick them. In our dealings with East German civilians we played it straight down the line. They respected us for that. Of course in the process we would sometimes take abuse and the odd aggressive response, but we could not be faulted for our honesty. Forty-four years of British presence inside the country amounted to a considerable sum of personal contact with the population, however casual. We found the average East German to be quite an honest individual, rarely cynical, and not terribly suspicious. They contrasted starkly with the average West German and even more so with the arrogant West Berliner. The straightforward and humorous characters that they encountered over the years must have grated sharply with the propaganda image of the 'villains of the piece', that they were told we were. Real life contact with Westerners severely contradicted the official view of the world that they were taught at school. They may not have believed or agreed with our version of events but it must have made them think.

We especially concentrated on the kids and young people. It was not a policy or a tactic that was directed from on high but rather an insight generated by Brixmis itself; be nice to them and they may be nice to you. If they weren't, fine. We hadn't lost anything. As a precaution we were always wary of any information given to us. It was quite easy to tell when we were being set up. Body language across Europe is not terribly different from our own. Additionally, people's knowledge of military equipment is vague. Their sense of timing inaccurate. They may have been trying to please. We never paid for information except where we were genuinely running an informant and even they often had motives other than money. It was surprising what a bar of chocolate or a cigarette could elicit from an East German. The odd Sov was not wholly immune to our charm either. Reggies, in particular, were regularly befriended and quite often fed, out of pity, while they endured days of being stationed on road junctions, waiting for a convoy to show up, with no rations and little way of keeping warm. In turn, knowingly or unknowingly, they supplied us with rare gems of information.

'How about a bit of sightseeing, boys? I'll treat you to an ice cream.'

'It's November, Boss.'

'OK, just the sightseeing then.'

Buying ice creams was a traditional Mission pastime. It broke up the intensity of a tour and gave us a perfect alibi for mixing with the locals. It was difficult to be accused of spying while buying ice cream. Like waving and stopping for coffee breaks, there was a hidden psychology behind the routine. It gave us an air of normality or, even better, slight eccentricity, sufficient to disarm detractors. We looked casual, somewhat inept and we stood out like a sore thumb. Surely these weren't the people that were sent to spy on us? The effect we created was semi-deliberate. We were putting ourselves on a pedestal, in a typically British self-deprecating way, for the local populous to see us, poke fun at us and feel more at ease with us. Just as suddenly, we would disappear and melt into the background, getting on with what they couldn't see us doing. The rest of the time we simply wanted an ice cream!

We drove down to the main road below and into the square. The large crowd took us rather by surprise. There were several hundred people queuing outside the Vopo headquarters as well as the local post office. Neither of them, normally, opened their doors to the public in these numbers. We were almost completely ignored. Ordinarily someone would have at least shaken a fist or waved a cheery greeting. They were completely preoccupied. We parked up and observed them,

Graham Geary on the East German border marker, pointing to the equivalent Czech marker. Borders were easy to cross in the right places.

trying to make sense of it.

'Wait here, Al, I need to find out what's going on.' I got out of the vehicle and walked over to the nearest line.

'What are you queuing for?' I asked in German, directing my remarks generally to the nearest bunch in the queue.

'We're getting our visas.'

'Where are you going?'

'West,' was the single response.

'What are they doing at the post office?'

'They're trying to get 100 West D-Marks, as promised.'

Visas and money. Even I knew that the average East German found it difficult to travel abroad. The bureaucratic hoops they had to go through, designed to mask the barely transparent political reasons for not letting anyone out, were inordinately frustrating. Several explanations crossed my mind. They might be raving mad, I might be misunderstanding their dialect and incorrectly translating, or else this was a rather large package tour getting under way. It also occurred to me that the unthinkable had happened and the Wall was open.

They were clearly very excited and actually quite difficult to talk to as a consequence. Practised in the art of queuing, taught to them at an early age by the shortages in basic provisions, they rarely took their eyes off their position in line for fear of being usurped by the person behind. I relayed my brief exchange to Al and Brian, completely stumped and with very little way of rationalising what I was hearing.

Subconsciously, consciously, or wherever realisation dawns from, I knew the answer already but couldn't bring myself to acknowledge it. We sat in the vehicle for a short while just watching them and making notes. I was aware that somehow these events were part of a bigger stage and that if my conclusions were right, and the Wall was coming down, then there was going to be very little point recording this sort of information. This was beyond my remit. Of all our possible explanations for this behaviour, the Wall being opened was the most difficult for us to deal with. So that was the one we ran with.

I decided that the best thing we could do was to get the vehicle on to some high ground and tune in to the radio for more information. We left Rudolstadt and kept a low profile, avoiding any more towns for the time being, until we could get a better picture of what was happening. If the Wall had come down, then reaction to our presence might change significantly, but in what way I didn't know. The German radio was no good in this part of the world because their accent was so thick it may just as well have been another language. It was almost Bavaria down here. The terrain prevented us receiving either the American Forces Network from West Germany or the French equivalent. Rudolstadt was the largest town in the area and that was pretty small. Leipzig was the nearest big city. We were due there for a target in the morning.

We changed things around so that we would hit Leipzig that night. The remaining few targets in and around Rudolstadt came and went, but we were so preoccupied with the events of that morning and trying to establish the best way of finding out if something was awry that we could hardly concentrate on them. It was strange that with all the intelligence-gathering equipment in our vehicle, the one thing we couldn't find out was what was happening back home in Berlin. Our bleepers hadn't gone off so whatever was going on was not important enough to warrant calling us in.

I considered telephoning back to the Mission House in Potsdam, in itself not an easy thing to do with the state of the East German telephone system. BT in its worst years would have knocked spots off this tin-can affair. But what would I have said? Are you all right back there? Just calling in for a chat and, oh, nearly forgot by the way, has the Berlin Wall come down? They would have definitely thought I'd 'lost it'. I wasn't aware that at that very moment on the morning of 10 November 1989 back in Berlin, they were having as much difficulty rationalising the ramblings of the DDR government spokesman, Günther Schabowski, at a late night press conference on the 9th, as we were having trying to rationalise what we had witnessed in Rudolstadt.

Leipzig was my best shot for information. I knew that with favourable conditions and in the right place under the overhead tramlines, where they converged by the main station, we would be able to pick up BBC Radio Four long wave and the World Service, while still watching the railway line for any military activity. The overhead tramlines acted like an extension of our own aerial. We didn't have to connect up to them, we just sat under them in the right spot. It was very faint but we could make out references to the Berlin Wall, which were oblique and in the past tense as though it had disappeared. The reception was very poor and large chunks indiscernible. It didn't really confirm what we needed to know but it was enough to make us think something wasn't quite right. The city of Leipzig itself seemed normal. If there was anything afoot then it wasn't immediately apparent among the locals here. Their recent human rights demonstrations had died down a few days ago and had seemingly moved on to East Berlin. Freedom of travel had certainly been one of their demands and some lifting of its bureaucracy had recently been allowed, much as it had been relaxed after the Quadripartite agreement of 1971. But they weren't going to simply drop all restrictions altogether, surely?

I discovered a few days later that Ian Cameron-Mowat, the Senior Tour Officer, was out on tour with the Chief and Kev Powell that same day and had been similarly surprised by the same Radio 4 broadcast referring to the Wall in the past tense. He was only three hours away from Potsdam, but fortunately for him the Chief decided that his best place was back in Berlin, and they hotfooted it there immediately. He was back in his office before midday.

We resolved to travel back to Berlin slowly the next day, which is when we were expected back anyway. We still weren't totally sure what was going on so we didn't want to get back too quickly. If there was something going on then our best place was to be out here, observing reaction. In this case any reaction would have been welcome to give us a better clue as to the cause. The DDR was as quiet as a mouse.

On arrival at the Mission House it was a chaotic scene. Normally church-like, the place was full of Brixmis staff, some not on pass looking for all the world as though they were recovering from the night before and preparing to go out on the town again. The three of us couldn't take it in. The Sovs on the Glienicke must have made a mistake letting non-pass people over to Potsdam.

We got hold of Tony Haw, the Mission House Warrant Officer, a former tour NCO and man of enormous sanity. Tony wasn't phased at all. He was his normal laid-back self.

'Yeah, they opened the Wall two nights ago, the 9th I think it was, and last night they opened the Glienicke Bridge. It was Keith Marshall's leaving do in the Cecilienhof and Rod and Trudi McLeod's party in the Mission House. Some of them are still on the bridge. You'll have a job getting back into the city I reckon.' It was just another incident in an already colourful career for him.

We left the Mission House and drove the 2 miles back to the Glienicke Bridge that we had crossed with all the usual formalities only three days previously. We turned the corner onto Route-1, Berliner Strasse, the normally deserted road that led to the Glienicke. The bridge was only 300 metres away but we could barely see it for the crowds filling the road, walking towards it. The scenes were extraordinary. This was the second night that it had been open, Tony had said. We pulled into the flow and inched forward slowly with people either side of us as we were sucked into the general movement forward.

The bridge of spies was open to the public. The bridge immortalised in 1962 by the swap of America's U2 pilot Gary Powers (the man who almost single-handedly turned the Cold War into something much hotter) for captured Soviet agent Colonel Rudolf Abel, had people on it. It was unbelievable. There were no Soviet sentries in sight but there was a light on in the box and I could see a clear area around their building which was being kept so by both East German and West Berlin police. Not normally renowned for working together, the enormity of the crowd and the danger to public safety that such large numbers can create forced them to pool their resources out of necessity.

The crowd around us were unanimously happy, most were crying or smiling, singing or shouting. They all wanted to shake our hands, talk to us and slap the vehicle in a sort of congratulatory way. There was very little we could do other than ride along with them. There was no malice or harm at all. The atmosphere was one of immense and profound joy, the noise incredible. We represented the establishment, but if they were conscious of which side of the fence we came from it didn't seem important to them. They were just happy that someone in uniform and therefore, de facto, in authority in this part of the world, was there with them to help them celebrate their freedom. This was an expression of the people for the people and in their good grace we, the policemen and the Soviet sentries, were all targets of their happiness. It was almost as though the establishment was being publicly forgiven for everything that had gone on before. Roses were given to us by some young girls who were making their way over from Potsdam. All the policemen received them too. I was standing on my seat with my top half out of the cupola in the roof, talking away to everyone who wanted to talk to us. The atmosphere was electric, the moment of crossing intensely emotional and dramatic. Years of misery seemed to be peeling off, washed away in a single stroke.

'It's all over,' I remember saying to Al and Brian as I ducked back into the vehicle and then out again. 'We've done it. We're witnessing history in the making. The Cold War is over and we've won.'

It was a terribly naïve remark and certainly very premature in the implication that all our problems were now solved. The Cold War was certainly not won and by no stretch of the imagination was it over. The fall of the Wall simply heralded in a new phase in the long and tortuous postwar history; yet another momentous landmark in the much greater ideological struggle between communism and Western-style democracy that had been littered with momentous landmarks since 1945. With hindsight, the fall of the Wall certainly seems to have marked out the first page in the last chapter, but it was by no means obvious at the time.

I had been very confident that this day would come and expected to see it in my lifetime, but not yet and not so suddenly. Curiously enough I had been sent to Leipzig when the first demonstrations occurred to try and gauge the feeling of the people partaking in the human rights marches. It wasn't really a Brixmis role. We were the military experts not amateur social psychologists, but as usual we were conveniently placed in country. We visited everything from shipyards and chemical factories to undiscovered war graves and misplaced relatives. In the huge menu that made up our target list, observing demonstrations was as bizarre and therefore, paradoxically, as routine as all the others. Furthermore, there were many demonstrations that the Mission had witnessed down the years.

We observed the demonstrations in several cities. The response was firm but inconsistent. In some cases it was touch-and-go whether or not the Vopo and local military would actually turn their weapons on the crowds. German killing German. In other cases where physical restraint merely involved tear gas and baton charges, there was little conviction in, or pleasure derived from, those dealing out the punishment. They had become as confused as the protesters, as quiet chats with them and video footage revealed. Between 21 October and

8 November that year, thirty-seven towns and cities registered civil rights demonstrations. They ranged in size from several thousand to a staggering 500,000 recorded on Saturday 4 November in East Berlin itself.

As always there was a funny side to touring for the Mission. We could always be relied upon to get a laugh out of the difficult situations we found ourselves in. During one of the major protests that occurred in Leipzig centred on the city's main church, Saint Nicholas, Ian Passingham, the Operations Officer, had gone down to see for himself what was afoot. There were some 250,000 demonstrators reckoned to be marching towards it. As the lead group crossed the deserted main square and approached the church a pedestrian crossing light changed from green to red, whereupon the whole protest march came to a grinding halt until it turned back to green and they proceeded. It was a highly incisive observation reflecting the power of the authorities and the total willingness to obey ingrained upon the national German psyche.

What was evident to us was the degree of support or rather lack of it that was forthcoming from Moscow. The iron glove response to these demonstrations, that many might have expected from Honecker's regime, was unsupported in Moscow. For some years now Gorbachev had been warning Erich Honecker in sensitive but diplomatically clear language that his methods had to change. Most recently, he had visited East Berlin on 7 October, the fortieth anniversary of the DDR, and quite openly warned its government that 'Life itself punishes those who delay', He was referring to delaying internal reforms. There was still no implication that it meant the Wall was coming down. No one was going round saying, 'Only a few more days now'. No one was taking bets on when the Wall would come down and certainly no one was preparing for, or even considering preparing for, that eventuality. We were all so familiar with the way of life the Cold War engendered, all too close to it and wrapped up in it, to make such a wild prediction that it really did catch everyone by surprise. Diplomacy and policy were made on the move and off the cuff during that next week, at all levels.

For the moment, I was revelling in watching a momentous piece of history unfold. The Glienicke Bridge, ironically named in German, Brücke der Einheit, the Bridge of Unity, was the epitome of everything that the Cold War stood for – mistrust, suspicion and nastiness. For a fleeting moment tonight, all these negative emotions and attitudes had been swept aside and we were able to glimpse a world that was hopeful, positive and convinced that it could do without the artificial arrangements of the Cold War. Our vehicle, the Mission, and everything we had striven for seemed suddenly inconsequential and I think that was right and proper. For a brief instant the whole game seemed very unnecessary and out of place. It was as strange and yet as necessary as the Cold War itself.

We finally managed to make our way to the cordoned-off section in front of the Soviet guard post. A very nervous Soviet sentry came out to inspect our passes. There was much laughing at the ritual from the surrounding crowds. It wasn't derisory laughter but an encapsulation of the absurdity of the scene. What had been impossible for them was looking difficult for us. Normally, West Germans would have only seen this act from a good 150 metres away on the West Berlin side of the Glienicke at the closest point. East German civilians wouldn't have been allowed to view it at all. Our authorised but highly regulated access into the

East and back again was looking a bit of a sham compared to these revellers who seemed to be holding an impromptu pop concert on the bridge. Their passage across was only delayed by the enormous press of people in front of them trying to get over. I couldn't make out any passport or visa control whatsoever. It was a free-for-all.

Thus far the general thrust of the throng had been westward from Potsdam to West Berlin. I could see now from the centre of the bridge a less equal but nevertheless opposite force trying to come the other way. In the middle of the bridge it created a whirlpool effect whose centre was firmly held by the police from both sides desperately trying to organise the relative flows. The automatic steel gates were half closed to help them.

At the far end of the Bridge an enterprising West Berlin taxi driver with his standard ivory white Mercedes was trying to make his way across from the West Berlin side, half-heartedly remonstrating with the West German policemen. He didn't make it. It would only be a matter of days before he would, and there were other access points for vehicles already opening up. There was a Bratwurst stall set up only yards from the end of the bridge, an area normally kept clear by routinely patrolling West Berlin policemen. The owner must have been doing a roaring trade.

Our own pass and vehicle-checking ceremony was gratifyingly short and sweet. The sentry wasn't prepared to stop and talk but the officer on duty came out, saluted me and wished me a very pleasant onward journey. That was indeed strange and very much out of character. I thought he looked frightened. My exuberance and abundantly plain delight at the surrounding mayhem was disconcerting to him. The attention this normally eerily silent and sinister outpost of the Soviet Union was receiving had not precipitated in him the same jubilant thoughts that I was having. Perhaps he was guilty or ashamed. Not for himself but for the side he represented. He was certainly vulnerable, both literally, as he stood there among the recently oppressed masses, shuffling and pulling themselves around his barriers, and more widely as his role in this 'Great Game' was unravelling faster than he could comprehend. What fate had put him there and me in the G-wagon was difficult to fathom.

In a moment of understanding between two former allies it was Germany, the pivot of mainland Europe about which so many conflicts of the twentieth century revolved, that had become the common enemy for the moment. How fickle alliances were. The Soviet contribution to the downfall of Nazi Germany had been inestimable. Our allies then, had been our enemies since. As I looked at the officer on the bridge I realised that it was Germany once again who we were both afraid of. The early postwar years, always so concerned about suppressing a revival of the fascist state that rampaged around Europe, seemed to have come full circle.

He was pained. Only individuals suffer pain. Governments and institutions of state do not. The powers that had put him in this position were amorphous and immune to these intense and confusing personal feelings which I could read in his face. Again in that moment we could both understand what was happening. The future unravelled in a single glimpse. The awful consequences for him, part of a country that had 'lost' a war, thankfully never really fought, and the uncertainty for me, 'winning' a war against a former ally, suddenly made me as vulnerable as him.

He would have to return to the Soviet Union, bankrupt by the struggle to maintain its equitable Superpower status. I would have to return to Britain where a less drastic response would no doubt be already under consideration in the treasury that very night, if not the previous morning. I was sorry for him but not for his regime. He was on the losing side. Not his fault, but certainly not mine.

We moved on as quickly as we could. Crossing the white line at the centre of the bridge that marked the East German–West Berlin border, I stopped the vehicle. Maybe because I was now back in West Berlin I decided to dispense with the normal formalities. Whether I couldn't contain the intensity of the moment or whether I simply still had an eye for a good shot, I don't recall. Brian and I got out into the crowd, it was quicker walking anyway. Brian took a photograph of me between a group of East German and West Berlin policeman while I stood astride the line and in the whirlpool that was the physical passing point of those trying to make their way to Potsdam past the larger number trying to get into West Berlin. I nodded to them, acknowledging the hopelessness of their task. They laughed and shrugged their shoulders. They were similarly enchanted by events.

The majority of people coming the other way were West Berliners. They were laden with all manner of gifts but principally foodstuffs which I assumed were for relations in Potsdam. East Germans were also returning from what resembled a Viking pillage at a January sale. They had clothing from C&A, food from Aldi and some had clearly been adventurous enough to get themselves round Ka De We, West Berlin's equivalent of Harrods or Macy's. Most were bearing packets of fruit, in particular bananas, which were in short supply in the east. Many others were simply curious and coming over to have a look. The West Berliners were easily distinguishable. Both the men and women wore long warm cloth or fur coats with fur hats on their heads. The East Germans were mostly in leather jackets, or more likely plastic imitations, the women wearing scarves rather than hats. The contrast was as stark here as it was when we observed them apart. The opulent, curious and arrogant West Berliners passed the poorer, humbler and indifferent East Germans. The two were united in their single-mindedness and determination to get to the other end of the scrum, preferably ahead of the person in front of them. The Germans were never very good at queuing, whichever side of the divide they came from. The West German was unwilling and too impatient to queue and went to its front as a matter of course. The East German had mastered the art of invisible queue jumping. You didn't know it was happening but if you turned your back the competitor behind would slip round you without you knowing and then probably berate you for not concentrating should you complain. Sometimes they didn't even know what they were queuing for, but that didn't seem to worry them.

At the far end of the bridge a double row of buses stretched all the way back to the turning onto the autobahn for the city centre. They were being filled up by the East Germans coming across. Quite quickly, and completely free of charge, the Berlin Bus Company had laid on coaches to transport people from here to the Blue Church[55] and back again. It occurred to me, as it had obviously occurred

---

55 Blue Church: West Berlin's main church centred on the Kurfüstendam. So called because the sun shines through the blue stained-glass windows and creates a blue light inside.

to the Berlin Senate, that they would not have a clue how to get from here, the outskirts of Potsdam, to the bright lights of downtown West Berlin. They had been forbidden maps of West Berlin for the last twenty-eight years. That night, and for several days after, what had been a privilege for servicemen in uniform was extended to anyone and everyone who happened to be in Berlin at the time; free transport on all public transport. We were crossing back at about 11 p.m. but the place looked as though it was just waking up.

We got back in the vehicle and proceeded into West Berlin. It had been a most poignant short journey across a structurally minor but politically significant bridge. The momentous symbolism of the occasion was stunning. The eerie, dismal silence of the bridge of spies had been shattered by the sound of party goers and merrymakers. The impregnable barriers made up of video cameras, raked minefields, dogs and armed guards, passable to a very few Cold War warriors, had been shoved aside with no higher authority than the will of the people. It was democracy, freedom and choice all rolled into one. And although something they were not themselves very familiar with, for once they were not afraid to exercise it.

It was an intense, emotional and moving spectacle. It was difficult not to be affected by the scenes around us. For the thousands upon thousands who witnessed those next few days firsthand, it will be indelibly etched upon their minds. Perhaps as the youngest of the three crew members I could be forgiven for having to wipe a tear away. I wasn't alone. There was a very down-to-earth, enormously resourceful Corporal, about to be Sergeant, Al Tipping who hailed from the troubled streets of Ulster and had completed well over a hundred tours in all conditions under enormous pressures and a very hard Brian who had done tours of duty in the SAS and 14 Company, and neither of them were prepared for this moment.

We drove back to USMLM in near silence, deep in our own thoughts as to the likely consequences of this day. There were Trabbies everywhere, their farting, gurgling, 2-stroke engines with smelly exhaust systems detectable a mile away. The roads were full of them. West Germans joined in their vehicular celebration. I didn't see any vehicles being allowed over the Glienicke, so these must have been coming through the Wall at Checkpoint Charlie or other crossings. The streets were full of Easties, window-shopping along the road on the way out to the Glienicke, a most bizarre sight as the shops here were barely patronised normally.

Brian and Al were both due out on tour in a couple of days time. I had a week set aside to prep for the forthcoming Ashford course. I was now the senior Army tour officer and as such due to return to the UK next year and instruct the Special Duties course for the new set of potential tourers. What on earth was I going to say to them? Sorry boys, there's no job for you. I was way offline with that thought.

We checked in at Spam house and simply put NTR[56] across the whole report adding at the bottom, 'suspected pop concert on Glienicke Bridge, attendance several thousand, probably worth investigating'. I wonder how many people around the world, one hour before it was announced that the Wall was going to be opened

---

56 NTR: Nothing To Report.

at the Brandenburg Gate, actually knew that it was going to be so. How many people one week before that event knew that it was going to happen? Probably no more than a dozen in the whole world. And it wasn't as if the announcement at the Brandenburg Gate was specifically arranged to tell us that the Wall was going to open. It was an error on the part of Schabowski, himself sent simply to make announcements of the easing of travel restrictions, who when asked when the arrangements would come into effect, replied rather sheepishly and clearly without higher authority that they were immediate. No one knew the date because a date had not yet been set! So much for the intelligence game. Just as in 1961 (although there were many more clues) when the Wall was put up so it was in 1989, that the intelligence community either didn't know or weren't telling anyone. Its construction and demise were two of the best-kept secrets of its history. We knew it would happen but we failed to predict when and the Mission was as culpable in that as probably every other agency.

We returned quite quickly to the Mission headquarters in Berlin. The roads were packed and the streets more alive the closer we got to the centre. It was not until I reached the Olympic Stadium, headquarters of the British Garrison in West Berlin, and noticed how relatively quiet it was compared to downtown, that a couple more glimpses of understanding became apparent. I began to consider the consequences for the British Army in Berlin, let alone Brixmis or the Soviets. How long would the Germans want us here now? The only reason for our presence in Berlin had just become finite. Taking that one step further it didn't take a quantum leap to imagine the consequences for the British Army and Western armies as a whole.

I didn't need to be told my future. Being at the eye of the storm it was only too obvious that the money and resources devoted to sustaining the Cold War would no longer be required. Within the year the 'Peace Dividend' would become a household phrase. It was benignly and euphemistically used to mean defence cuts. (It was a most cruel and deceptive title for the round of redundancies, mergers and savings that would emanate from it). There was no peace and certainly no dividend. The so-called peace that broke out after the Wall came down was as phoney as the war that had raged during it.

For the time being I knew the Mission would be safe. The West didn't yet trust Gorbachev, however much they wanted to believe he was an 'honest injun'. At the very least we would still need interpreters. The only doubt was the timing and that would depend on how long the Soviets would stay. I reckoned that there was still another year left and it would probably take longer than that to move 300,000 Sovs out of the DDR, even if they started the next day.

I went to the mess, dumped my kit and made for the television. The place was deserted. Everyone had gone out to the Wall to see it being opened up. I caught a glimpse on the news of the first section of wall to be hoisted away by a huge East German crane under the guidance of the Grepos[57] and East German engineers. They might very well have been some of the ones that had chased me out of

---

[57] Grepos: Grenzschutzpolizei. East German border guards responsible for the security of the IGB and Berlin Wall.

Storkow so many months before. It was an extraordinary scene. The crowds on the western side were being kept away from the Wall by the West Berlin police who seemed to barely manage or control the urge to push forward.

On the East Berlin side the crowds seemed fewer and were being held back at least 100 metres from the Wall. The mere presence of the border guards was enough to control them. How long would the border guards last? Would they last the night, even? They looked terribly nervous and very uncertain of the changes going on around them. These were the same border guards that had shot so many innocent civilians as they tried to escape over the Wall. Why didn't the crowds turn on them? I only just noticed that curiously, they were no longer carrying weapons.

I saw clips of the first East Germans to come through the open wall. They tried initially to control the flow by requesting passports but the tide of people was simply too great and the enthusiasm, joy and unbounded happiness overwhelmed the crossing point. The guards just gave up and let the masses have their head. Again some were very nervous of their situation. It showed on their faces. Better I thought that they might be feeling some guilt rather than smiling and laughing and joining in the festivities as though the last twenty-eight years of the Wall had been irrelevant. Were they delighted that it was all over or did they think that soon they would wake up from this horrible nightmare? Were there any good guys among them, the border guards who, in the last twenty-eight years, had been responsible for killing eighty of their own kind, attempting to flee communism for a better life in the West? I couldn't tell. Only on 5 February that year the twenty-year-old Chris Guffroy became the last person to be shot and killed on the Wall at Treptow while attempting an escape. On 8 March Winfried Freudenberg's escape attempt in a hot air balloon failed tragically at Zehlendorf. And only in October, some twenty days ago, shots were fired as escape attempts were foiled – three weeks before the Wall was broken! It was almost the 1,700th time that would-be escapees had been fired upon since 1961. Clearly, when taking their chance, they had no inkling of the momentous events that were about to unfold. Had any of those guards on duty tonight been there when they died? Were any of them there responsible for this year's batch of shootings? Were the nervous ones feeling a sense of shame at the atrocity of the Wall or were they only worried about their own skins?

Then I saw the highly-charged scene of the little old lady who walked out across the open square of the Brandenburg Gate from behind the barriers. She was afraid of the guards no longer and could not wait to be reconciled with her family in the West. She was not interested in the formal bureaucracy that restricted her at this particular crossing site. She wanted to go through the Wall now. One of the guards showed some compassion and walked her around the square and led her back to the barriers. It was a momentous event, like the young man who defied the tanks on his own in Tiananmen Square. I wandered how much Honecker would have wished for a resolution of the recent protests like that one. This single old lady expressed a national rage at discovering forty-four years of her life had been nothing more than deception and lies. Her frailty and her tears, so infectiously moving, symbolised the realisation that for her those years had been a sham. The frustration she felt was so overwhelming that at last she dared to challenge the authorities and the authorities could do nothing for her. It was compelling to want to hit the guards but this time it really wasn't their fault that she couldn't cross. They were as much caught out by events as the rest of us, whatever was in their hearts. It was one of several unequivocally passionate scenes that I witnessed over the course of the next couple of weeks and in the subsequent year on tour. There were many occasions over the next few months when, particularly the older generation of East Germans, would come and talk to us in various parts of the country and finally burst into tears as they tried to come to terms with the complete waste of time they had endured.

I had to get down to the Wall myself and see what was going on. I was annoyed that I had missed the first two nights, but I was going to make up for it. Bryn Parry-Jones and Lawrence McCourt were in the bar, having just returned from being out all last night. Bryn was a Royal Military Police (RMP) officer and Lawrence a Royal Signals officer. I persuaded them to come back down and show me what they had seen the night before. As it happened Walter Momper, the governing mayor of West Berlin, and I think Helmut Kohl were intending to speak outside the Reichstag that night, so we decided that we would make for there.

Bryn commandeered the local RMP patrol vehicle right to the Brandenburg Gate and took us through the cordon that protected the massed hordes of satellite trucks and major TV companies from the crowds outside. They had arrived in Berlin only two days ago, just as caught out as the rest of us. They were encamped at the Brandenburg Gate in anticipation of this part of the Wall being opened up. It was surreal. I wandered among the trucks as the anchormen from around the world practised on raised platforms that gave them a backdrop of the famous Brandenburg Gate. Trevor MacDonald and John Simpson, among many others that I recognised from television, were all there to report on events. Behind them was the very spot where the old lady had demanded to be let through the night before.

It took me a few moments to take all this in as Bryn guided me through the trucks and nearer to the Wall. He pointed out all the big news broadcasters on the way. It was the second night they'd been here. Bryn had been responsible for setting this lot up so he was able to wander anywhere with his RMP authority. The RMP had also been responsible for keeping the peace at the nearby Tiergarten Soviet war memorial. One of many curiosities of the divided city, the Soviet war memorial was in the British Sector. While it was permanently guarded by Soviet ceremonial soldiers, it was out of bounds to people on foot and watched by our own RMP. It had been put out of bounds since someone took a pot-shot at the Soviet guards. Now it was under threat again as a potential focal point for anti-Soviet protest.

There was security everywhere, whether it was RMP, British soldiers from the infantry brigade or various units of the West Berlin police. I just kept flashing my Soviet pass and British ID card. Like all Germans, East or West, the West Berlin police respond positively to officialdom. If you have an ID card then that will do. Most riots in West Berlin, and there were many, were caused by students who used confrontation as their first weapon. They didn't have the brains to play the police at their own game. Bryn took us through the news compound and towards the back of the Reichstag. I could hardly see the Wall because the crowd was so dense.

I noticed two things. The first was obvious. There were people on top of the Wall as far as you could see. Bryn said there had been even more on top of it yesterday. Miraculously none had been injured falling off. It was easily 12 ft high at this part. I gathered that British personnel were now forbidden to climb on the wall because several soldiers had climbed on the night before and created a 'scene'. It later transpired that they weren't British soldiers at all, but the damage had been done. It didn't stop them anyway.

The second thing I noticed but couldn't work out so quickly was the constant tapping sound, rising above the noise of the crowd. I had to ask Bryn what it was and he took us closer to the Wall. All along its base the West Berliners and now many tourists were chipping away at the concrete sections that made it up. It was man-made and it was being man defeated. The West Berliners, keen not to prevaricate any longer, were helping their East Berlin neighbours to hasten the fall. It was an extraordinary sight. The frenzy of destruction ranged from sledgehammers and picks being wielded with passion to gentle hammer strikes from tourists keen to secure a souvenir. The Berliners, who had nicknames for everything, called them the 'woodpeckers'.

What three or four days ago would have been an arrestable offence was now completely ignored by all the authorities. I wondered how long it would be before the gypsies would move in and start selling bits of the wall to the tourists. Almost without a gap along the entire length of the Wall between the Brandenburg and the Reichstag the 'woodpeckers' were at work. I stopped Bryn and turned to the nearest guy hacking away and asked him if I could have a go. All three of us joined in and symbolically chipped out little bits of concrete to retain. For good measure we also defiantly clambered up onto the Wall, just to say that we had done it.

The police concern for public safety was far greater here than at the Glienicke. There were hundreds of thousands of people moving round the Wall. Once outside the news compound we could hardly pass through the swell of people. We tried to stick together shouting to each other to give direction. At the back of the Reichstag Bryn led us in through a back door, past some rather heavily-built West German plain clothes policemen. I waved my ID cards again and just continued walking as though I had every right to be there. This was nothing new to me. I'd been conning Sovs and NVA all over East Germany for the past year. Anyway, I'd got into much more secure places than this years before joining Brixmis. I recalled my time at university when I gatecrashed the Miss Europe contest with a fake ID card, a monkey suit, speaking in German and pretending to be Miss Austria's bodyguard. Getting past a checkpoint in this chaos was easy.

We'd lost Lawrence in the crowd. I think he saw someone else, turned to talk to them and that was it. He was swept away by the surge of people. Bryn and I swept past what appeared to be several more plain clothes policemen. I knew that Kohl was possibly speaking but they didn't seem to have that on their minds at all. They appeared to have been here a couple of days already. Bryn explained quickly that they were BfV[58] and were here just in case of any trouble.

---

[58] BfV: Bundesamt für Verfassungsschutz. Federal Office for the Protection of the Constitution. West Germany's counter-espionage agency, loosely equivalent to British MI5.

One of them came forward to meet Bryn. They obviously knew each other. I was introduced and Bryn succinctly explained what I did in Berlin. The German guy was very interested, but I was sure that he probably already knew what we got up to in East Germany. Within the year they would certainly know and be forced to take up where the Allies were obliged to leave off. He took us to another guarded door in the corner of the Reichstag and led us up some winding stairs, explaining that we would get a better view from the top. It reminded me of the innocuous back stairs up to the Brixmis office in the furthest corner of the very grand Olympic Stadium headquarters.

At the top of the stairs our host knocked on the door and we were let through, out on to a corner parapet of the balcony that circled the roof of the Reichstag. It was like a small turret at the top of a castle, sectioned off from the rest of the balcony by two end walls. Whether there was one on each corner of the building or whether it had been especially built for the purpose it was now being put to, I didn't know.

Out on the parapet, which resembled a box in a West End theatre and was about the same size, there were three BfV guys, dressed in black, kneeling down and watching the area over the Wall back towards the Brandenburg Gate. At first I thought they must be here as security for the political speakers but these guys weren't armed and I could only see one radio between them. There were several long lenses, high-powered binoculars and viewing devices. Their interest on the Wall and behind it back to the Brandenburg seemed too precise when from here they could also see a great deal further round back into West Berlin towards the opera house. Slowly it dawned on me that I was in an OP. They too were watching. I couldn't get away from it. How many similar spy versus spy situations were present in this city and who was watching who? It seemed countless. The BfV would probably be concentrating on the East Germans and secondarily the Sovs. We watched the Sovs in East Germany. Loosely organised Flag Tours, centred on the Int Corps, overtly toured East Berlin. MI6 operated out of the Olympic Stadium in West Berlin as well as the Embassy in East Berlin. The French and Americans had similar set-ups and then of course the Sovs and DDR had the opposite teams. It was a curious way to establish confidence measures but it seemed to work if you thought the success could be measured by the number of wars we didn't have.

We were motioned to stand near the back and handed binoculars to have a look. We must have been one of many sets of visitors they had seen this last two nights as the guys carrying out the observation totally ignored us. Cups of coffee were provided, a sure sign that they were expecting people and had to cater for them. The watchers were scanning the Wall on both sides. Bryn explained to me that they had used this OP on top of the Reichstag for many years to covertly watch East Berlin activity at this politically and diplomatically sensitive spot. There were many overt watching points, in and around the area of the Brandenburg Gate. Quite naïvely I had assumed that these were sufficient to cover everything. It never really occurred to me that we were doing the same to the East Germans as the Sovs did to us with the hidden cameras in the old schoolhouse on the other side of the Glienicke.

It felt very odd to be introduced to someone else's spying operation with only a cursory check as to who I was and a good word from the local 'bobby'.

I suspected they were not looking at the wall-chippers or those making a fool of themselves on top of it. I didn't ask what they were looking for. I wouldn't have expected a straight answer and I wouldn't have answered their questions about the Mission. The intelligence world is deliberately partitioned to avoid such unnecessary leaking of information. It would not have been professionally astute to ask another intelligence officer what he was up to.

My best guess was that they were looking for those who might exploit this chaotic movement of people across the border. Whether they might be terrorist or other spies, I didn't know. Alternatively they might have been using the chaos to bring their own people in who might have been seriously exposed in the heat of the moment. There were many East Germans and Soviets in East Berlin working for the West. In this massive rupture to the normal routine of spying, it would be inevitable that some would be revealed sooner rather than later and in the unpredictable events of these two days, agencies had to work fast to protect their agents.

It was a most curious few minutes, the atmosphere so different to that being created down below on the streets. Up here it was cold and calculating, an icy ruthless demonstration of duty, undertaken without emotion and without prejudice. Down there it was passion, emotion, anger, joy, sadness, tears and laughter. It didn't seem that there was anything necessarily wrong in the contrast between the guardians and the guarded. Unlike the people down below, up here they were already forcing themselves to think, beyond the fall, to what might happen next.

Even now in this very public and very visible outpouring of emotion on such a massive scale, where tears and laughter filled the streets below me, there were still those who exploited the event for all it was worth. From the 'wall-sellers' who would emerge over the next few days, to the West German spies up here, the opportunities that this almost spiritual occurrence threw up were not squandered. I wondered if suspicion and mistrust were still the guiding principles. Was I any different and were those in charge above me any different? I hoped that Reagan, Thatcher, Kohl, Mitterand, the four leaders of the Western World and Gorbachev, who between them had inherited what Churchill, Roosevelt, Stalin and Hitler had left for them, would be moved to act in a different way to the madness that had created the Cold War.

Down below us it was possible to sense the energy of the crowds. The atmosphere was highly charged, a concentrated mixture of emotions that made you want to laugh and cry at once. I couldn't do either. The Glienicke had already had my emotional attention. I was simply mesmerised by the events unfolding below me, able to watch history being made in high dramatic style from my box in the stalls.

We left the BfV to whatever they were doing and went back to join the crowds below us. We forced our way round to the front of the Reichstag to try and get a position for the speeches. I can only think that the crush we experienced in these crowds was similar to the large football crowds that sometimes got out of control. I would not have been surprised to hear that someone had been killed. The only difference that prevented people from getting killed was the enormous area in which these crowds were able to move. The only barrier against which they were pushing was the Wall and that wasn't going anywhere – yet.

The Reichstag was the only place throughout that night that we encountered any hostility. Some young West Berliners squashed in front of us were clearly the worse for drink, (not that you needed to drink alcohol in this atmosphere to become intoxicated) and were deliberately pushing this way and that for a bit of fun, moving the crowd around them. Bryn, conscious of the effect that would have at the front of the crowd, tried to stop them. They recognised him immediately as being British and started to swear at him, telling him to go home. The idea that our time was limited was clearly not mine alone. The speeches were short and not very interesting.

We decided to move on round the Wall to Checkpoint Charlie, the first crossing point that was opened on the 9th, the night before. Here there were many more East Berliners than West Berliners. They were so easy to spot. There were also many more tourists and the camera crews were present again to witness the cars as well as the pedestrians that were now coming across in their hundreds. They were singing, honking their horns, waving flags and banners. In the background there was the regular slapping of hands on metal as each and every car that crossed through was greeted and pushed through into West Berlin. There were scores of old East German flags with the central compass and circle neatly cut out to signify their instant conversion to a West German loyalty. It was a marvellously joyful scene. I had never been caught up in so much emotion before and was unlikely to experience it again. If all this energy, wrapped up in such emotion and happiness, could have been bottled and put to good use then many more of the world's problems might have been solved during the course of that week alone. It was the biggest and largest street party and it went on and on for days.

We left Checkpoint Charlie at about 4 a.m., the party atmosphere still going strong. Ian Wellstead, a Brixmis tour officer seconded from the SAS, stood and watched helplessly as the Wall went up in 1961. Powerless to do anything about it, when he could have kicked over the still wet mortar, he would have treasured this moment. He may not have realised then that the monstrosity started in his lifetime would come down, also in his lifetime. There were many who didn't. Within the year I would be present at its official decommissioning, amid all the pomp and ceremony that the Allied powers could muster.

I will remember those few days, and crossing the Glienicke in particular, for the rest of my life. There were two curious things I recall about that night. First, there was not the anger from the East Germans one might have expected, given the length of their incarceration behind the Wall. There was no apparent malice or retribution. The sheer joy of being released overwhelmed all other feelings. The anger unfortunately would come in time as the state system slowly unravelled its trail of deceit, dishonesty and nastiness. But even then there would be no bloody revolution as there would be in Romania when Ceaucescu and many of his secret police were killed by the crowds. Most people simply wanted to see the lights and riches that they had been missing. Everywhere the East Germans asked for maps to get them round the shops of West Berlin or asked for directions to Ka De We and the Kufürstendamm. Second, was the chanting. Everywhere East Germans and West Germans alike were chanting, 'Gorby, Gorby, Gorby' for Gorbachev. They didn't shout for Kohl or Thatcher or Reagan or Mitterand, all of whom had played their part. They identified Gorbachev

Closure of the infamous Checkpoint Charlie on 22 June 1990. The world's press corps are assembled – they had been in the city since 9 November 1989.

as the man who had really been responsible for delivering them. At the time I thought it a bit rich, not to mention ironic, that the leader of the country that had subjugated them in the first place should now be so universally acclaimed. Furthermore it was Gorbachev, in the next few months, who would have to be persuaded of the wisdom of reunification and a full withdrawal from the DDR because it certainly wasn't forthcoming at this moment.

Over the next few days the Mission would become heavily involved with the ramifications of the Wall coming down. Most prominent of these was reassuring the Soviet armed forces, almost immediately, that we would do everything in our power to preserve the integrity of their interests as the fourth allied power in West Berlin. This was quite a feat given the last forty-odd years of unyielding Soviet reluctance to guarantee the Western Allies their interests in East Germany. At the same time we had to point out to them that it was the East German government who had instigated the fall and presumably provision had been made with them for such an occurrence. I was in the Chief's house on the morning of Sunday 12 November, ready to accompany him to the annual Remembrance service as duty interpreter, when he took a personal call from General Boris Vassilievich Snetkov, Commander-in-Chief GSFG. Snetkov was most pressing to enlist support from the Allies at this worrying time, keen that we would ensure the safety of Soviet troops on ceremonial duty in West Berlin and almost refusing to acknowledge that what was happening was really happening.

It was clear that it had been as much a shock to the Soviets at the very highest levels of their military government in East Germany as it was to the rest of the world. In this fact alone it was possible to see the early seeds of the difficulties that the Mission's final year had to endure. There was a clear dichotomy of view between the political and the military. They were unaware of the looming change in their status and its consequences. It quickly transpired that the Wall coming down was as far as the Soviets were prepared to go and in many respects it was merely a response to the already growing number of refugees leaving around the sides of East Germany that prompted them to act. As much as the Wall was put up in 1961 to stop the haemorrhaging of the country from the massive exodus of refugees, so it was quickly brought down for the same reason. Both were embarrassing but this time they had learnt from the last. There was no decision to withdraw more Soviet forces from East Germany for several weeks and there was certainly no truck with the call for the reunification of the two Germanies. That was going too far. A period of purgatory followed while negotiations at the highest levels persuaded Gorbachev that having come this far he should go the extra mile for a lasting settlement. Once the rapture and partying died down and politicians examined its wreckage in the cold light of day, the Germany question was no further forward at the end of 1989 than it was in 1946. A major sore had certainly been lanced but it was unsure who was now going to be responsible for cleansing and healing it.

'Business as usual' was a phrase I coined for the benefit of the course and this was also the instruction for Brixmis. There were three compelling reasons why it was very much 'business as usual' for Brixmis for a further year after the fall of the Wall. First, the Soviet military machine was still present in East Germany and, with or without political direction, it remained a very dangerous animal indeed. It had to be watched and courted as much now as it had ever been, if not more so. The number of previously unseen and technically advanced pieces of military hardware coming into East Germany during 1989 increased rather than decreased, a trend that was apparent throughout the 1980s. The Soviet equipment procurement programme made ours look like a Saturday afternoon shopping trip to the supermarket. This huge tunnel into which money and resources flowed, once committed, couldn't be that easily switched off. Second, the Soviet military in East Germany became confused, vulnerable and frightened. Very rapidly they realised there was nowhere for them to go – certainly not back to the Soviet Union. What would more than a quarter of a million extra troops do back there, apart from be disbanded? Furthermore in the immediate aftermath of the fall of the Wall, it was not clear, either to them or to us, that they would have to go back. No one was talking seriously about reunification. It was enough that the Wall had come down. It was enough that border controls would become less stringent. But there would still be two Germanies. This enormous uncertainty proved very destabilising. Finally, if the pressure brought to bear upon the Soviets had got us to this point then now was not the time to let up. The tourers in the Mission took the view that it was time to pursue them harder than normal and exploit every opportunity while they were still in contact with us. A unique opportunity existed to continue looking through our window onto the Soviet Union, before it withdrew for good and became even more difficult to observe.

I managed five minutes with the Chief later that week to check with him that I could proceed under my new slogan. I sensed it rather gave him something to hang his own hat on amid the more pressing problems of the realities of the situation on the ground. The Chief was under pressure from the diplomats and politicians to handle the Soviets with care and consideration in our observation role as well as our liaison function, but this didn't square with the situation out on the ground as the next few months were to reveal. The extraordinarily mighty Soviet military presence was still on the border of Western Europe. Sure it had been getting numerically smaller in recent years but it was also becoming more potent as new and more advanced equipment came in. Now, above all other, was the time to watch them in case they turned nasty out of fear or frustration.

At the same time it was equally imperative that our liaison role should emerge as the parting *raison d'être* of the Missions. The very reason why Brixmis had been set up in 1946, to promote and foster confident relationships in place of mistrust and language barriers in the turmoil of postwar Germany, was just as necessary in the turbulent and unclear post-Wall Germany. The difference now was that the technology of 1989 compared to that of 1945 made the risk of failure more catastrophic than ever before. The privileged resource provided by the Mission's twin roles of liaison and observation remained highly sought-after.

Within a fortnight the Chief chaired a tourers' meeting himself. He had been given guidelines for the way ahead and uniquely he proffered them with his own interpretation for us to digest and consider. We basically threw our cards on the table in order to thrash out a way forward. Business as usual became our guideline. As ever the diplomatic and political interpretation of events contrasted deeply with the picture on the ground. They were way ahead of themselves.

If ever there was a delicate moment in the Cold War then this was it – the last bit. The Berlin airlift in 1948–9, the Bay of Pigs and U2 debacles in 1961 (not to mention the Wall itself), the Cuban Missile crisis in 1962 (itself uniquely allied to the Berlin crisis at the time), the birth of the concept of Mutually Assured Destruction, Philby, Burgess, Blake and Maclean, not to mention a host of less infamous traitors, the invasions of Hungary and the near invasion of Poland in 1956, Czechoslovakia in 1968, Afghanistan in 1979 and all the other incidents that went to make the Cold War, each in their own way provided a degree of worldwide tension, reaction and threat. This was something new and yet nothing new.

Once the Wall came down the next phase of the Cold War proffered a wholly different set of circumstances. Most people thought that it was the end already. To coin Kenneth Wostenholme's marvellously understated phrase of 1966 – they thought it was all over. There was still much to be done before the whistle went. This was about coming to terms with a new world order peacefully, with dignity on both sides and without loss of face on the Soviet side in particular. And let's face it, it wasn't as though we had really been given much warning of these unfolding events ourselves. It wasn't easy for them or indeed for the Mission to come to terms with it all, in a calm and considered manner. Worldwide disasters, epoch-making events and international political crises very rarely flag themselves up for future attention. They don't bring themselves forward to a conveniently free moment in the world calendar.

They just happen and they have to be dealt with here and now, in the best way possible, with all the mistakes and flaws that real life is made of. Two steps forward for one step back would do for the moment until the situation stabilised.

As far as our own situation was concerned where violence did occur after the Wall came down, it was as much a reflection of their own nervousness as the presence of our tours. They were scared and afraid for their situation. They were pariahs in the country that for the last forty-four years had accepted them as a necessary occupying power. Now they were no longer required. The authorities they had erected to front for them were instantly discredited. From Honecker and Marcus Wolf down to the local Stasi and bus driver turned informant, they were exposed and vilified. Ironically, in time, some of the authorities that performed the day-to-day running of the country would be recalled to carry on their jobs in the complete absence of any one else competent enough to perform the duties. Former communists would be back in power, calling themselves democrats or reformed communists. The one-party state did not have an opposition party to step into the government's shoes. There had to be put in place a period of stability to allow change, an unfamiliar phenomenon for this people, to take effect slowly. Few of these revelations and insights came to me as I crossed the Glienicke or witnessed the scenes along the Wall but the sights on the bridge did open my mind to the future course of events, that yesterday I had not even considered possible.

The whole episode had been personally emotional for every serving member of the Mission. East Germany was our domain and our area of expertise. It was with selfish sadness that we knew things would change but it was also exceptionally rewarding to have been part of it. That things would have to change was obvious, that the Mission would close next week was ridiculous. The fall of the Wall, although symbolic, did not mark the end of the complex and involved situation the last forty-four years had created. There was much to be done now to ensure a safe transition to whatever lay ahead. Germany was divided long before the Wall went up. In the weeks and months to come, for as many who were joyful on 9 November 1989, there were an ever-increasing number who were frightened and wary of the enormity of the task to deliver a lasting solution to a divided Germany. The recovery phase of any operation is always the most difficult.

After all the excitement and upheaval of a long endured normality there would still be a long way to go. The Mission was to operate for another year under the most difficult and complex circumstances and its work was to continue a further year after that under a different name and under slightly modified rules of engagement. The Soviets would not withdraw for a further two or three years and the problems of Soviet internal unrest would manifest themselves most violently around the former Soviet Union and its satellite states. As each day went by, post-9 November 1989, the lid slowly came off the boiling cauldron and it was not a pleasant sight. The forty-four-year peace, inadvertently brokered by the machinations of the Cold War, as turbulent and unsteady as they were, suddenly looked enormously attractive and stable to many seasoned observers around the world. Pandora's box, closed at the conclusion of the Second World War, had been reopened and many would contend that it is still not yet shut.

Brixmis continued business more or less as usual. The fall of the Wall was simply another momentous event on the historical path of its operation.

CHAPTER SEVEN

Detained

'Christ! There's kit everywhere.'

We were moving almost due east along tac-route 5 towards Neustrelitz garrison, making for the track north that would take us out of the top end of the 'Rheinsberg Gap'.[59] There had been a kit explosion that morning. Everywhere we turned there was some unit or other from the local area being deployed to their respective EDAs.

It was 25 January 1990, over two months since the fall of the Wall. I was now deep into my first East European winter, looking forward to spring and the chance to warm up. Five tours in a row in the first weeks of January saw me at Gollmitz, Luebben and Cottbus, watching the railway lines out of East Germany into Poland. Withdrawals had started on the 2 January, only to end on the 15th. They didn't resume again until late August, another indicator that a final solution of the Germany question was far from obvious. Each tour was only forty-eight hours and conducted in relays with the other Missions to ensure complete and total coverage. The only task was to watch the railway line for that forty-eight-hour period before being relieved. The days were still very short, the nights dreadfully monotonous and indescribably cold. The cold more than the boredom made it thoroughly demoralising. I did it but I didn't enjoy it. The rest of the tours were fairly routine as we settled back into near-normal activity after the Wall had come down.

We'd just run a vehicle column prior to entering the Gap. We took it from behind, overtaking each vehicle and pulling back into the column when oncoming traffic demanded. It was a dangerous tactic, much more so than running columns on the nose. Quite apart from anything else it contravened East German law to insert a vehicle into a military column. More importantly it gave the Sovs every option to sandwich us from front and back. Our drivers really had to be on their toes for it. The other two in the vehicle would be constantly watching for sudden moves from the Sov vehicles and possible ways out. Once a vehicle had been overtaken the G-wagon would drop back from the one in front to try and maintain a safe gap. The overtaken vehicle would invariably close right up and threaten the rear bumper, flashing his lights to attract the attention of his colleague in front. Often the vehicle in front would fail to spot the overtaking manoeuvre. If we maintained a safe but close enough

---

[59] Rheinsberg Gap: a strip of land sandwiched between two PRAs in which tours occasionally came to grief.

gap the driver in front could only see his colleague's lights flashing in his wing mirrors. He wouldn't be able to see us. All the time the camera would be going and the vehicles would be called for the tape. It was a very busy and mind-concentrating tactic, not rashly undertaken.

There was an anti-aircraft deployment down in the south of the Gap which we circled, photographed and left. As we made our way up the Gap more and more Sov kit started to appear. Our current target was a regimental size deployment of T-80 charging across the top of the Gap's training area from east to west. We had stopped for a brew overlooking this transverse tac-route, more for a breather than in the hope of spotting anything.

Kev Powell, the driver, was outside, undertaking the ritual and oft performed window-cleaning routine. The G-wagon may have gone through a hedge backwards and up to the engine block in mud pools but the windows were always spotless all the time. Taking photographs through windows added yet another layer that light had to penetrate through. Having dirty windows to exacerbate the situation was inexcusable. Every time we stopped the windows would be cleaned. Before going on to a training area the windows would be cleaned and whenever we were stationary in a target OP the windows would be cleaned. With the 500-mm and 1,000-mm mirror lenses it wasn't even advisable to attempt taking photographs through the window. The mirror reflected an image back onto the glass of the window and back to the lens. This created an intensely blurred effect in the final photograph. The long mirror lenses were always used with the window wound down. Given that they were used for long-range targets or anything flying the danger posed by having the window down was slightly mitigated.

Cleaning windows was the only other opportunity, apart from breakfast, when the driver could stretch his legs. Exceptionally he would be allowed out to buy ice creams in town but this usually only happened to new drivers who hadn't been nobbled by the senior drivers' Mafia and told who did what and when on the social front! He would also have checked the number-plates to see if they were dirty and if they weren't he may accidentally have flicked some mud onto them to disguise the Union Jack and number. It all helped to lengthen detection time just that fraction longer and thus maintain the element of surprise for the moment that you might really need an extra second or two.

Kev must have heard them while outside the vehicle just as Brian and myself inside the vehicle saw them. He came scampering round to the driver's side to confer. Through one of the many shallow valleys that filled the area, ideally suited for late twentieth-century tank runs, a column of T-80s could be seen and heard making their way towards us. They were some way off. Brian confirmed T-80 through his bins but couldn't confirm type or number, simply that there were more than ten. The dust cloud set up by the lead vehicles was enough to mask the remainder. Spotting them far enough in advance and fortunate to be in the right place at the right time meant that we only had to manoeuvre slightly to put us in best cover for their approach.

We were high on an overlooking ridge to the north side of the run. It gave us a good view down on them and to their front when they came past. This would be a useful series of shots which would give us a front three-quarter profile as well as a hull perspective, normally reserved for the Chipmunk. The only other way to achieve a look at kit from above was to photograph it as it went under you on a train from a bridge over the line or similarly from a bridge over a road. Both of these were rare opportunities but highly valued. Most of the sexy technical scoops that we would be looking for, extra antennae, modified sights, range finders, new hatches, were usually bolted on to or somehow incorporated into the top of the hull. A profile shot might reveal it but not really expose it in the way a top down shot could. More often than not we found ourselves side on to armoured vehicles and on the same level. Normally this meant that the top of the hull was slightly higher than the G-wagon.

There was another way to get hull shots and that was to get on the vehicle. Not impossible but very dangerous and very much asking to be shot at. I had done that recently at Falkenberg sidings, also with Brian, when the train started moving and the driver and myself followed the train until, confident that he'd got sufficient detail from the vehicle in question, Brian jumped off. The risk had to be worth it though, given that kit trains were usually guarded by armed troops and watched by railway staff.

This angle would still give side-numbers for the particular regiment, updating records from their last sighting and would also allow Weapons to scrutinise each vehicle for any slight modifications not seen before. To my knowledge this particular set of tanks had not been seen out of barracks for a good few months, ample time to fit some new gadget somewhere. We knew they were likely inhabitants of 16 Guards Tank Division, but which ones only the side-numbers would tell us. Given that there were so many of them it would also usefully demonstrate how and where the command and control element might be deployed in such a manoeuvre as well as allow us to identify which were the actual command and control vehicles in the column. The T-80Ks (K being the universal identification nomenclature for Command) were easily identifiable from the rest by an extra aerial. This second aerial indicated communication up the command chain as well as down. Close examination of a particular command vehicle's camouflage pattern might possibly identify that vehicle again when associated side-numbers were not visible or painted out. The extrapolation to identifying it in the heat of battle might be a little tenuous but at least the information was there to nail it if necessary.

Anti-air protection in the form of ZSU-23-4 or the more recent 2S-6 would probably denote divisional command travelling with that particular regiment and that in turn would tell us that this regiment was probably the lead regiment for the division. It would be unlikely that this exercise was much higher than divisional in scale because it would have been notifiable under CSCE confidence building measures, as well as warranting imposition of a TRA, which in turn would have been communicated to us by the bleeper. Furthermore we would have hopefully been tipped off by our own Sigint that something was up before we tackled this particular area. It's difficult to conceal a divisional scale exercise from the signals world.

There were a lot of things to think about when observing kit move on training areas. It wasn't just sufficient to get yourself and the vehicle in a position to observe and record events. They had to be interpreted and linked as well. Over the years touring with the Missions had become immensely sophisticated. Logistical support for up to six days out on the ground had been ironed out. The armoury at our disposal, ranging from vehicles to cameras, were proven and reliable, incorporating the very latest technology. Knowledge and experience, passed down over the last forty years, had been expanded and built upon. The people chosen for the roles were of the highest calibre and special-to-role training was tailored to get you on the starting blocks. But simply taking photographs and recording side-numbers would not do. Crews had to know what the required intelligence was for each and every piece of equipment spanning both the Soviet and East German arsenals, from helicopters and aircraft to rifles and anti-personnel mines. It wasn't sufficient to be able to recognise equipment as they flashed past on a train at 40 miles an hour in the dark. We all, and the NCOs in particular, had to know what the Defence Intelligence Staff (DIS) and respective Technical Intelligence branches as yet still didn't have proof of and find it for them.

Additionally, there was scope for expert interpretation and informed comment. We would assess the training and activities of the troops and equipment on the ground as well as being able to link it to activity seen miles away or on a previous encounter. An observed occupation of an EDA in one location would prompt exploration in an associated five others. A chance sighting of a comms rebro[60] antenna would prompt a lookout for another within line of sight. Seeing a tank meant it had to be compared with known varieties of the same series. Was there something different, an extra grenade launch tube and if so what was it for and why was it separated from the others? Bolts coming out of the hull with no obvious attachments, what were they for and were they uniformly distributed? Lugs for mine ploughs, were they the same as the last recorded sighting? Could you remember? If not, the only option was to get after it and get the imagery to compare later. The state of their equipment, the perceived state of morale, their drills, competence and efficiency were all things we had unique access to. We had Russian and German speakers on board, for goodness sake, and when it was safe, or even when it was not, we spoke to them asking them direct questions. Why not? The accuracy and effectiveness of drills, the use of initiative and flexibility, always a big criticism of Soviet troops by Nato, was it really true? We had the opportunity to find out.

The list was endless. The recording was just the basic requirement. Being in the right place at the right time was essential but only the start to getting the job done. We were able to provide added value to the intelligence gathered. We had the opportunity to do so much more because we mixed with them at close quarters. We were able to bring a three-dimensional image to the intelligence picture as well as the further dimension of being able to observe them over time. We were drawn from so many different areas of expertise from our own armed forces. I understood bridging operations and engineer operations generally. Brian understood infantry and special forces tactics and Kev knew more about vehicles than the two of us combined. We covered the complete gamut of our own armed forces from armoured corps representatives and RAF pilots to naval chief petty officers and Intelligence Corps corporals, all of whom had experience

---

[60] Rebro: rebroadcasting station. Usually sited high up to create 'line of sight' communications.

A regulator enveloped by dust and completely oblivious to the tour crew behind him as he ushers a BTR-80 across a main road from one tac-route to another. The latest and most capable of wheeled infantry personnel carriers were hunted down throughout the late 1980s.

in their own arms and disciplines which, when mixed with a thorough education in the tactics of the Soviet armed forces, made for a very comprehensive tool that could be applied right to the heart of GSFG in East Germany. We were a complete spanner in their works.

'I reckon that's the last one. What do you reckon, Brian?'

Thirty-two T-80 had rumbled past and below us.

'Battalion strength, Boss?'

There was a single command vehicle, eighth in line from the front. That was probably the battalion commander. But there was a spare T-80K at the rear and he signified a higher level of deployment. Somewhere there would be two other battalions deploying into the area. Spacing was good and they didn't seem worried by the tight twisty track through the wood. This was not driver training but a route march to contact.

'Yep. Thirty seconds then we'll go.'

We all prepared to move. The brew, like so many before it, went out the window virtually untouched in the activity of observing the column. It was a hazard that was worth the loss. I could have lost every brew in the day for that sight. Film was quickly stowed. New film was put in the cameras. It wasn't worth the cost of film to run out on a new sighting. If I'd only used four frames I would change the roll for a new target.

'OK. Kev. You happy?'

'All right, Boss.' Kev Powell, alias Brummie Powell, was from Birmingham, proud of it and like many Brummies displayed enormous reserves of the black humour that they are famous for. He was a delight to be on tour with. Nothing was too difficult for him and nothing got him down. He was still a relatively new driver, having been at the Mission only a few months longer than me.

This was my sixth tour with Brian, not his real name given that he was from both 14 Intelligence Company and the SAS. Brian had been on the Ashford course with me, completing our final exercise in the same crew and then touring together on many occasions after our initial probation. A more accomplished soldier I had not met – softly spoken, highly intelligent, self-effacing and humble. He contrasted starkly to the latter-day, popularly contrived version of what a special forces soldier should be. He was as vulnerable to error as anyone else and no less or more competent than the other NCOs who toured. What was noticeable was the occasional flash of determination and aggression to see something through, together with the ability to look out for others having first got his own act together. Brian and I got on particularly well, partly as a result of being on the course together and partly because we had similar ideas about touring. We represented a new generation of tourers, responsive to the wisdom handed down, keen to try out new methods and tactics and sympathetic to the changing world around us. If someone ever said to us 'this is the normal route in, Boss', or 'this is how we did it last time', then we would immediately change it. We always looked for new ways. Above all else it made good tactical sense. As a result we worked well together with many dividends.

From the map we established an open area that the tanks were likely to cross and hopefully fan out over into some sort of tactical deployment. There was an OP we could use to observe them from there. It was close country they were traversing, slightly wooded in some places and heavily planted with young conifers in others. Together with the steeply undulating terrain this channelled them into single file to make the crossing from the eastern training area to the next one further west. There were only two reasonable routes across to it. They were on one of them and we had come off the other to make this stop. We could see both.

'OK, let's go.'

Kev Powell launched the vehicle out of the wood line that we had been using for cover and joined the second and parallel track. It was out of sight to the tanks and a much flatter route, not the undulating tank tac-route that could make you seasick as you repeatedly crabbed up on to a crest to minimise sky lighting and rolled into the swell, to remain hidden from view. As they picked up speed the tanks simply crashed from one crest into another, almost leaping the gap in between. It was an awesome demonstration of their power seeing these vehicles in full flight down the tac-routes. It was also a reminder of the danger we faced trying to outmanoeuvre them, not just to get away but also to avoid inadvertently being hit by one of them in their haste.

We weren't doing too badly ourselves down the flatter route, touching 60 or 70 m.p.h. in order to catch up with and get ahead of the column. The G-wagon loved these sandy woodland trails. There was no chance of traffic so Kev was able to put his foot down and drive like the rally drivers but without the backup team.

More damage to a tour vehicle. A bullet has penetrated the boot leaving its mark and an all too familiar story. Violence was rare but did concentrate the mind when it happened to you. Every tour crew was rammed or shot at some time. Occasionally some were physically assaulted and tragically, two tourers were killed in the mid-1980s.

About 2 kilometres further west down the track the woodland became more sparse and the shallow valleys flattened out. We could see the other route that the tanks were on but no sign of them. We were ahead of them already. Other routes going north to south started to cross this one. Ordinarily each crossing would have been carefully negotiated for fear of something else being out and about, but we were now in a hurry to make the OP before being spotted by our intended victims. There was still another kilometre to get through before the land became completely flat and we would become vulnerable to the open ground. We flew over the crossings, looking left and right down each one but not stopping or slowing.

'Clear left,' from me.

'Clear right,' from Brian.

Kev was looking forward, his eyes not deviating from the track as he worked the wheel and span the car round the corners. It was an exhilarating run.

'9-T-31-NTS on the right, Boss.'

'Seen, Brian. You take the map, I'll make a note to come back. Keep going Kev.'

Kev had instinctively started to slow as Brian called the vehicle to our right. A slow lumbering wheeled vehicle with a gantry-type construction was just visible pulling out of the wood line into a small clearing no bigger than half a football pitch about 150 metres away. It was hard up against PRA and seemed to be on its own. I made a mental record of its position, noted its proximity to the no-go area and left it for later. 9-T-31-NTS was a signature vehicle for Surface to Air Missile (SAM) or Surface to Surface Missile (SSM) systems and as such was high priority for the missions. On its own it was pretty harmless but its association with missile systems made it a key vehicle in the missile set.

Taking the map meant that Brian was to continue the navigation. We routinely swapped between front and back seat. If there was kit to be photographed while on the move it was impossible for the tour officer to read the map as well. The tour NCO would call the kit and read the map. Although he had as much to do, being in the front seat gave him an edge over the tour officer's rear seat when it came to navigating. Close in to a target, both would read the map, the officer the immediate target and the NCO the strip map, allowing him a bigger picture for routes out in an emergency. Again this would swap around as both gained experience until such time as it became second nature to chop and change seemlessly. There were no hard and fast rules. Everyone in the Mission could navigate to an exceptionally high degree. We altered responsibility as we felt like it. Quite often the determining factor was familiarity with the territory. Each tourer had a favourite area that they had become acquainted with in detail. Again the man with the most experience took the lead. Towards the end of my posting there were areas in the DDR that I could navigate without a map and probably knew better than my own home town. But it was a foolish crew who didn't have one of their number with a pinpoint on their exact location.

The track ended abruptly, together with the trees that offered the last remnants of protection. The land in front of us was snooker-table flat. We nosed out of the wood line and into the open area that constituted part of this western training area. The parallel track emerged about 200 metres to our left. Nothing had come through it yet. To our 11 o'clock position, about 300 metres away, was a small hollow in the otherwise flat, bare landscape. The hollow, gifted with short steep sides, sprawling shrub that masked the true depth of its bottom and in size not much bigger than a tank itself, was warily avoided by rampaging vehicle commanders and thus protected from the incessant traffic that scarred the rest of plain into virtual desert. But it wasn't impregnable to the G-wagon. The forward slope was sufficiently shallow to allow the G-wagon to back down into it, covering it from view as vehicles streamed past on either side.

A little oasis of green, it had become a highly prized OP that only a few brazen tourers would use and then only sparingly to avoid it being detected. Some former tourer had probably spotted its potential when all was quiet, investigated the possibility and reported back that it was a goer. It was on the file for the area but it was annotated 'balls-up'. If you were here then you were committed and you'd better get it right. It was a high risk if a tank crew saw us creeping in or if one of them, unaware of the relatively minor belly flop leaping the hollow might have caused, decided to cross it for a laugh to complete the final obliteration of the landscape. Either way they could flatten us and claim complete ignorance. Then it was G-wagon pancake with us as the stuffing. If they saw us on passing, through the clouds of dust, assuming one of them was out of the cupola at these speeds across country, and if they could detect us against the backdrop of dense thicket then, knowing these boys, they would probably swing that tank round so fast that it would be fairly obvious what their intentions were. Flushing us out would result in a straight motorised fox hunt back to the cover of the wood that we would win, providing the car didn't bog down in some of the churned up mud and sand that constituted good going for tanks. Hopefully as always, their minds would be concentrating on other things and would not be expecting us in the first place. Once they were past this OP the initiative was with us.

We checked the area was clear. The tank column was still some way off, neither seen nor heard. We sprinted across the open ground, cursing the dust that we spat up, its effect more visible than the vehicle creating it. Hopefully it would be passed off as yet another vehicle on the area. We snuck backwards into the bushes and waited.

The first tanks thundered past about two minutes later, fanning out all round us as they passed the hidey-hole. It was a marvellous sight and noise. The rear-mounted turbine engines threw out so much hot air they created a false heat haze across the open expanse. The noise from their rear-mounted turbines was awesome. Thirty-two tanks passed us, every one on video as well as stills. Brian was shouting at the tape recorder to make himself heard and Kev was as tense as a Formula One racing driver in pole position being held on red before the lights turned green. It was a petrifying experience. The intense noise made it difficult to concentrate. As frightening as it was we wallowed in this awesome demonstration of power that washed around us. It was such a ridiculously exposed position there was nothing we could do other than enjoy it. They flew past us, fanning out into three separate columns as they emerged from close to open countryside. The speed was impressive. This was an unreserved charge to build up momentum and knock everything reeling in their wake. They must have been exceeding 50 m.p.h. across this flat expanse.

The unhealthy impression among Western military professionals that whatever advantage was conferred upon the Soviets by dint of numbers they lost in technical knowledge and professional skill, was a view brutally shattered by anyone involved with the Missions and privileged to have witnessed this sight. In later years the volume of arms sales Russia now enjoys with the rest of the world vindicates the reality that their equipment was competent, reliable, simple and effective. If there were differences then they were not significant enough to warrant the near complacency surrounding the threat lectures that I recall from my early army career. The technology was adapted to the battlefield where 'think simple' is by far a better maxim than being fancy. The T-80 was a most impressive beast as anyone who had been chased by one could vouch for. It was agile, fast and sleek. It had reactive armour, a snorkelling capability and gas turbine engines all of which were unheard of in contemporary Western equivalents.

Once the noise had died down and the tanks disappeared from view we just sat there, stunned by the magnificent spectacle that we had been sitting in the middle of.

'Marvellous! Marvellous! Marvellous!' I kept repeating until the noise finally drifted away. We were completely transfixed. I thought about some of my colleagues who would have to face them on the open northern plains of West Germany and considered myself very lucky to be this side of the IGB, if and when they did decide to thunder across.

This French tour crew are caught in a classic 'mission sandwich'. The two attending Soviet vehicles have rammed the French vehicle front and rear to prevent them moving anywhere at all.

'I think now the NTS please, Kev.'

We tentatively left cover ourselves and proceeded back to UV 669 190, the last recorded sighting of our tell-tale missile truck. I still had the video out on the pole to record our route back. We often recorded the more tricky training areas for the target files. It allowed less familiar crews the chance to prepare their tours more thoroughly.

'Nice and slowly back, Kev, I'll comment on the route back for the benefit of the video. Take the tac-route.'

We were cock-a-hoop at our last sighting. Little did we know what was still in store. The Rheinsberg Gap had not finished with us yet!

The Rheinsberg Gap, 50 kilometres to the north of Berlin, was so called by Brixmis because the lakes that hemmed its western side and the railway line that ran part of its eastern side effectively constrained touring there to a strip of land running north to south about 20 kilometres wide at its broadest point. To complicate matters it was bordered on both sides by PRA which, together with the terrain, narrowed the southerly entry point to less than 6 kilometres and the northerly exit point to less than 3, thereby creating a funnel effect at both ends.

To put it in Mission jargon there was only one way in and one way out. It did have its advantages though. Every conceivable line of communication had to come out of the same funnel. At the north end, the tac-route ran parallel to the only railway line and was crossed by the only road. They all converged out of Neustrelitz within a few hundred metres of each other. There were several

This was the classic detention pose adopted by the Soviets. Two soldiers were positioned at the front of the vehicle and two at the rear. They knew that we would not deliberately run them over.

OPs that boasted views onto all these major arterial routes into and out of the Gap that avoided a crew having to commit into the Gap unnecessarily. The best was the north–south bridge over the railway. The only road to the bridge was bordered by PRA for 3 kilometres on its western side and dense coniferous woodland to its east. The wood was not passable even to the G-wagon. From the bridge, the tac-route and training area were in full view to the west and the road had sufficiently long views up and down it to anticipate any reaction to our presence. The bridge itself was wide enough to U-turn on. It was in full sight of the high concrete viewing tower that itself commanded a lookout over the whole training area but there was very little they could do about us. It must have infuriated them, to put it mildly.

Like several other key Soviet military concentrations, the density of barracks, training areas and equipment centred on Neustrelitz was of the highest priority for the missions. This was where 2 Guards Tank Army, consisting of three tank divisions and two motor rifle divisions, faced the northern defensive positions of 1 British Corps, having the area between Hamburg and the Kiel canal as its primary objective before holding ground against Nato's northern flank in Denmark in support of its southerly neighbour 3 Shock Army and its punching drive to Belgium, Holland and the Channel. It was often difficult to comprehend from the relative safety of West Germany that there were another three armies within GSFG besides those two; five divisions to the south in Czechoslovakia and a further two divisions to the east in Poland.

Although rather uninspiring, these comms box-body vehicles were key targets. The aerials, attachments and even the generator would be closely scrutinised by analysts in the Defence Intelligence Staff. An army marches on its stomach but it can be stopped by lack of communications.

The Rheinsberg Gap was like a giant pinball machine with buzzers and bells and stops and rebounds that represented all the various installations, barracks and training areas that were 2 Guards Tank Army's domain. The Mission cars were the little silver balls that rebounded off them. The only difference was that while we controlled the timing of pulling the lever back as well as when it was time to leave the table, the buzzers and bells sometimes came after you!

We proceeded back up the track that the T-80 regiment had just come down. It was about 30 metres wide, bordered by thick woodland which every so often revealed tracks off to the side that we could use to escape down if necessary. If I thought that they petered out into dead ends then I would comment to that effect for the video. We zigzagged across the width of the track partly to stay close to likely escape routes and partly to backtrack the tank route on the off chance of finding anything that might have fallen off one in the rush. A piece of Explosive Reactive Armour (ERA) would have been a prize possession. We also carried a specially hardened tool for scraping the armour of any tank that might have been left broken down and abandoned. It was quite feasible that the crews would walk off and leave them. You just didn't know what opportunity was around the corner.

On anti-tank ranges they used old hulls for target practice. On research ranges they test fired against the most up-to-date armour. We investigated and sampled all of them, sometimes retrieving huge lumps of metal in the process.

We pulled off the north side of the tac-route and into the last bit of wood line before it emerged into the large desolate plain that was Neustrelitz's back garden. We were about 300 metres from the chance sighting of the NTS, back inside the cover of the sandy floored forest, at a confluence of several small tracks and one minor tac-route.

'Stop and listen please, Kev.'

There was distinct movement to our north and east. From where we were I couldn't clearly match the location on the map. There were several open areas that were possible. To our front, running nearly north to south and about 100 metres away, was the main route out of the northern end of the Gap. On the other side of it the Neustrelitz PRA started, which meant that the track itself was in bounds but all routes off it to the east were no-go areas. It seemed as though the noise was coming from the far side of the track, about 250 metres away to the north-east. We were pointing in its direction, exceptionally well concealed from whatever it was but rather unguarded on our southern flank to anything that might come up the tac-route we had just left.

'I think we should take a look on foot, Brian, what do you reckon?'

We were at the very top end of the Gap. We'd played the whole pinball machine and were now trying to get past the flippers when someone had placed an additional stop, right in the open jaws. Firstly we had to determine its exact location and also ensure that our only vehicular access out of the Gap wasn't blocked. The exit route narrowed down to a single track that twisted and turned back on itself, sandy hillocks topped with thick tree growth that conspired to pen you in. It was only a short dash down the track to relative safety but it was easily blocked or ambushed. The banks and trees either side prohibited even G-wagon movement. Normally we would have run the gauntlet relying on speed and surprise but it wasn't worth running straight into trouble when we could have detoured back to the south and left the Gap at its southerly entrance.

'I think you're right, Boss. What do you want to take?'

'You take a tape I'll bring the 85-mm and 180-mm lens. Kev, should you need to move then circle back to the track junction we're on now and pick us up.' I oriented him on the map and left it with him.

'We'll come back through your 10 o'clock and won't be more than twenty to thirty minutes. OK?'

It was almost noon on a bright winter's day, great photography weather but bloody freezing outside the vehicle. We both put on Canadian parkas. They didn't rustle as much as the Gore-Tex jackets that we were also issued with and were much duller than the Gore-Tex sheen. They were big, bulky and knee-length. You could easily hide under one. I had lately taken to sleeping with it on inside my Arctic sleeping bag, inside my bed roll on these cold winter nights that were now plummeting to -10 degrees and more. The parkas covered the bright Union Jack Brixmis flashes and badges of rank on our jumpers. To all intents and purposes we looked like a pair of local East German farmers. Theirs too was a uniform of black boots, green trousers and green jumpers. Unfortunately this was nowhere near farmland, completely off limits to the local population. We were the only two peas in this particular pod.

Leaving the vehicle so close to obvious military activity was always risky and certain precautions were taken before doing so. The minimum amount of kit was taken in case anything was dropped in a hurry. Anything that could be tied on was. A compass or a torch was fitted with a loop, the loop threaded through a buttonhole and stored in one of the big pockets. The driver was always briefed for actions-on with a simple point for him to make for in the event of being split up. Out of military contact, leaving the car was a relatively safe option, usually employed to search an area that a troop concentration had just left or to offer the tour officer a better camera shot or more practically still when we had to go on 'shovel recces' in answer to the call of nature.

This particular dismount was not a safe option but necessary before going any further. The area had been bursting with kit all morning. We had been going since about 5 a.m. and were having difficulty avoiding the stuff. The ball was bouncing around the board quite nicely. I had already shot thirty-odd reels of film and it was only our second day. It was becoming quite clear that we were probably in the middle of a divisional exercise. The chance of a SAM or SS missile sighting was therefore not unlikely and certainly not to be passed up lightly. Our luck and timing was impeccable. It was considered worth the risk.

Brian and I got out with as little noise as possible and made our way through the cover towards the target. It was dense young pine forest only about 10 to 12 feet high. It provided excellent cover but lousy fields of view. We couldn't see what was going on without getting right to the edge. The wood line was buzzing with soldiers preparing shell scrapes, unloading stores and running communication lines between vehicles and comms boxes. We had arrived just as they were deploying. Soon sentries would be stationed, patrols sent out and we would be engulfed in their expanding perimeter.

The last time I had been out on foot in such close cover was on a recent tour of the Haufeld training area, the summit of which was a large open plateau completely ringed by densely wooded, steep sides. I was with Martin Brain and we had spotted an open signals wagon parked alone on top of the hill that was part of 97 GMRD. It was clearly a 'rebro' vehicle and as such would contain significant comms intelligence. We watched it and watched it and began to realise that it was completely unoccupied. We decided to go and pilfer what we could. We clambered up the hill towards it, stopping every few metres to check and confirm that it was still unoccupied. It was quite possible that the occupants, if there were any, would be armed and therefore have us at a distinct disadvantage if caught. As we neared the top a Soviet signals officer bobbed up out of the scrub not 2 metres off, facing completely away from me and just as suddenly bobbed back down again. He had earphones on his head, which accounted for him not hearing us at such close quarters. I looked across at Martin, both of us stunned at the emergence of the guy so close to us. We slowly crouched down, trying to work out our next move. He couldn't see us and he couldn't hear us but he was only a long arms length away. The reason for his curious position became clear as grunting noises revealed that he was performing the necessary bodily functions that strike all of us on a regular basis. He was obviously savouring the moment

Narks in a UAZ-469, this time trying to video us.

as he then proceeded to smoke as well. We sat there with him for almost twenty minutes, almost in agony trying not laugh. Eventually he got up, slung his rifle and walked back up the hill, completely oblivious to our presence. If I'd had a long-handled shovel I could have retrieved the droppings. As it was I retrieved the customary signals paper wipes and we scurried back to the G-wagon, absolutely pissing ourselves laughing.

However, this situation was entirely different.

'Boss, look 10 o'clock, far side of the open area.'

Through the open area I could just make out a pointed nose cone of a SAM system looking suspiciously like SA-6 and therefore really not worth the risk. Behind it, but not hidden by it, was an altogether much bigger and more rounded cone similar to one of the SS systems. The view was almost completely obscured by the foliage, let alone the SAM-6. There was no point taking a shot from this position. I motioned to Brian that we would move closer when a noise off to our left froze us. A couple of Sovs were laying line about 10 metres away. They were barely visible, only their noise and movement giving them away. They were taking it from the deployment we were observing to an adjacent position, either another unit or a sentry position.

It was time to leave. We let them get as far away as possible before we felt safe to move and yet not delaying too long before the next party turned up. We headed back to the vehicle on the run, holding the sides of our parkas to prevent anything falling out. The consequences of being caught out in the open with binoculars and a couple of grand's worth of camera equipment did not sit easy. I tried to remember what other things I had on my person that could possibly incriminate me. Dumping them would have been a pain in the arse. If we had thought that there was no chance of getting away then we would have hastily stowed or buried them in whatever cover was available, remembered the area and come back for them at a later date. I'd had to do that with some film several tours before.

We got back to the vehicle. Kev had clearly moved it further back into the scrub for some reason. He unlocked the doors and we climbed back inside the vehicle, locking them behind us.

'The place is crawling, Boss.' Kev confirmed my suspicions.

We still didn't know whether the run past was on the cards because we hadn't been able to determine whether they had blocked the exit route or not. Common sense told me it was time to leave, but the sighting of a possible SS system was holding me back. I started to plan our next move based on the recce.

Suddenly there was a whack on the rear of the vehicle as though we'd been hit by a sledgehammer. Two Sovs appeared from our rear three quarters and stared right at me from outside my right-hand window. Where the hell had they come from? Kev floored the accelerator.

'Go right, go right,' Brian commanded urgently. Kev turned the vehicle back towards the tac-route that the tanks had gone down previously. More Sovs on foot poured out of the wood that Brian and I had just walked out of. The track behind was blocked by two huge KAMAZ trucks who acted in unison to block our path.

'180, Kev.' Me, this time.

Kev spun the vehicle round again to head for the PRA boundary track that would take us away north. Once more the route was blocked. We started doing pirouettes on the confluence of the tracks. Fifteen or more Sov troops on foot, all of them armed, quickly closed us down by surrounding the vehicle. Outside the ring of Sovs there were two vehicles to our rear and another blocking the path further ahead, which looked suspiciously like the NTS that we had spotted in the first place. They had us good and proper. It was a new experience for the three of us. Not one of us had been detained before and although we were clearly up shit creek without a paddle I was not in the least bit frightened but rather felt as though I was witnessing a dream that sooner or later I would wake up from. Suddenly touring had become deadly serious. All the training, all the planning and all the caution were designed to avoid this moment. Getting caught was not getting the job done.

'Doors and windows.' I forced myself to think and do something rather than freeze.

They were all locked tight. We didn't make that mistake in this sort of area.

The soldiers were armed and very slowly advancing towards us, some already touching the vehicle. Most were shouting, pointing and waving their weapons wildly in our direction. They were well aware of who we were and what they'd caught. What they would do next, once sure that we couldn't get out, would be critical. They were very agitated. It was time to be passive. The more we riled them now the more excuse they had not to control themselves. This was not like Salisbury Plain and these were not Paras playing a role.

'Check on, Kev.' Kev paused the vehicle. They were as unsure of us as we were of them at the moment. I was very keen to keep it that way. Even when caught we had

FLOGGER-C firing unguided air-to-ground rockets during the range training day. The camera work has stilled the rockets sufficient for them to be designated and the rates of fire determined.

to remain in control of the situation. Anything that might influence that, particularly our vehicle and body language would help now. It did not appear as though this was a coordinated effort or being deliberately led. That might bode well for our safety.

'Don't switch off. If an opening appears then go for it but for fuck's sake don't run anyone over,' I said. It wasn't going to happen. They were too close to get out of the way quickly enough. We were now curiously responsible for their safety while hoping to God they would be thinking of ours!

Brian was looking around desperately to see if we could reverse out. At the same time he was recording everything that was going on, the tape thrust down his right side into the well of the passenger door. There was another whack on the rear of the vehicle. Somebody was clearly sticking tight to our back end. These guys certainly knew what they were doing. Two of them had now put their hands on the front of our vehicle. That action alone was enough to effect a detention for their safety's sake, but I was more concerned at the frenzy they were getting themselves into. It reminded me of the excessive jubilation displayed by gangs of Moslem gunmen in the Lebanon that constantly seemed to capture the news. Self-preservation was sharpening the brain without doubt.

'Drive forward slowly, Kev, at walking pace, try to walk them off the vehicle.' Sometimes a gentle nudge forward could persuade the most ardent protesters to slip to the side. The G-wagon inched forward and the two soldiers started to walk back with it. Suddenly there was a shot from my right rear three quarters and at the same time one of the guys at the front slammed his RPK-74 assault machine gun onto the bonnet, the barrel supported menacingly on its bipod in line with our front windscreen. I whipped round to see who and what had fired the weapon. Not 5 metres away a young soldier was lowering his rifle and looking at me quite openly, acknowledging the source.

'Shit! Cut the vehicle. That's enough. Everyone sit back and relax.'

There was another whack at the rear, this time duller as an SA-6 transloader slammed into the rear of us. We were quite definitely surrounded and they knew it. Kevin and Brian held up a single hand, as if to acknowledge that we weren't going anywhere. An officer appeared and motioned the NTS to come over and position itself in front of us. They didn't take any chances, the truck manoeuvred right up to us, rear end on, before the officer would allow the two on our bonnet to move away.

There was still more sport to follow. One of the soldiers hooked up the crane to the vehicle and proceeded to winch us off the ground. Having established what he was capable of doing he dropped the G-wagon and took up the slack to prevent us from moving at all. At this point Kev came out with a line that I shall take with me to the grave.

'Shall I show them my knife, Boss?' with which he pulled from some scabbard down by his left leg a hunting knife that must have been a good 10 inches long. He put it on his lap so that no one outside could see it. Whether he was serious or not or whether the heat of the moment got to him, I'm not sure. I put it down to his extremely dark sense of humour. But it took the tension right out of the moment. We chuckled at the possible good it might do in our predicament, which in turn confused the hell out of the Sovs outside.

'Thank you but no thank you, Kev. Let's just sit back and make the most of it.'

'OK, Boss.'

'25 Jan, 12.00 hours. Grid uniform victor 669 190. First vehicle 9-T-31-NTS. VRN 92, 79, M, Z, H. It's hooked up to us! Approximately fifteen troops, artillery on black, all armed, thirteen AK-74s and two RPKs.'

Brian was still recording everything he could see. No sense in wasting this valuable opportunity to get some detail. He recorded the number, type and state of each vehicle, the number and type of weapons, the condition and appearance of the soldiers as well as any other vehicle that appeared in the distance trundling down the track.

The mere action of sitting back in our seats and demonstrating that we had accepted detention seemed to allay their worries that we might still try to escape. We were so precariously balanced, literally, that it seemed highly unlikely anyway. A smile crept across some of their young faces as they realised what they had achieved. Just as quickly they stiffened up and parted ranks.

A lieutenant-colonel equivalent stood legs astride, hands on hips, beckoning me to come over to him. I declined the offer, motioned that he should come over to me and then promptly ignored him. I was more prepared for this chance meeting than he was. The likelihood of him having met a Westerner, let alone a Brixmis tour officer, was remote indeed. Furthermore there was no way any of us were leaving the vehicle having witnessed the reactions of the surrounding soldiers so far. He came over, I showed him my tour pass, requested the immediate presence of the Neustrelitz Kommandant, leant back and ignored him. My irritation was not feigned by any means. Being detained was one thing, being shot at and then hoisted was not in my book a particularly friendly action from an allied force with whom we had liberated Berlin and certainly not in the spirit of the Robertson-Malinin agreement. As a Jewish saying puts it, more succinctly than the English, I was working up a good hootspah. I was also conscious of the double standards I was now about to employ and was considering my story for the Kommandant if and when he arrived.

Priority number one was to avoid being compromised, that is to say to avoid being put in an incriminating situation that could be photographically recorded and used against me or someone else later on. It was very unlikely that they would take a photo of the current situation as this wouldn't help their case at all. It was quite possible that they might conjure something up later. I rather gambled that, in the absence of taking responsibility for any further precipitous action, this lieutenant-colonel would seek help from an authority who knew how to deal with us. He was unlikely to lose any face, quite the contrary, he had captured a Mission crew and that would go down well on his record. Had we been captured by a Spetsnaz team then no doubt we would have had a much more robust welcome. The officer disappeared. I was desperate for a chance to get my camera out and photograph the offending crane and jib on our bonnet but he'd posted a Sov at each window and one on each wheel.

It was a further hour and forty minutes before the officer came back with two Vai marked[61] cars following behind him. It wouldn't be long before we would be breaking out the emergency plastic bags for this sort of occasion, having not stopped since 5 a.m. The Vai vehicles were in the direct employ of the Kommandatura. Although Neustrelitz was only 4 or 5 kilometres away I thought the response rather quick and immediately became suspicious that we perhaps had been set up after all.

The Kommandant was a major with a captain in tow, probably his deputy. Additionally the artillery colonel had brought along his officers, three senior lieutenants, a major and four praporshicks[62], numbering eleven officers in total to deal with. We had certainly attracted attention. The Kommandant came over and identified himself with his ID card and papers pressed up against the window. Major Borisyev was his name and not surprisingly in this area, he was a tank man. He introduced the captain as his deputy, Alfontiyev, also a tank man. Major Borisyev seemed almost as unfamiliar with this routine as I was. I showed him my pass and wound down the window.

'Good afternoon, Major. I am sorry that you have been called out to this incident but regrettably the Colonel of Artillery has prevented us from proceeding along our chosen route.' I spoke in Russian and deliberately avoided telling him where we were going. He would probably think I was lying if I did and totally ignore it anyway. He studied my pass.

---

[61] Vai: in Cyrillic it looks like 'VAU' and is pronounced 'vye'. Vai marked vehicles indicated that they were part of the Kommandatura's own military police. As such, we were always on our best behaviour for them.

[62] praporshick: Soviet Warrant Officer.

Stephen Harrison looks on almost indifferently as he is detained for the third time in one day. He was a highly successful tour officer and for a while became targeted for special treatment by the Sovs, including villification in the Soviet press. He finished his tour and went on to become Military Attaché in Moscow, where he would get even again.

'Captain Gibson, regrettably I must inform you that you have been prevented from proceeding because you are in PRA,' he responded.

This was not going to be straightforward.

'Let me interpret for the benefit of my crew,' I remarked. He nodded. I bought a little time. This was a serious accusation and while I knew what my reply would be I wanted to be sure. I did not want to give ground and I also did not want to give cause for a PNG.[63]

'Brian, check our grid and check that we are not in PRA. Keep the tape running.'

I gambled that he didn't speak English and then returned to him.

'Major, I can assure you that we are not in PRA. Perhaps you have a map that would allow me to verify our position.'

My Russian was quite formal because this was now a formal meeting. I was speaking with the authority of the Chief of Mission and he with the authority of Chief SERB, undoubtedly he would have called him before leaving his office to establish who was

63 PNG: Persona Non Grata.

If a long lens couldn't capture the necessary detail, then the camera had to be taken nearer. This tour managed to get exceptionally close to a lesson being given on the mortar-locating radar 'TALL-MIKE'. The soldier with his back resting against the tree gives the unnerving impression that he has heard something behind him.

out here. We were also taught that way at Beaconsfield. I had enough difficulty with the correct Russian without having to delve into slang and vernacular. I found it easier to say, 'Let me verify my position' than to say, 'We're here, mate!'

The Major turned to his deputy and asked for the map. He produced a 1:1,000,000 scale map. Basically a map of East Germany on one side of A4. He pointed to Neustrelitz and its associated PRA and repeated the accusation that we were detained because of inappropriate activities inside a restricted area.

'What activities, Major?' As soon as I said it I knew it was wrong. I should have concentrated on our position. In he waded.

'You have been observed photographing and filming Soviet military equipment, installations and training. All of this in PRA.'

I should not have given him the opportunity to add to the list of charges. I had been put straight on the spot and my only defence was to lie. It would have been better to avoid the issue altogether.

'I can assure you, Major, that we have been doing no such thing.' He knew I was lying because he knew what all Mission tours got up to. He didn't have to see me and he didn't have to prove it. What else was I here for? They knew the rules of the game as well as we did. Catching us was the prize because then they could do something about it. Over the years they had gained enough knowledge of our methods, techniques and equipment to convince anyone of our activities. Equipment and techniques they weren't sure of were gained by forceful means. There was no point asking him to prove his allegations. The front two soldiers, still on the bonnet, now with weapons slung, had seen me frantically disconnect the video from the pole in such full view that I could have given them a lesson on it. I switched back to the PRA issue.

'Major, with respect, the map you have there would mean that the thickness of a pencil line would represent 2 or 3 kilometres on the ground.'

Brian whispered quietly for me to hear.

'Boss, there's no way we're in PRA. The track to our front is definitely the border and it's about 80 metres away.'

I had a blank 1:25,000 target map in my case. Blank in that it had no detail that could compromise future operations. I pulled it out.

'I'm getting out and showing them where we are,' I said to Brian.

I opened the door and got out of the vehicle, careful to lock it behind me as I did so. I was committed now. No need for a forced entry on their part. I walked over to the bonnet of the Kommandant's Lada, spread out the map and asked them all to gather round and have a look.

Certainly the majority of them were surprised at the detail and scale of the map, about four A4 sheets with individual tracks and vegetation features in clear detail. I have no doubt that the Kommandant had brought his particular map to argue his own case. He wasn't as impressed or swayed by my map as the other officers from the missile deployment seemed to be. They gathered round, marvelling at the OS detail. I pointed out our exact location on my map, which he quickly refuted saying that our maps were incorrect. It was stalemate and we were now going round in circles of charge and denial. He was very effectively keeping us from getting on with our job.

'Major, it is clear that we disagree. May I suggest that we proceed to Neustrelitz and call Colonel Polozov, Deputy Chief SERB, Potsdam, for further guidance.'

The reaction was electric. I'm not sure whether he was surprised that I knew Colonel Polozov, surprised at my cheek or concerned that I was calling in higher authority. He suddenly motioned me into his car and abruptly dismissed the gawping artillery officers. He sat in the front and I sat in the back. Captain Alfontiyev got into the passenger seat. If it was a trap then I had just walked right into it. I suspected Brian and Kev were wondering what was going on. I trusted that they would keep calm about me getting into his vehicle. Ten further minutes of inane accusation followed, which I simply denied without offering any reason for my presence other than it was the Mission's right to transit the country as we pleased in support of our official duties on behalf of GSFG.

I'd been sitting in the car for twenty minutes, subjected to this quasi-interrogation. I could still see the G-wagon and occasionally glimpsed Brian watching me through a pair of small bins that fitted in the palm of his hand. I was sure they would be concerned but while I remained in view there was no danger. I was a little more reassured by now. If they had decided to drive off with me then they would have done it by now. I realised that this was indeed a rare opportunity.

One of the last detentions (March 1990). Flight Lieutenant Mark Knight has emerged from his tarped vehicle to exchange passes with the Kommandant (far left). An interpreter is in between them. They knew they were being photographed with the Mickey Mouse, what they didn't realise was that the camera was working its way round to the BTR-80, a relatively new vehicle, over Mark's shoulder. Tarping a tour vehicle was common practice but also highly dangerous, especially when summer temperatures outside the vehicle were in excess of 40°C.

I was inside a Kommandant's staff car. I scanned the inside, looking for anything that might be remotely useful. There was a secure radio in the vehicle designated 'Lyon-V', which I memorised. I noted details of its frequency bands and general layout. I noted the number of switches on the dashboard and memorised their titles. I even noted the number of gears. The Kommandant could see what I was up to and uncomfortably tried to progress the discussion.

'You will wait here. I will go to Neustrelitz and ring Potsdam. But first you will sign this document.'

He produced the 'Akt'. It was a standard document, more a sign that the meeting was nearly over, bar either the shouting or the handshake. An Akt was a document for the Kommandant to entice a tour officer into signing. It was essentially a confession. They were not very subtle documents and the inducement was not too subtle either. It was a propaganda exercise in very basic form. In this particular case it was a blank form with the usual opening paragraph generalising activities inconsistent with the Robertson-Malinin agreement. They knew we wouldn't sign them but they persisted anyway.

I took the document, scanned it and returned it to the Kommandant.

'I can't sign this. It's not true.'

'But we know what you were doing. You are a reconnaissance officer. You were observing our troops. You are spying on us.' This was the captain in the front seat and suddenly he was speaking in English, which took me by surprise. He was unlikely to be the tank officer that his epaulettes and insignia of rank showed. This was the one to be wary of. I translated his comments back into Russian for the Kommandant's benefit. Unintentionally, this proved a rather shrewd move on my part. I was merely being polite to the senior officer present assuming, quite correctly now, that he didn't speak English. The captain repeated the accusation in English and I repeated it in Russian for the Kommandant. The effect was marvellous. The Kommandant was not amused with the new line of questioning or with who was leading it. These two clearly did not share a good working relationship, if they had ever worked together at all. Whether he was KGB or GRU, I couldn't say. The captain pressed on regardless, now accusing me of using a video camera specially mounted on a pole. He had been sharp enough to get round the soldiers who had detained us and quiz them on our activities.

There was no doubt that I had been seen using the video but that was something I wouldn't or couldn't admit. I recalled my final words with my commanding officer in Hameln. Back on the course these very situations were dealt with. Under no circumstances was it permissible to admit to spying or anything remotely akin to spying. I had no doubt that a tape recorder was running somewhere in the vehicle otherwise they wouldn't have bothered to ask me into it. Maybe that was what the Kommandant thought I was looking for. I simply replied, 'No, that is not true. Kommandant, you stopped my vehicle for being in PRA. That is not correct as I have discussed with you.' My words were carefully chosen and directed to the Kommandant alone. 'Your colleague is now accusing me of spying. That is quite incorrect and I intend to take it further on my return to Potsdam.' I didn't stop there. 'Furthermore, I wish to know who fired the shot toward my vehicle and who was responsible for the damage to the rear. Which officer should I hold responsible?'

The Kommandant had had enough. He motioned me out of the car and the two of them got out themselves. The Kommandant walked away, indicating the captain to follow. They left me standing alone so I walked back to the G-wagon and spoke to Brian to let him know what was going on. I recalled the conversation for the benefit of the tape that was still running in Brian's lap, described the contents of the Kommandant's vehicle and gave a description of the officer who had spoken English.

The conversation between the two Soviets was clearly fractious and barely disguised. The Kommandant walked back to the vehicle. I made him walk round it to look at the dents that the rifles and transloader had made, persisting with the business of who had fired at us. He couldn't ignore the damage but he flatly refuted the shooting. There was no bullet hole in the vehicle but he was not to know that. We afterwards surmised that it was a blank round and that his so-called deputy had probably ascertained that already. I looked round for the Sov who I knew had fired the weapon and saw him sitting in the second Kommandatura vehicle, another soldier standing outside almost acting as a guard on him. He had two weapons slung over his shoulder. I was in no doubt that one of them was the offending weapon. He was in the shit. I dropped the line of argument. There was a spark of understanding between us.

Soviet 'paras' detain a tour at Cottbus by wrapping barbed wire around the axle. This detention became an incident as Tour bags were also 'removed' from the vehicle. Here, Corporal Mick Rostrun RAF is now overseeing the 'paras' take it off in front of a growing crowd!

'You can go now. You will follow us out and we will put you on the right road to continue your journey out of PRA.'

'But, Kommandant, I must protest that I am not . . .'

I was cut off before finishing.

'You will have the opportunity to take that up with both our superiors later. Just follow me.'

I got back into the G-wagon, still very cautious of his intentions. It was not unknown to be led out of a detention straight into PRA, usually where the Kommandant's office was located, or alternatively to be photographed on exit in front of some compromising installation that had a Mission restriction sign outside it. The NTS was unhitched and the troops retired. The Kommandant provided us with an escort out of the detention area and back towards the track out of the Gap.

'They're going to take us straight past the deployment, Boss.' Brian was incredulous.

I had the camera out in no time and photographed the entire lot as we were escorted through. The SS system, if there was one, could not be seen. We'd all won in the end. We got to see the deployment and they got to remove the most important equipment before we saw it.

CHAPTER EIGHT

2A-65

'OK. Last target coming up. Marienburg training area. It's usually very quiet, more often used by the East Germans than the Sovs. It's not very big as training areas go and only a couple of miles from the Czech border.'

I was repeating myself I knew. We'd gone through all this back in Berlin before coming out, but that was four days ago now. This had been a long tour, from Görlitz in the extreme south-east through Dresden, Karl Marx Stadt (its inhabitants now preferring to use its pre-war name Chemnitz, while we called it simply KMS), Zwickau, Plauen and finally Marienburg. The drive back, from Marienburg to Berlin, would be about the same distance as Amsterdam to Hannover but not quite the same standard of road. A real slog for the driver.

'We'll circuit first, see if it's active or not before making the next move.'

My tours, since being detained two months ago, had been conducted slightly more cautiously. The jury was still out as to whether or not I was inside the Soviet's version of PRA or outside our version of it. Chief Brixmis and Chief SERB were still discussing it. Furthermore, the incident had coincided with the visit of Commander BAOR to the Mission, General Sir Peter Inge (later Field Marshal, Chief of the General Staff and Lord). He asked me about my most exciting time at the Mission to date. With the shooting fresh in my mind, I recounted it. Clearly, he hadn't been made aware of the incident yet and as our direct commander I'm sure somebody would be hauled over the coals for the oversight!

I had still managed to tour effectively, revealing a new avionics jammer at Schoenwalde, known as HEART ACHE, filming SCUD-B TELs at Wittenberge and PMP bridging rigs on the River Elbe at Appolensdorf. The last two were filmed for analysis of drills and competence levels as much for technical detail. The highly dangerous antics of the HIP-C on the Buchholz–Schwerin road occurred in this period and were logged by the Chief and used as ammunition during the detention 'discussions'. It was conceivable that I was being targeted and set up for provocation. It was a common tactic and many tour officers were subjected to it down the years.

February saw me take a week off touring to prepare more material for the Ashford course in June. It was also convenient to keep a low profile for a while. I finished off a series of two-man tours to Halle, with Dave Collins as driver, ostensibly to check out some basic mapping details but actually to measure certain key bridge spans, in and around the strategically and industrially significant city. RAF targeteers were worried that their calculations for bomb payloads were inaccurate against some of the newer bridges and they needed their records updating.

In broad daylight I clambered around them one by one with nothing more than a tape measure, tape recorder and Mickey Mouse camera. To my complete amazement no one stopped me or even batted an eyelid. My approach was so ridiculously audacious and direct it must have appeared completely kosher. The precious few people that did pass me and saw me must simply have assumed that I was from the local bridge-measuring department!

It was now early March. This tour of the south-east DDR had already been rewarding from a technical as well as from an orbat point of view. We had recorded the first sighting of T-72 in the hands of the NVA in Military District III, the district that centred on Karl Marx Stadt. To our knowledge they had only ever had T-64s in this southern division of East Germany so it was a good sighting for us. The Sovs did not feel comfortable with their satellite states being as well-equipped as themselves. Now that they were mostly armed with T-80, it was only right that their East German brothers should receive their next upgrade, or cast-offs, depending upon which way you look at it. Military equipment exported from the Soviet Union prior to the Wall coming down was rarely the top-drawer item; ever mindful that it might be turned against themselves, it was reserved for the home market. Nowadays they only export their very best technology in an effort to secure hard currency. The T-72, although a later model than the T-64 and therefore theoretically more capable, had its own technical difficulties and thus rapidly became the favoured export model. It would satisfy the requirement of developing countries abroad while boosting coffers at home, either monetarily or in other goods.

The proximity of the Czech border was also influential in Soviet military policy at the southern end of the DDR. No need to frighten them anymore. They did that in August 1968 when Prague was rolled over, almost thirty years to the day after Hitler invaded in 1938. The East German-Czech border was a sensitive area. Military activity was curtailed. Both Soviet and NVA barracks were discreetly positioned away from the border. The Polish border was similar, whereas, not surprisingly, the IGB between East and West Germanies was so intensely patrolled that even passing tourists reported information to the Allied control points as they crossed through. Of all the satellite states of the Soviet Union the East Germans were probably the most reliable, despite being the newest. However, reliability was not to be confused with trust if the transfer of military technology was the measure. Khruschev himself had probably inadvertently summed up the dichotomy some years before when he described the DDR as 'our most respected but least trusted ally'.

During its last year the Mission was to observe a curious dichotomy in the DDR that complicated matters further. In 1990 the Soviets had announced the phased withdrawal of WGF forces from East Germany to take place over the next few years as a result of the Wall coming down. These were on top of the already planned withdrawals from the Warsaw Pact countries as outlined in the 1979 Stockholm agreement on Cooperation and Disarmament in Europe. A new Brixmis role became the independent and unbiased observation of Soviet troop withdrawals as well as the reorganisation of both NVA and Soviet orbats. While withdrawals commenced in January 1990, watched around the clock for several months on a tri-mission basis, the Missions also observed an almost feverish introduction of new equipment.

As fast as troops and equipment left the country, there was still an extraordinary volume of new equipment systems coming back the other way. It was as if WGF already had in mind a desire to make their forces in the DDR a leaner, meaner machine by the introduction of new sophisticated technology – and more of it. (Curiously enough the 'leaner, meaner army' was a phrase already being used at the time to describe the seemingly endless defence restructuring being undertaken by the British Army.) The transfer of Soviet T-72 into the hands of the NVA could have been part of an already scheduled hand over or simply a cheaper solution to transporting them home as part of the withdrawal plan. So why were they re-equipping as well? Why, nine months after the Wall came down, did we still continue to observe new variants, completely new items of equipment and old fleets still being replaced by the very latest upgrades? It was certainly confusing. Restructuring and withdrawals were very conveniently being mixed up. Ours was not to reason why, as the saying goes, ours was to observe and report. There were plenty of people queuing up to do the analysis on our observations, particularly at this more interesting of times.

'It's got one entrance into the artillery live firing range and from there it takes you on to the rest of the training area. If it's not in use we'll use the front door and update the files if nothing else. Graham, there's an OP at US 747 068 which should give us views on to the area. Happy about that option?'

'Fine, Boss. You to take us in?'

'Yep. OK.'

To be honest we were knackered. It had been the usual run of events, two Tommies – one on each of the last two nights, rail watches each night prior to the Tommy and an unusually heavy driving burden for Al. Although one of the best drivers in the Mission, he was only human. We had had two rather exciting incidents already. Firstly, the occurrence of narks: contrary to popular reports that the Stasi had been disbanded, their presence had been particularly high and secondly, we had had a close shave on the Czech border. The narks, or whoever it was that was tailing us around the city of Dresden, had been abnormally persistent. We'd deliberately gone through the city centre to shake them off. The abundance of streets and other vehicles would help to lose them before leaving the other side. But they had been difficult to dislodge. In the end we parked in one of the main squares and let them watch us. We had a brew and ignored them.

Dresden at the best of times was not an easy place to venture into with a Union Jack on your number-plate. Memories of the bombing campaign were long and minds resentful. They could recognise an RAF uniform a mile off and further still distinguish it from an Army one. It was doubly difficult when you were there to spy on them, as well they knew. Dresden housed a sophisticated but embittered population.

We had narks with us all the way down the Leipzig–Dresden autobahn, had taken them for a detour round Meissen where we lost them, doubled back on them and appeared up their chuff, much to their surprise and considerable annoyance. They disappeared, only to reappear back on the autobahn where we ran into an East German police roadblock. It wasn't a set up but a routine East German police speed trap that we had the misfortune to be followed towards. We would not be stopping for them and I instructed Al to drive right through it.

Our intention was very clear and the message equally clearly received. In a frantic scamper they withdrew to the sides, getting out of the way just in time to see their flimsy red and white traffic barriers being removed to the side of the road by the G-wagon. Had it been a Soviet block then we would have swung off the autobahn and disappeared into the woods rather than take them on.

Whether our tails were the remnants of the Stasi or freelancers who had nothing else better to do was unclear. It was not yet certain that the MfS really had gone out of operation. Even if they had there would be no doubt that someone like the KGB, GRU or Spetsnaz would take up the challenge of watching the Missions in the front line, now that their subcontracted agencies were no longer doing their dirty work for them. What was clear was that whoever they were, they were a pain in the arse and very effectively stopping us doing our job. The last thing we could do with this incessant presence was to get annoyed with them. That had been tried before and while it had been got away with many times, on at least two occasions an act of vengeance invariably born out of sheer exasperation had resulted in a *persona non grata* for the tour officers concerned. One had actually been photographed exacting retribution in his own way and regrettably these photographs had been used by the prosecution. The greatest difficulty this presented to Missions was the fact that they would lose a highly-trained individual while his successor was still halfway through training. Getting the right person with the right combination of skills, including languages and Special Duties, was a tall order and there simply were no reserves to call upon. Once again it simply meant that we couldn't get the job done as effectively as we might with the full complement of tourers. In the end being provoked by this attention would always backfire somewhere. The key response was to stay calm and not react but beat them at their own game.

Our other incident was right on the Czech border itself. It was frustrating in its own way, completely self-inflicted and amusing with hindsight, but not at the time. We had gone to look at the tri-border road and rail crossing between East Germany, Czechoslovakia and Poland near Zittau, partly out of our own curiosity and partly for professional reasons. We had found a small forest track that gave us access across country to the border, off the main road about a kilometre before the main vehicle crossing point into Czechoslovakia. Although Czechoslovakia was strictly off limits to Brixmis, (military attachés at the British Embassy would cover that option) it was always useful to monitor crossing points for equipment coming in or out of country. Border crossing points are few and far between the further into eastern Europe one goes. Because there were so few they became obvious targets for watches as they were the only likely access points. The Szczecin (Stettin) railway crossing into Poland where it met the E74 autobahn from East Berlin to Warsaw and the Mukran ferry crossing from Rügen Island to Kaliningrad on the Baltic were two other such targets.

This crossing, at the confluence of three countries, was not on our scheduled list of targets, but given that we were down here and given that there were no other operations going on that we might possibly compromise, we decided to take a look anyway.

The track down the side of a gentle slope in among the dense conifer growth was uneven and narrow. That alone should have set the alarm bells ringing. We reversed the vehicle off the track and into a small break in the dense forest. We were out of view from the main road and off the track should anyone be using it. Graham and I left the vehicle and made for one of the red and white border crossing markers not 20 metres further down the track. We crossed into Czechoslovakia, making a bit of a show to each other pretending not to see the crossing post. We were trying to get a better view of the border crossing post and the railway line. There was nothing moving on either so this would be a useful opportunity to recce the ground for the future. We found a good spot that could be filed as a future OP, obscure and remote enough to do on foot. We observed proceedings at the checkpoint for about twenty minutes before returning to the vehicle.

We could hear the revving long before we got back. Not being able to interpret this unlikely commotion we crept up on our own G-wagon. The vehicle was revving away but the sound didn't change. It wasn't actually going anywhere. A previous tour in the early 1980s had been surprised when they woke to find that they had been chained to a BTR-60 during the night. My first thought was that somehow Al had been jumped and the vehicle had been chained to a tree and he was desperately trying to get away with the tree as well. But we were nowhere that could conceivably have been contentious.

When we spotted the vehicle we could see Al in the driving seat wrestling furiously with the wheel and transmission. He was clearly on his own and for all the world looked as though he was having a fit. The problem was obvious when we reached it. The vehicle was slowly sinking. The forest track we had followed down was a covered stream. It was early March and the whole area was sodden. The weight of the G-wagon was slowly defeating the upward support of the ground. Al was flooring the vehicle to try and carve his way out, but to no avail. There were two schools of thought on extracting the G-wagon from a bit of soft going if you had the misfortune to get bogged in. One was to try and leave slowly, automatic first gear and gently climb out, the automatic transmission would control revs to the wheels better than the most experienced driver could derive from a manual gearbox. The other theory was to put the vehicle in drive and floor the accelerator, delivering maximum torque to the wheels. The wheels would slice through the mud to a harder layer where it would grip and ease the car out. If it didn't work inside thirty seconds then all the attendant problems of wear and tear would take over. But it was impressive when it did work.

Al Tipping was an exponent of the latter method. It was an amusing moment and we both split our sides when Al caught sight of us watching him. But again it was not very clever as it simply delayed us getting on with the task in hand. Furthermore we were over 300 kilometres from recovery, not to mention several kilometres from the nearest telephone, wherever that might be. Graham had broken down in this part of the world during his last posting eight years ago and had somehow persuaded the local Kommandant to recover him. In the process he had broken two of the Kommandant's ZILs but made a lifelong friend when a few months later he returned with a couple of bottles of whisky and the Brixmis first eleven drinking team. He probably learnt more about the Soviet way of life in that short encounter than you could in a year at the Russian embassy.

Flooring the accelerator wasn't working and re-calling the Kommandant for the second time, so close to the Czech border, would have set off a few alarm bells even in his amiable head. Calling back to Berlin and requesting recovery would have meant being stuck here for at least a day and quite possibly two if the recovery vehicle was already deployed. By that time there may not have been anything left to recover in this ground. We quickly rigged up the electric winch fitted to the front of every G-wagon, put down logs and our own trackway (carried in the back) in front of the wheels and applied some fairly nugatory, but good-for-the-soul pushing from behind. We got out after some struggle and several winches from one tree to another. The only benefit was that the vehicle was completely mudbathed. It was difficult to tell what it was, let alone whose it was. We made for Marienburg, having lost the tail back at the Vopo speed check and recovered Al's sense of humour after sinking.

We made the OP on the far side of the circuit.

'Nothing, Boss.'

'What about a quick trip up the front drive before leaving?' I suggested rather than directed.

'No problem.'

Some eight months and forty odd tours previously, when I was still very new at the game, I had persuaded Graham against his better judgement to humour me in a little hunch that had paid off. I had spotted a Sov vehicle broken down on the other side of a main road and suggested that we turned round to investigate. He thought it was a one-off and wasting time but I insisted on being proved wrong. It resulted in several columns and me understanding what making your own luck meant. His willingness to try anything once made him an ideal touring companion. He was always prepared to continue beyond what was reasonably expected or acceptable in terms of risk or degree of difficulty. He was always willing to follow a hunch.

The circuit round the training area, about 7 miles, had been uneventful. It was particularly difficult going on a rough track full of potholes, with constant deviation to avoid fallen branches and streams. Mindful of our recent sinking swamp we were careful not to get caught out again, particularly as we were now on a Soviet training area. We had seen nothing from the OP so we decided to call it a day and head home. It was about 3 p.m. and we were each out with different crews again in three days' time.

We returned to the front entrance having decided to simply scan the firing points, cover the training boards and perhaps have a wander round the range control building. We were very relaxed about the place having circuited it, cut into it and seen nothing. This, on top of what we already knew from the rather drab write-up that it had received from previous visitors in the target file, rather dismissed any real hope of seeing anything at all. The main entrance on to the training area was a single lane tarmac road about 150 metres long and flanked by thick coniferous woodland. It was on a slight incline with the usual red and white barrier pole at the far end of it, denoting the official entrance into the open training area. Unusually the barrier was up. Ordinarily this would indicate a presence in the area but we'd seen nothing. We would have expected to see the barrier down in the closed position and probably padlocked to the short vertical support pole in order to keep vehicles out.

Soviet soldiers being moved on exercise by cattle truck.

'Hmmm!' Graham leant forward, already on the look out for danger.

This was more like it. The normal tour pre-engagement checks routinely rippled around the vehicle. Door locks were checked, windows were wound up, the driver's seat belt came off, cameras were checked for light levels and new film, a date, time group together with location grid reference and target description were put on tape. All spare kit was stowed in the event of it being flung around should we meet anything unexpectedly. There was no need to say anything. Something was up and we instinctively knew it.

The road was so tight that we decided to reverse up, trusting to wing mirrors but preserving the fastest means of getting away down the only route we knew to be open – forwards. This was a normal option for a target with only one entrance and exit route where we suspected a military presence. Had we not been alerted by the barrier we would have probably nosed into the area. It had the distinct advantage of greater visibility over backing on. But if we were jumped going backwards then we would now be facing the right way to make an exit rather than be faced with a high speed reverse or worse being forced into the open ground of the training area and the only entrance/exit route being closed off behind us. There was the option to dash round the perimeter to find our incision point and get out that way, but if we'd been seen then there was the possibility they had it covered themselves already. Furthermore, diving into the lion's den was not done lightly. It had to be worth it. If there were other vehicles in there then it would not be so easy to get out again. The resulting action would have to be outweighed and justified by the gain.

We eased up the road, nice and slowly. I was watching the front, Al and Graham the rear.

'Wait, Al.' Graham had spotted something out of his wing mirror.

We stopped slowly, not wishing to draw any attention with sudden movements.

'There's a Sov on the gate. He's walking away from it back to the control building.'

'Has he seen us?'

'No, Boss, he's got his back to us and is walking away. He is armed. I reckon he's going for his replacement, or a piss or something.'

'OK, let's give him a few seconds to get out the way and then keep reversing up.'

I maintained my watch to the front for anything coming up the drive behind us. If anything did come up then we were going to lead it on into the open area. Nothing dramatic, it wouldn't recognise us, particularly down here where they probably didn't see Mission cars the whole of their conscript days. Furthermore, the vehicle was covered in mud, the number-plate indiscernible, let alone readable. We would just let it follow us in as though we were backing up for it, like two vehicles meeting on a narrow road, allow it to pass and then dart out behind it as it came through the barrier and away. Alternatively, it may have done the same to us, which would have been a sweeter option. It was not unknown for the Sovs to unwittingly let a G-wagon through all sorts of gates, barriers and road blocks thinking it was a senior officer's vehicle before realising what they had done. A double flash of the headlights sometimes prompted the duty sentry to raise the barrier. Usually right behind us, several pursuit vehicles would come into view a few seconds later, the vehicle commanders shaking their fist at the poor sentry who'd made the gaffe.

'Still clear to the front.'

The familiar tension crept back into the vehicle as we drew into the danger rather than away from it. We crawled very slowly under the raised barrier, exposing our back end to the open ground, pausing as the wood ended and the training area stretched behind us. We were just cresting the incline, testing for a reaction from anybody we could see and anybody who might be able to see us. The range control building came into view about 200 metres away. A group of Sovs were standing around the building facing up the range and looking away from us. There were two old ZIL-131s parked up. A pair of armed Sovs were walking across the open ground about 400 metres away, again with their backs to us and moving away from us. We were sitting in full view of the group at the range building but they simply hadn't noticed us. We sat motionless for about three or four seconds watching them as they huddled together and chatted, completely unaware that we were there.

'What the hell are they?'

Graham had been concentrating on the retreating Sov at 9 o'clock out of his left window and the Sov patrol further round to his left and almost behind us at his 7 o'clock position. Al was being careful to avoid attracting any attention with the noise of the vehicle or its sudden movement. The Sov sentry had nearly rejoined his 'oppos'[64] at the building. I was watching the drive to our

---

[64] Oppos: slang for colleagues.

front as well as keeping an eye on the control building. All the action was on the left side of the vehicle, we were using the right-hand wood line as cover and manoeuvring closer to it, all the time keeping our flank perpendicular to their line of sight to us. Graham had flicked an eye over to the right, probably conscious that we were neglecting the less obvious for what we could see on the other side. Suddenly he twisted right round staring at the wood line immediately to our right as he made the remark. I saw them in the wing mirror. Not expecting to find anything at all and just about ready to leave anyway we could see, 20 metres in from the wood and only 30 metres away form the G-wagon in our 5 o'clock position, a monstrous artillery piece completely tarped up. It had only become visible as we crested the incline.

'Shit, there's loads of them, Boss. I count sixteen.'

We all craned round to the right. At 30-metre gaps or so, stretching down the wood line on the reverse slope away from us, a further 16, possibly more, similar bits of kit were each 'tarped' up. They stretched into the distance and down the incline away from us. The position of the last visible one indicated that the line probably extended further. Graham was sitting up in his seat to try and see where the last one was. My immediate thought when he counted them was that there should have been eighteen for a battalion. The main bodies were all covered, but neither the barrel sticking out nor the box trail towing arms were familiar to me. I could see the wheels but they looked oversized for anything I knew.

'Reverse up to it, Al, nice and slowly. Graham, see if we get a reaction. We've got time to get a shot of this one nearest us and still get away if they spot us.'

Al backed further into the open ground, swinging left hand down, away from the wood line but putting our rear momentarily back on view to the control building before squaring us up again as we positioned alongside the gun and parallel to it. Anyone observing would by now be wondering why this UAZ-like vehicle had reversed on to the training area and was now snaking around one of the guns. We were really pushing our luck.

'Way out is still back through the barrier, Al.' The plan was developing off the cuff quite nicely! We probably wouldn't have planned it this way had we known they were here. But an opportunity like this didn't present itself very often. We would run with the luck while it stayed with us. I took a quick couple of shots for reference but the breach, working parts and main features of interest were under cover.

'I'll get out and take it off.' Graham was halfway out the door before there was a chance to think about it.

'OK. Al, keep your eyes on all round.' What the hell, we were in there now and our escape route was still clear. An artillery piece that none of us could identify was worth the risk. Graham got out of the vehicle and started to lift the tarp.

'Boss, there's another patrol on the end of the gun line coming this way.'

Al had his bins out and was scouring as much of the 270 degrees available to him as he could. At the far end of the gun line two armed Sovs were moving towards us about 600 metres away. They had their heads down in the biting wind that swept down the hill and across the open area towards them. It was the same pair that had been walking away from us. They were patrolling the area in some sort of circular fashion. Maybe there was other kit beyond the range building. That would remain a mystery. We had been quite lucky with the weather and the daylight so far. It was overcast but not dismal. It was cold and windy but the threatening rain, or more likely snow at this time of year, had not yet materialised. This patrol was probably cold, wet, miserable and completely switched off, just when real soldiering really begins. Anyway, from that distance and in this light they would probably also mistake us for a visiting UAZ-469.

I wound my window down and took a further two or three shots of the uncovered working parts while telling Graham what was happening behind him. It was time to go. I motioned him to get in giving him the thumb down signal for enemy spotted. Graham replaced the tarp and got in. We moved slowly away, no fuss, no attention drawn, just pulled forward under the unattended barrier and drove out. As far as the patrolling Sovs were concerned, we'd never been there. No one saw us come in and no one saw us leave.

That we did not immediately recognise the exact designation of the artillery piece while standing on top of it was worrying. The three of us discussed all the possible combinations as soon as we had cleared the entrance and were back on the main road. This really only left the possibility that it was something we didn't know by sight but knew of by reputation from the hours upon countless hours of recognition training both at Ashford and every single day that we were back at the Mission.

We went through every single artillery piece that we could think of but there was no match. We even confirmed that the soldiers we had seen were Soviet and that we hadn't strayed by some fluke into Czechoslovakia and into a whole new collection of weapon systems. Eventually the only conclusion we could reasonably come to, and that instinct probably told us in the first place, was that it must have been the only-once-ever glimpsed, unidentified 152-M-1987 field gun. During recognition lessons we had only sketch drawings and a very poor photograph of a completely tarped possible sighting from a French Mission crew that had baffled them on a kit train almost three years previously. Again it was an inability to recognise and identify it that drew their attention.

Most equipment types and even specific equipment could be identified, whatever their tarping or indeed whatever their packaging. We trained our recognition skills extensively on poor camera shots, long-range views, tarped vehicles and even vehicles packed into crates. 'Tarpology' and 'crateology' were specialities of Weapons. Years and years of similar sightings allowed them to categorise and even identify vehicles or equipment inside large crates using various methods: mensuration against the known size of a flatbed precluded certain items, distinguishing packing and loading insignia sometimes narrowed it down further, comparisons with other recognisable vehicles on the same train together with its route and any observed soldiers accompanying the cargo provided collateral evidence. It was a forensic and scientific analysis of what it was not that could finally lead you to what it was.

We knew that the gun we had seen could not be matched to existing known inventories of equipment in WGF. The French had seen it up in the north of the DDR, not down here in the south. But then the train wasn't followed, why should it have been if there was nothing apparently special on board? It might have been coming into or going out of the north. Their imagery subsequently confirmed it as an artillery piece and, because it had never been seen before, was given the curious nomenclature 152-M-1987 identifying it as possibly

152-mm bore, that being the next logical size up in the towed artillery world and 1987 being the year of its first known sighting. The possible bore size alone made it a very high priority target indeed. If it was 152-mm then that would certainly match and potentially out-gun any Western equivalent.

We went about a mile down the main road and pulled in. It was quite normal to stop after a target and quite randomly at that. It was always interesting to see who stopped with us further back up the road. It was a great trick to play, especially if you could combine it with a sharp bend in the road. A tailing car would come round the corner, the searching looks on the faces of the occupants already giving themselves away, would be compounded by the uncertain vehicle handling as they passed us by, not sure whether to stop or continue. There was nothing. More importantly we had to discuss what we had just seen.

'We've got to go back and get more detail, Boss. If it's U/I then it's worth the risk of a second visit.'

Graham was absolutely right. That we had spotted it and possibly found its home was achievement enough but this beast had been eluding all three missions for nearly three years now. We may never get the chance again. Already the detail we had shot had significantly improved upon the last sighting but had it not been for the roving patrol we could have got so much more.

'I also need a look at one of the attendant vehicles to get a VRN.'

Graham knew I wouldn't be able to pull a VRN, even with the 2,000-mm lens in this rapidly deteriorating light or at the range we might reasonably expect to get to. He would have to call it with a 'swifty'. Even the bins in this light would not do it. VRNs could help pinpoint the unit that held the gun. Seeing it down here, not to mention so many of them spread out in all their glory, did not mean that they hailed from this part of WGF. It may have been that the regiment had come down for training. This was a live firing range after all. The impact area was well known, miles away from here and in theory would have been the next target on our list. (It made good sense in anyone's army to check that they weren't firing first before venturing out there.) It was off the itinerary now, that was for sure. It was crucial to know the unit in order to know where they fitted in the overall WGF orbat. Were they an army-level asset or divisional level? Graham was saying the right things, not that I needed a lot of encouragement. I had to weigh up the fact that the gun line was being patrolled with armed sentries, that there were a further dozen or so loafing around the control tower and that for all our confidence on a clean sheet so far for this target we may very well have been spotted. However, if we were right then it was a significant find.

'Right, we'll go back. We need a different approach though. On foot.'

We got a blank target map out and started to plan quickly. It was only 4 p.m. but light was starting to fail rapidly. This would partly be in our favour for getting to the guns but definitely not in terms of photography. I had already decided to take the Micky Mouse, a simple point and press plastic camera with built-in flash plus the 85-mm lens on one F-3. I wouldn't need anything else. I took two spare films, one for each camera in case one jammed or I took more frames than expected. I wasn't intending to go back a third time.

We plotted a route in through the wood to reach the wood line directly opposite the ninth or tenth gun in the line. This would give us excellent cover from view of the control building and put us midway between the armed patrols that we had to assume were regularly patrolling up and down the gun line. With a bit of luck they might take a break at either end or both. We thought it unlikely that they would break for any reason in the middle.

We isolated the key components of the gun that I would photograph and the order in which we would do it. Timing would be critical and tight. Graham would take down any serial numbers and physically remove anything from the gun that might be of use such as instruction or warning plates. We established that patrolling 800 metres, roughly the length of the gun line, would take about 4 minutes. This would give us about 2½ minutes on the target, 30 seconds to get out to it from the edge of the wood, 30 seconds to get back and 30 seconds for any cock-up. The difficult bit would be getting the G-wagon to a suitable lay up point. We decided to drive from where we were now by compass bearing and try to weave our way through the wood, the distance of about 1½ kilometres, to a possible lay-up point.

This hot planning took us about fifteen or twenty minutes. We had to get on quickly. The more elaborate the plan in these opportunity situations the more likely it would go wrong. The real value in stopping to think about it was to eliminate anything that we may have overlooked, regain a little calmness and consider more carefully the options and actions-on. Ultimately, speed would be more important now than being watertight. If they had seen us and recognised us then they may be already getting themselves sorted out for a return visit. If they had just finished a day's firing then they might be packing up and moving off already. Either way we needed to get back quickly while they were least expecting us or unable to react quickly enough if they were expecting us. On top of all that the light was against us and there was no artificial light out there to use. We would be into the realms of driving back on to the area and taking II pictures with the IR spots, which would have been wholly unsatisfactory and improbable.

'OK. Al, you stay at the lay-up point unless you have to leave. If you do have to leave, then we'll RV here exactly where we're parked now, back on this road. Leave quietly for a controlled exit and noisily for a forced one.'

We moved off when the road was clear, slowed for the first trackable route breaking into the wood and U-turned in the road to take it while the road was still clear. No one saw us enter the wood. So far so good.

'Another 50 metres should put us about 200 metres away from the edge of the wood line.'

'Roger.'

This track wasn't marked on the 1:50,000 and the target map didn't extend this far down. We were flying by the seat of our on-board compass. They were notoriously inaccurate and had to be recalibrated constantly. Not surprising, given that they were bolted to the inside of a 3-ton lump of metal that was regularly flung about the countryside. Although fitted with counter-metallic effects, the delicate little thing was very vulnerable to its environment and handling. It was good for giving general direction when all that was required was a confirmatory heads-up but otherwise rarely used. It had an unnerving tendency to spin erratically in the vicinity of nuclear power stations. Consequently, when it span in an area that was not really recognisable as a nuclear power station it was quite alarming.

'Stop here, Al. Let's listen.'

We had gone about 500 metres into the wood, creating our own path on the direction of the compass.

The customary feelings of apprehension and excitement returned. I was trying to remain as calm as possible, not for the benefit of Al and Graham, but for myself. We were very frank with each other as to when the going was getting scary. If we had concerns about what we doing we were very careful to make sure they were aired generally. There was nothing worse than to go touring with someone who wasn't frightened by doing these sorts of things. It was a lack of fear that was usually a precursor to a lack of concentration that got people caught. Being unlucky was acceptable, mistakes did happen. Being reckless was inexcusable.

I had already trodden the very fine line between recklessness and bad luck while looking for a particular kit train at Falkenberg railway sidings. We were traversing the sidings very late one night by crossing the tracks. It was a well practised manoeuvre but not at night and not at all by Mac, who was driving. Completely unseen by us, we were nearly run down by a locomotive engine changing tracks. Its foot-guard brushed the wing mirror as we manoeuvred in time to get out of the way. I frightened the life out of Mac and received a thoroughly well-deserved bollocking from John Buchan, the tour NCO. We'd pushed our luck too far, beyond the risk versus gain equilibrium. It was a very salutary lesson.

We were back in the danger area with patrolling armed guards and a potential artillery regiment's worth of men somewhere not very far away. It was quite permissible to be terrified, but it was not permissible to pass up the opportunity if the gain outweighed the risk. That was my judgement at the end of the day. We moved another short distance along the bearing. The wood line against which the guns were backdropped was about 150 metres away, the light from the open ground visible beyond it. We could discard the compass now. We swung round to point at the wood line perpendicular to it and hopefully in line with the ninth or tenth gun in the series.

'We'll lay the vehicle up here.'

We stopped and listened again. Another twenty or so minutes had passed since leaving the main road, almost an hour since leaving the area the first time.

'OK, it sounds quiet enough. Let's go, Graham.'

I had my parka on, carrying the Mickey Mouse and the 85-mm in separate pockets. Graham got out of the vehicle with just his shirt on under his parka. This was quite normal for him. He was a big man and could beat off the cold better than me. However, the weather was not looking great and I looked bemusedly at him. It was getting gloomier. The sky looked heavier and more threatening. He clearly had no intention of running around the countryside if we were spotted.

'We're coming back here, Boss,' he emphasised as if reading my mind.

'Whatever you say, Graham,' I mocked, easing the tension somewhat.

We moved quietly to the edge of the wood line, having to pause as we saw the patrol between us and the guns walking towards the building. We were still some 50 metres away from the wood line, so time was already lost. Taking the opportunity to time them over half a run served only to confuse our calculations. Looking at each other we both motioned to get on with it. We moved quickly through the last bit of cover, the wind masking any unsolicited noise that we were making. We paused only briefly at the edge, checking up and down. The patrol

The first untarped sighting of 2A-65, a towed artillery piece. This and accompanying photographs worryingly revealed the weapon to have a 3-km range advantage over its Nato counterpart.

were more than a hundred metres away. As we dashed across the open ground towards the gun of our choice, Graham diverted us to the next one down and away from the Sovs to give us a bit more time.

'Good thinking,' I said, as I ran alongside him.

Halfway across the open ground the already grey skies had gone horribly black. The first few flakes of snow were already falling.

'Shit!' came the response from the short-sleeve-shirted man.

'Shit!' came my reply as I had brought only 100 ASA film for both cameras. He was going to freeze and I had left the 400 ASA film in the vehicle, not believing that it could get so dark that I would need it for the 85-mm.

'At least I won't get cold,' I said to him as we made it to the gun. Quick as a flash he responded, 'At least I won't fuck up the photography!'

We slipped blind side of the patrol. Graham stripped the tarp off and I took some general shots with him adjacent to it before going into the planned detailed shots. Fortunately I didn't need depth of field at this range, therefore I could really stop it down giving me one sixtieth of a second exposure. Ordinarily this should have been adequate, I was able to hold an 85-mm lens sufficiently still for up to half a second, but in these conditions my hands were already numb with the cold and I was having difficulty holding it steady. I couldn't stop it down any more to give me a faster shutter speed to compensate. The snow got thicker and thicker. We'd nearly lost visibility to the next but one gun in the line.

'We'll complete the shots and then do it again with the Mickey Mouse.' If I couldn't have any 400 ASA to compensate for the dark then I was going to add some light to compensate for the film. 'Two minutes left, Boss . . . maximum.' Graham rolled his eyes and smiled as he realised that I was going to double the time on the target and set off the flash into the bargain. There was a strange feeling of complete invulnerability once out on the target and working the camera.

'Open the breech.'

Graham pulled the obvious lever and the back plate swung open. I photographed all the workings of the mechanism, the fixed metal plates that gave instruction on bearing and elevation settings, the recoil dampers, levers and every single rivet that looked important or remotely attached to the firing of the bloody thing. I then went to the towing arms and did the same there, went to the business end and photographed the barrel support plate and finally the barrel opening from the muzzle break back towards the firing pin. In other words, looking right down the barrel. It was rifled, and detail of the splines running the internal length would be of enormous importance.

'One minute left, Boss!'

The heavens opened to the most ferocious snowstorm. Visibility was no more than 50 metres.

I changed cameras and went through the same procedure with the Mickey Mouse. The Mickey Mouse flashed when the light conditions told it that it needed to. Every now and again as I moved in for detail the available light would be so limited that it would go off. Each time it flashed we paused, checking for a reaction from the Sovs. The roof of the control tower was barely visible in this light and only just in view anyway as a result of the upward slope towards it. God knows if the flash could be seen from that far in this light or whether the gloom and falling snow accentuated it. I was frantic now as this little camera took forever to wind on to the next frame. The whirr of the flash building up charge seemed deafening so I smothered it between shots with my Canadian parka. Graham tried to mask the flash with his body as I took more frames. Finally I repeated the shot down the barrel with the flash to try and reveal more of the spline detail for the boffins to wet themselves over.

'OK, let's go!' Graham was aware that I had lost concentration of our immediate predicament in an effort to get the best possible shots. He grabbed me by the arm, replaced the tarp and left. We made the wood line and waited for the sentries to come past. They were not happy chappies in the snow. It seemed like an eternity before they passed the gun we had shot, but they carried straight on, not noticing that the tarp was slightly askew.

We walked back to the vehicle, not wanting to run and draw attention. We were absolutely frozen but extremely pleased with performance. There was a very unfortunate piece of mission jargon known as 'raping'. It was poorly used to mean that we had taken someone to the cleaners, did them over, stuffed them good and proper, rather than any sexual connotation. We had certainly done them over that afternoon. We could probably have gone on another two days after that, the nervous energy of the day's events recharging our batteries. We knew we had found something of considerable importance.

It was about midnight before we got back to the American Mission to file our initial report. There was much excitement there because the French local tour had been rammed and seen off during an attempt to obtain imagery of a previously unsighted BTR-80 variant. Apparently the imagery obtained was very exciting. Graham and I said nothing and filled in our scant report: SCUD-B TELs, PMP Bridging, T-72s in East German Military District III and 152-M-1987 at Marienburg casually thrown in at the end with enormous understatement. We left outwardly smiling and inwardly gloating. Completing a tour highlight at USMLM marked the end of a tour. The fear, apprehension, uneasiness and need for incessant vigilance were suspended and replaced with relief, elation and adrenaline-busting excitement in anticipation of the results. Coupled with weariness, fatigue and a constant pressure, this rollercoaster of emotions was repeated every tour, twice a week for three days at a time for months on end. It was a punishing yet thoroughly gratifying experience.

For me the thrill and the reward always came with the imagery. Was it in focus? Did it show enough detail? Could I have done it in stereo to allow photographic interpreters the opportunity to lift three dimensional images? What had I missed out? As soon as I got back to my pit in the mess I would start to think about it. I always found it difficult to sleep the first night back.

We got back to the Mission at about 2 a.m. I'd telephoned ahead from USMLM to call out Special, again with a lack of sympathy for the backroom boys who shared very little in the glory but suffered the worst of all the shift patterns. Al took the car away for cleaning, they were never left until the morning because it was never known whether one would be required at short notice for a recovery or emergency. He would log all the faults and repair work necessary and be back at 8 a.m., ready to be briefed on his next tour.

The tour NCO and tour officer would commence writing a report on the tour the next day. All tour reports were credited to the tour officer in their onward transmission to the various agencies, not by name but by code. My own codename was Red 41. It prevented names being released to the wider world, partly to prevent compromise and subsequent targeting by the Sovs as well as to guarantee anonymity outside the Mission, within our own intelligence community.

The call came at about 7 a.m. I was ready for it this time. I knew we had got something good. As usual I had hardly slept, waiting to see the developed imagery.

'Meet me at eight before recognition.' Adrian Pryce was coming towards the end of his posting as Weapons Officer and he was on a roll. The amount of new equipment he must have seen in the course of his two years was astonishing. The amount captured by Brixmis and therefore his responsibility to promulgate to a wider audience was considerably more than half the tri-mission output. He must have loved going to the ALTWIC conferences, the annual intelligence community's 'Summer Ball' where they swapped war stories and intelligence detail. Lots of blurry pictures, barely audible, half-garbled, loosely translated Sigint messages, our contact said this and that but we can't tell you about it type rubbish and then a burst of sharp, frame-filling imagery complete with date, time, location, holding unit and likely effectiveness from the Brixmis Weapons Officer. He must have been in heaven as slide by slide, he was able to reel off a new, unseen bit of kit in full colour, close-up and with enormous detail.

Everything we photographed, excluding the product from 'upstairs' by Chipmunk or recovered from Operation Tomahawk, was graded Confidential,

Detail of the breach mechanism of 2A-65 taken in the snow with the Mickey Mouse and flash.

the lowest classification we could possibly put on it. Most other intelligence sources were Secret at best and further restricted for handling and access. It was inherently self-defeating. The idea behind our discoveries was to advertise the resulting information as widely as possible in order to prepare troops on the ground with the latest and best information possible. Because the Mission was not truly under the auspices of the Foreign Office or Military Intelligence we were very much loosely controlled and as much self-tasked as tasked by other agencies. The value of our product gave us the perpetual license to operate. This quasi-independence, together with the quality of work, was a double-edged weapon that created as much friction as congratulations. We were very much a surviving relic from the end of the Second World War, quaint and gallant on the surface but ruthlessly incisive underneath.

Adrian was in punchy mood when I met him in the corridor. He was with Ian Passingham and Graham. He grabbed me by the shoulders, put his hand over my mouth and kissed the back of his hand. He was absolutely delighted. 'I've got to go to an extraordinary tri-mission weapons meeting this morning to be told by Frogsmix[65] what wonderful boys they were yesterday. I can't wait.' He must have seen the imagery already, he was uncontainable. Graham shrugged his shoulders

---

65 FMLM: French Miliary Liaison Mission. The French equivalent to Brixmis, nicknamed Frogsmix.

behind his back and performed the universal sign for early senility, his finger pointing to his head. The French sighting of a BTR-80 variant was a considerable coup, worth getting a tri-mission response for further targeting action, but the artillery piece we had uncovered would steal the show.

He was skipping away down the corridor when he turned and said, 'You didn't take a ruler for the photographs then?'

'Bollocks!' I'd forgotten to mensurate the shots. That is to say if you put a ruler against a particular part of the equipment to be photographed, the photographic interpreters and DIS analysts can accurately determine the length of the item in question. I thought that putting Graham in the shot would have done the trick. Adrian was a perfectionist. I'd been touring for nearly a year and still hadn't attained the perfect photograph for him. I was quite dismayed and explained to Pass what the particular circumstances were. He wasn't in the slightest bit worried and took me into the Ops room for debriefing. Inside was Keith, the SAS Warrant Officer, whom I had also completed Ashford with, Sandy, the SAS tour officer, and Al Tipping.

'Morning, Boss, just going to finish it off for you. Tell me all about it!' Keith was ribbing me for all it was worth. He had a big smile across his face. Like all the SAS tourers he was a thin wiry individual, extremely self-effacing and modest. You would pass him in the street and never look twice. He would relish a chance to go and see the gun for himself. We went off to recognition after the debrief. Pryce was so keen that he had already got a slide of our imagery into the carousel for general viewing.

There was a note from Adrian attached saying that initial analysis suggested that the gun's range was in excess of 2, maybe 3, kilometres beyond that of Western equivalents, which meant that Soviet batteries could adopt stand-off positions without fear of counter-battery fire. Originally estimated at 52-plus calibre barrel lengths it was likely to be far greater. That such a range could be achieved on such a light gun was an extraordinary discovery.

It was a useful find but now that they were withdrawing, perhaps not relevant on this battleground. Nine months later Brixmis would be undertaking its last mission. That night Graham, Al and I went to the Brixmis Club where I repaid Graham the many beers that I owed him. Three weeks later Graham Geary left the Mission, having undergone the traditional last tour with myself and Ernie Wilson, complete with silver service barbecue in the middle of the Rheinsberg Gap served by Ernie in black bow-tie. Graham was awarded the BEM in the Queen's Birthday Honours list, Al was awarded the same distinction in the New Year's Honours list.

CHAPTER NINE

The Last Mission

Crossing the Glienicke Bridge from West Berlin to East Germany must have appeared a rather intimidating affair to the tourists who watched the procedure from a discreet distance. It was a fairly clinical, set-piece process for the Missions. The G-wagon would stop on the West Berlin side at the huge electric gates, which only recently replaced a simple barrier. (In March 1988, a civilian W-50 van with three East Germans inside crashed through the barrier into West Berlin without any shots being fired. The rolling gates and concrete block chicanery was the response.) A sentry would step out of the guard post situated just beyond the middle of the bridge. He would look at the vehicle quizzically as if he'd never seen one before. The automated gates rolled back on his nod, then he would motion the G-wagon to come forward and stop at the cantilever barrier adjacent to the guard post. The tour NCO would get out of the vehicle, careful to lock the door behind him, and present all the tour passes to the Soviet officer on duty, returning to the vehicle with them once checked and after several rounds of saluting. After the Wall came down, and a civilian lane was set up on the bridge, the routine changed slightly to avoid the somewhat embarrassing formality in front of the common enemy. Passes were simply handed to the sentry through a narrowly cranked slit in the window, the rear curtains drawn open showing that we had nothing to hide. Either way the passes were examined inside the guard post and records made of who was on tour, the number of the car, the state of the vehicle, the composition of the crew and so on. The passes having been returned, the barrier was raised, a little more saluting and then forward to the next automated gate which would start to open as we approached it. At no time were both gates at either end of the bridge open together. It was very much like passing through an airlock from one atmosphere of pressure into another. The Glienicke was our version of the Tardis time machine.

The Glienicke took us back in time when entering the DDR and returned us to our own time when we came back a few days later. This passage between the two different worlds and two different cultures was extremely abrupt and brutally stark. At the home end of the bridge, a large tarmac turning circle allowed Western tourist buses to come within 50 metres of our regular performance. Holiday companies used the bridge as a tourist attraction, a sort of freak show. If there was also a tour crossing at the time then it drew all the spectacle of the changing of the guard at Buckingham Palace but without the glamour.

Of the millions of visitors to the city who viewed this and other famous Wall landmarks from behind their cameras or videos, very few really saw what was in front of them, let alone understood it. So many were anaesthetised to the reality of the Cold War game by the fetish to record it on film. Only when they came across part of the Wall that bore memory to someone having lost their life there, did people really begin to understand. A recent death in 1987 or 1988 made them realise that this was no relic but a living monument to man's inhumanity to man, a place of misery and suffering that might record another tragedy right where they were standing, in two days time, or in the next ten minutes.

Occasionally you might witness true understanding. Someone would shed a tear as they looked across the Wall from the viewing platforms over the rows of barbed wire, the lanes of mines, the dog runs, the hordes of patrolling armed guards and sentry towers. They might have read below them on a small brass inscription, accompanied with fresh flowers, how an eighteen-year-old was shot and left hanging on the wire without medical attention to die a slow and lingering death. It took Peter Fechter nearly an hour to die in 1962. He was in full view of the Grepo, West Berlin police and American soldiers on duty at Checkpoint Charlie. They were unwilling or unable to help. Only then did the tourists begin to glimpse what really lay behind the wall. This was Berlin's daily existence. It was not history.

At the other end of the Glienicke, in Potsdam, there were few street lights, the road was still cobbled and the old tram lines, that had gone straight across the bridge before it was partitioned, stopped abruptly. They served as the end of the line and turning circle for the Potsdam tram system. The first house on the right as you crossed into Potsdam was GRU and Stasi occupied. It used to be a schoolhouse in the 1960s. Remnants of a children's playground could be seen in the back garden but no children were ever seen arriving or leaving. The adjacent houses between the school and the bridge were demolished shortly after the Wall went up. The resulting open ground gave good fields of view and arcs of fire onto the breadth of no man's land and the Havel River that was the Wall here. Like so many other sections of the Wall, a house's proximity to the border presented an opportunity for escape to the West and was thus removed. Tunnelling, death sliding or jumping were all to be prevented.

The school now housed an arsenal of cameras, listening devices and videos. Every crossing that took place was recorded. Apart from ours and the odd diplomat, the only other crossings that occurred on the Glienicke, were one-way affairs. This was the bridge of spies. The whole area could well have been a setting for any one of Le Carré's novels; dim lighting, oppressive smog-filled skies that met the rising morning mist from the Havel underneath and the odd Volkspolizei vehicle patrolling the empty street on the far side. Strange figures lurked at nearby street corners with issue raincoats turned up at the collar and we, the heroes of the piece, looked to get away from those prying eyes as quickly as possible.

But it was no novel. It was very real. The novels were written around this bridge not the other way round. It was here, throughout the Cold War, under the auspices of the relevant embassies, their agencies and agents, that people and equipment were swapped in tit-for-tat arrangements or simple hard currency. Clandestine swaps in the small hours gave way to our early morning Mission spy runs, which in turn gave way to more official business. As the sun rose on the bridge, the animals that favoured the dark disappeared; it seemed an unfortunate correlation.

It was gloomy on the bridge, the light was poor and quite often in winter the Soviet sentries on duty used torches to inspect our vehicles. They were looking for damage on our return. It was useful corroboration for them if we raised a subsequent complaint about our treatment in the DDR or if they complained to us about our conduct. They recorded the state of the vehicle on the way out and then compared it on return. They knew in advance if we had been involved in any fracas, but the bridge was not the place to dispute it. However, it was the last place they could get substantiating information for any subsequent discussion.

It was even darker in Potsdam itself. Its bright and historically significant past had, like much of East Germany, fallen upon hard times. Formally the film capital of Europe, host to the Olympic village in 1936, proud owner of Sans Souci, the former palace of Frederick the Great, and the Cecilienhof where Churchill, Stalin and Roosevelt met to determine the future of Europe. The housing was falling to pieces; plumbing didn't work, sewage leaked, the electricity supply could be erratic and telephone connections were a lottery. There was very little street lighting, no advertising hoardings or paint to brighten up the blocks of flats and houses. As an oil-based product, paint was a rare commodity. Oil was more urgently required for military purposes. Its scarcity was exacerbated by the oil price boom of the 1970s. It was imported and virtually unaffordable, but the military got it. The smell of lignite smoke from Potsdam was just perceptible on the bridge. It lingered and hung like a pall on the other side of the bridge, creating a downward cone of light around each individual street lamp. Even the pollution was not permitted to cross without the necessary authority. This was 1990 and yet still barely different to 1945. Every tour was a constant reminder of how lucky we were in the West, not 200 metres away.

There was a DDR presence on the bridge to control diplomatic and other crossings pertinent to East Germany and by 1990, civilian traffic too. As always we ignored their authority but scrutinised their activity thoroughly. The lanes were so close that we could talk to whoever was going across with us if we chose. Occasionally it would be Western diplomatic staff having to renew work permits, this being one of the official crossing points for them. More often than not it would be DDR officials. We would simply stare at them, wondering what their business was that allowed them to cross here in such exalted surroundings. They would shift uncomfortably in our presence. Why? What were they afraid of? Did they know they were wrong? Were they intimidated by us? Probably a mix of all these. Perhaps they knew we were right and had very little moral conviction of their own. How ironic that forty-four years of stand-off could be summarised in a single fleeting expression. If they had just toured through West Berlin then maybe forty-four years of isolation was rather depressing by contrast to what they were returning to? They looked spineless and gutless.

The people in charge of East Germany, the authorities, the minority entrusted or empowered with the secrets and mechanisms of socialism, were afraid of change, behaved like sheep and were out for themselves. The ordinary people were very different and we met hundreds and hundreds of them during the course of our time in the DDR. The nearer we got to the towns and cities, the drudgery of factory life, the hustle and bustle of living in the city and the proximity to all sorts of seen and unseen authority, our observations made for a pretty depressed and downbeat populace. We came across the state bus driver of Halle, the postman of Schwerin, or the local council official of Dresden, all of them wrapped up in their own self-importance, all of them in uniform and therefore with status, and all of them privileged by virtue of being part of the state machine. They reminded me of school bus-monitors. The willingness to talk was countered by the degree of difficulty they perceived in doing so. Nowhere among the ordinary people of East Germany did there seem to be a genuine support for communism. In the rural areas, the farmers and farmworkers lived a very simple life and on the whole were content with it. They were very happy to talk to us and keen to make their feelings known, often very emotionally.

On one occasion, very early in 1989, I recall a ninety-year-old man stopping us as we were trying to take an inconspicuous route across farmland. We thought he was going to berate us like all farmers do for trespassing. Instead he said he knew who we were and wanted to tell us about the way his life had been ruined over the last forty years and how everything he and his family had worked for had been taken away by the state. He had nothing to show for his years of working the land. He went on at length telling us how things had changed in his lifetime. He was in tears at the end of his long speech, some of which we couldn't understand his accent was so thick, but it was a picture that symbolised the dreadful condition the East German state had been subjected to in the name of socialism. The infrastructure was barely functioning, the people were downtrodden and all the time the state wanted more. Things were changing for the worse not the better and people were unhappy about it. He needed to get it off his chest but above all he needed hope that things were going to change. How utterly powerless we were to help.

It was some three or four months after this encounter that I was able to make sense of what he was getting at when I witnessed for myself the human rights demonstrations and protests in the cities of Leipzig and Dresden. Our observations and conversations, although anecdotal, were highly illuminating and replicated in varying degrees what he had said. The pressures of the state had simply become too great for them to bear and they were showing it. They were helping themselves to create their own hope. The main expression of their new hope and their number one demand was the freedom to travel.

With hindsight, a key landmark on the road to the end of the Cold War can be associated with Gorbachev's accession to power and the launch on to the world stage of his doctrine of perestroika (restructuring) and glasnost (openness). Not just a new man on the scene and therefore a fresh start, he was also a relatively young man by Soviet leadership standards. He simply stood back, surveyed the situation and realised that the Cold War was not a battle his country was able to win. Furthermore, it was plain to anyone taking even a tourist's eye-view of the Soviet Union that it was causing them great economic pain and suffering. That pain was being felt by all but a handful of Soviet people. He called a stop to it and asked his country to change direction. It was so simple to see and yet so very difficult to deliver.

In addition to his significant contribution there were two other very strong and highly convicted world leaders that were able to grasp the significance of the opportunity: Margaret Thatcher and Ronald Reagan. Both very different in background and style but both conviction politicians who were able to nudge the Western world back to some degree of stability. Some say that when Reagan came to power in 1980 he spent too much on defence which led to the American budget deficit problems of the 1990s. His detractors now argue (not at the time), that he knew in the 1980s that the Soviets were financially crippled by their excesses in trying to match the military capability of the industrialised West. So why did he increase defence spending instead of reducing it? He was putting the pressure on. In 1979 Margaret Thatcher declared to Lord Mountbatten that the Cold War was over, and later, when she met Gorbachev, that he was a man she could do business with, but added, 'that she was sure that deterrence must continue to lie at the heart of our defence'. Maybe they had spotted the end, way ahead of anyone else. But 1979 was not the right time to slow down military spending simply because the early signs of exhaustion at the race were being displayed by the Soviet Union.

The average East German had certainly latched on to Gorbachev. They identified readily with the terms glasnost and perestroika and used them freely from 1986 onwards. That they would mean the Wall would come down or that the Soviet Union would relinquish East Germany and the two Germanies would be reunited was not part of the equation. They were simply expressions of a new way of understanding and dealing with society as seen from the Soviet point of view and a means by which the Eastern Bloc might extricate itself from the self-defeating spiral of the Cold War with the West. Reunification and a final resolution of the German question were agenda items that the West strongly urged the Soviet Union to address in late 1989. A cold hard look at economic realities in 1990 forced them to be addressed.

The difficult question that troubled the Western powers was whether or not they could trust Gorbachev. He in turn, unable to make progress under those terms, was forced, or chose (the distinction is unclear) to take his country and its satellite states forward in his own way. He must have held his breath every day as he followed this course of action. Not only did he have to convince the Western world of his genuine desire for a new world order but he had to convince and carry his own people. Gorbachev's role in successfully concluding what the poor economic prognosis of an escalatory arms race must have made all too apparent, the end of the Cold War, was no mean achievement. His attitude to the Wall and the division of Germany was an enormous reversal of traditional Soviet intransigence and bullying. The job of the diplomats and politicians in his wake was to ensure that the transition was as ordered and calm as possible. Brixmis' role in the end game was as vital as ever before. The parameters by which we operated responded to the changes around us as they had always done. The twin roles of observation and liaison were as important after November 1989 as they were in 1946.

The fall of the Wall was not the end of the Cold War or the collapse of communism as many in the media understandably portrayed at the time. It was merely the symbolic close of one chapter, albeit a very substantial one. There was still a very short but delicate chapter to come. The Wall was erected in 1961 as a direct response to the exodus of the clever, the skilled and the disenchanted of East Berlin. For many in the West, let alone the East, it was a welcome solution, however inhuman, to a very problematic and worsening refugee crisis. The Cold War had started fifteen years before that event. By the time the Wall went up, it was already in advanced stages of stalemate. It came down in 1989 to prevent another refugee crisis that in October and November had seen many thousands of East Germans 'leaking out' around the sides of the DDR. Ideologically it solved nothing.

There were many issues yet to be addressed after November 1989. Clearly there had to be a new order for both Germanies (a regular call since 1945) but its composition and construction were as much a mystery to the Allied Powers as it was to the Soviets. It was as though no one had really thought beyond bringing the Wall down, much as no one had really thought what might occur beyond the airlift in 1948 or the Wall's construction in 1961. Was this just another change in the Berlin weather or was this the final catalyst in the quest for the elusive German solution? The truth was that no one was really sure.

It certainly wasn't obvious from the Russian side. They were at their wits' end. They still wanted to preserve the two German states but had no idea how it could be achieved. They found it unacceptable that the West Germans were already trying to dictate terms to a sovereign state. They wanted the DDR to be allowed to work out its own political and economic reforms. That was wishful thinking! How could a near-bankrupt country tackle all the problems of inflation, price control, savings, subsidies and unemployment that would emerge as it was released from Soviet support (a country in dire financial straits itself) into some sort of quasi-independent state still loosely tied to the Soviet Union. We saw East German poverty every day. They couldn't survive on their own. Financially there was no alternative to West German help, and lots of it.

The fall of the Wall presented Gorbachev with other political worries. By changing the character or even removing a frontier in Europe, a precedent would have been set with dire consequences for other parts of Europe. (How right he was to be proved when Yugoslavia finally erupted.) In stark contrast to the disposal of the British Empire, which was largely overseas, the Soviet empire was bolted on to its own land mass. Strategically, politically and geographically it was not an easy thing to give up. Furthermore, anything that exacerbated fears at home of a Fourth Reich emerging on their doorstep might presage the end for Gorbachev. The reunification of Germany was certainly not on the agenda when bringing the Wall down.

On 18 October 1989 Honecker resigned to be replaced by his shadow, Egon Krenz. Krenz, deeply unpopular from the outset because of his connections to Honecker, was soon replaced on 7 November by Hans Modrow, considered the safest pair of hands around at the time. Refugees were arriving in the West at alarming rates, estimated at about 200 an hour, more than the average 2,000 a day in 1961. Soviet troops had been confined to barracks and training areas from the 6 November, coinciding with my very poor showing out on tour with Brian and Al. They were being kept well away from the demonstrations and unavailable for use by the East German government. Gorbachev had threatened not to interfere with their internal affairs and was now showing it. He did not want to be involved or implicated in possible shooting matches between East German civilians and their authorities. It wasn't a great clue for us that anything was afoot as we still saw them on training areas, much as we always did, and it wasn't unusual in times of tension for them to be confined. It was certainly a tense time. The East German population was in open revolt and the East German government was panicking. But still no one knew, thought or predicted that the Wall would come down. Schabowski's shambolic afterthought at the news conference late on 9 November after promising free elections, itself enough of a revelation, was the first anyone knew of it. It was symptomatic of the lack of control the DDR government now exercised. If for no other reason than public safety it should have been more controlled than that. The rest is history.

When the dust finally settled on the longest party in Europe, people started to ask the question – so what? At a meeting of the deputy chiefs of Embassies (held the day after the first meeting of the Ambassadors of the Four Allied Powers since 1971) on 11 December 1989, Maximytschev, a Soviet minister, agreed that there was a need for a transition to a new order but that it should be accomplished peacefully and by agreement between the Allies. No mention was made of unification. In December 1989, Erich Honecker was arrested, his SED politburo resigned and the Kampfgruppen were disarmed. The governing mayor of West Berlin, Walter Momper, was predicting political breakdown and a deteriorating internal security situation for East Germany. Our own tours, retasked from 14 November, revealed that the political crisis now defining the phrase 'centre stage' had not really permeated down to street level. People were essentially calm and still trying to take in the enormity of what was happening.

My own first tour after the Wall came down was a town tour to Magdeburg on 14/15 November with Adrian Pryce, Brian and Stan Matthews. We went specifically to gauge reaction from the Soviets. We were invited to dinner at the Interhotel by the Kommandant and deputy Kommandant. They were so keen and pleased to see us that they totally overlooked the fact that the hotel was in PRA. I recall that they spoke nervously of the future as they saw it, in particular the prospect of being sent home, which they had already figured a certainty. I also recall the degree of difficulty and the amount of diffidence the Kommandant received from the receptionist at the hotel when making his reservation for a dinner table. I had to help translate from the Russian to German although his German was quite understandable. The receptionist was simply being obtuse. It was almost as though the tables had been completely turned. Only one week before the Kommandant was a feared man, the military governor of the region with several thousand troops at his disposal.

On 19 November Helmut Kohl, the West German Chancellor, visited Dresden. It was a tense visit. The Soviets were worried by an opportunity for enticement, not to mention the significance of the presence of the German Chancellor. The Chancellor outlined the patient steps necessary to achieve unity. He deliberately avoided the emotive phrase reunification. He talked of the security needs of others, referring to the Allied Powers, and that any future German house should be built under a European roof. It was a tactfully worded speech and a very successful visit. He was already being hailed as the candidate they would be voting for, regardless of whether his Christian Democratic Union party was standing or not. Once again the people were way ahead of the politicians. By December 1989 unification had already become a reality in their minds.

On 22 December 1989 the Brandenburg Gate was finally opened to pedestrians. If the old lady had waited until then she certainly wouldn't have been the last one to turn the lights out! In the first two weeks of January 1990 alone, 15,000 DDR citizens emigrated to the West. But now this was being countered by the odd (as in few!)West German moving East and many more speculative West German businessmen looking at commercial prospects. Hard currency, from US dollars to West D-Marks, became readily acceptable. The total East German debt was revealed

The Mission's drivers posing in front of the border line on the Glienicke Bridge. The greatest drivers anywhere.

to be in the order of 22 milliard (a thousand million) marks. Who needed East Marks? Also early in 1990, Modrow sacked the official in charge of dismantling the Stasi. However, demonstrations and strikes continued as it became known that wages and payments were still being made to former Stasi employees. MI6 in Berlin warned of plans for a counter-revolution by the Socialist Unity Party (SED) based on the fact that they still had the monopoly of political assets and an internal 60,000 strong security structure still in place. The SED themselves argued that rising fascism was threatening their country. MfS offices were already being guarded by the Vopo as civilians continually tried to gain access to their own files as well as discover exactly who was reporting on them. Revenge was in the air and many of the Stasi operatives still retained small arms. The Stasi touched the lives of every ordinary East German and as a result there were many scores to be settled. There was a very real concern that events might slowly gather a dangerous momentum now that the initial euphoria had worn off. In 1990 the Mission was beginning to receive open comment from officers in SERB, together with many reliable and informed reports from other agencies, that the Soviet military would not stomach this revolutionary change of events, either here or at home. These were thoroughly loyal men, either to their country, the army or their party and usually all three. It was confidently predicted that there would be a military coup in Moscow before the end of 1990 and that Gorbachev would be deposed. If the Soviet military machine was getting involved, then these were indeed worrying and delicate times. We needed to know as much about the military and their motives as ever before.

In outline the Mission's objectives changed little to what was yet another crisis in the long saga of postwar crises. We would have to adapt as we had to adapt when the Soviets invaded Afghanistan in 1979 and the Foreign Office suspended all formal contacts. Informally, Brixmis would prove vital in maintaining lines of communication. As always things could be said or expressed through the Mission that would not give offence, would convey intentions and explore opportunities. The change in emphasis for the Mission was most marked in our key role of observation. A slightly more subtle approach was required. We were no longer to take columns from the rear. OPs were to be far more discreet. We should not provoke reactions. In short we were to tour less aggressively and even more inconspicuously, if that was possible. These precautions were taken much as a sop to the Foreign Office who always panicked when things got tense, thinking that somehow the Missions' presence would create insoluble situations. We knew how to conduct ourselves in front of all the various audiences that watched us because it had never been and never was in our best interests to create a scene. We had to go back time and time again and sometimes the lessons of that had been dearly learned over the years. Out on the ground, very little actually changed. Tomahawk continued, the Chipmunk flights continued, new and even more sophisticated equipment was observed, we trialled new techniques and equipment ourselves, training areas, installations, road, rail and airfield watches continued as normal. If anything there was an increased intensity and urgency about the crews. More targets and more ground were covered to compensate for the more subtle approach.

Modifications and refinements had been going on from the day the Mission started in 1946 and the first tours were conducted. Interestingly enough the very first tour was detained within hours and our card marked from the outset. There was not much we hadn't learned about avoiding trouble since then. The previous Chief, Brigadier Foley, had already instigated a more subtle approach to touring long before there was the slightest indication that the end of the Cold War was in sight. As a former director of the SAS he had already changed the emphasis with the immortal lines, 'see but don't be seen, hear but don't be heard'. By the time the Wall fell we had already become phantom-like and less confrontational, yet more robust and still turning in ever-increasing and ever-better results than before. The suddenness of the change of events complicated matters. It put us on the back foot slightly. It was undoubtedly a difficult time to operate in, with so many conflicting signals to interpret and vacuums to make decisions in, not least from our own side. But the product continued to flow unabated and touring continued with all its customary professionalism and intensity.

The number of incidents of violence rose in 1990 compared to 1989 on all three Mission fronts. Shootings and rammings were no less common in 1990 than in almost any other snapshot of Mission history. It never reached the proportions of the late 50s and mid-80s and certainly no one was killed but it was no less frightening for the tour crews concerned. In many ways it was testimony to the evolving sophistication and expertise of the Mission that in its last few years violent and close contact with the enemy had been kept to the absolute bare minimum. The principle of 'see but don't be seen, hear but don't be heard' put us in the driving seat.

In March an air tour crew of Flight Lieutenant Mark Knight, Master Aircrew Ray Parnell and Corporal Pat Thomas was aggressively detained and 'tarped' for several hours at Moehringen while quite innocently transiting between airfields. A local Potsdam tour conducted by Major John Walker, Staff Sergeant Mick Camp and Pat Thomas (again) was ambushed at Satzkorn by a wire hawser stretched across the road as they passed. Fortunately the momentum of the vehicle broke the steel rope and absorbed the damage. It was a highly dangerous practice which we thought we had suspended two years earlier when serious crew injury had been sustained. Curiously, also in March, the French ground crew of Girardet and Perez were detained violently at Neu Bukow and then immediately taken to dinner in Rostock by the local Kommandant! A few days later Girardet, this time with Brunel and Contant, were literally jumped on by troops from a passing truck at Angersdorf railway sidings. They managed to get away – without dinner that time!

In June the ground crew of Colour-Sergeant Jim Edgerton, Staff Sergeant John Buchan and Corporal Dave Collins, some of the most experienced tourers in the Mission, were shot at five times by an SA-11 sentry on the Euper training area. It was the subject of another vigorous protest that year by the Chief of Mission to SERB. Curiously it wasn't denied by Colonel Polozov, deputy chief SERB. He was more upset that he hadn't heard about it, given as he said himself, that it was routine procedure to report the shooting of even a single round at a military Mission crew. It was an interesting admission.

To confuse the signals there was a marked increase in friendliness from various Sovs. There was no pattern and it only served to necessitate more caution in our dealings. Soviet reaction to our presence on the ground became less easy to predict and we had to be more prepared for the unexpected than usual. Narking continued for quite a while after the Wall came down until they were finally flushed out in the summer of 1990, despite assurances, press reports and our own informants within the MfS that they were being rapidly disbanded. Some worked unofficially on a freelance basis to keep their hand in for future employment with the BND, Americans or Soviets, whoever got to them first. Others were recruited by the Soviets to maintain a watch on us and there is some evidence to suggest that they still operate today under the auspices of the reunified Germany.

Two comments helped crystallise Brixmis' role in the end game. In March 1990 the Deputy Commander for British Forces in Germany stated in a letter to the then Minister at the British Embassy Bonn: 'It is my belief that there will be a role for the Missions as long as Soviet troops remain on German soil, although the way in which they conduct their affairs will evolve with the changing situation.' At last a solid endorsement and a very clear and straightforward message to carry on.

The other was more prophetic. In October 1987 General Konovalyenko, Chief of Intelligence Directorate GSFG, said to Major General Joulwain, G3 Ops USAREUR,[66] and himself destined to become a future SACEUR:[67] 'We all know that the Missions have become involved in intelligence, but we must remember that they were set up for liaison.'

The Soviets were very worried about the future position of their troops in the GDR. By early 1990, criticism was already mounting about low flying, environmental issues connected to training and, in particular, nuclear weapons on East German soil. The criticism rose sharply through the year. Troops were confined to barracks in their spare time, families and officers were abused outside. Their formal relationships with the now discredited DDR authorities suffered similarly. They were not sure who their interlocutors should be in this new situation. They were isolated and in many instances in 1990 they turned to us.

Uncertainty among Mission members about our own future was equally apparent. A change in style was difficult to come to terms with, particularly among those who were in the Mission for their second tour, their first probably conducted in the difficult days of the Afghanistan invasion in the early 80s. Some thought it a weakness to have to change. Most got on with the job, adapting very well to the changing circumstances. Several new tourers arrived in the summer of 1990, their fate already sealed, having spent all that time studying and undergoing the Special Duties course, just in case things in East Germany didn't work out as planned. They must have felt terribly cheated out of one of the most intense and demanding jobs the British Army could offer.

I was sandwiched somewhere between the two. On the one hand the old guard were reluctant to adjust to the change. On the other the new team were not even going to get their feet under the table before their services would no longer be required. For me and several others who had experienced a year's touring before the Wall came down and would experience the last year before the Mission closed, the position was clear. Things would have to change in line with the changing world and in particular with the changing circumstances in the DDR. What had not changed was the fact that 300,000 Soviet soldiers remained stationed in the DDR, the very reason for our existence in the first place.

Many new opportunities also arose under the changing circumstances. Soviet officers, perhaps trying to save their skins from going home or trying to earn some hard currency to go with, were flocking to Western intelligence services. Efforts to recruit them were increased and Brixmis became involved. We would endeavour to gain more intelligence through liaison than I had witnessed previously and we would do more liaison while out on tour.

In many ways, the Mission had simply come full circle as its founders had envisaged in the Robertson-Malinin agreement and General Konovalyenko had

---

[66] USAREUR: United States Armed Forces in Europe.

[67] SACEUR: Supreme Allied Commander Europe.

so recently predicted. Born out of a need to communicate in the uncertain and confused postwar period of central Europe, at its simplest to overcome language barriers, at its most complex to put across grand and detailed argument reflecting our respective political masters' views, the Mission was once again required to be spokesman for the sane and calm transfer to another new world order. Reassurance and communication remained imperative. In that vein it was perfectly legitimate to use the opportunity to reassure one's own side that what was being promised in theory by respective governments was really happening on the ground. Reassurance worked both ways. We were able to verify that proposed subsequent Soviet withdrawals actually did take place and we were able to comfort the Soviets that every effort would be made to help them withdraw peacefully and with dignity. Liaison and observation were merely a means to an end as they had always been and the end was now more in sight than ever before. All means at our disposal worked towards securing it. Germany, ever the pivot about which European history has revolved, once again became the flashpoint for yet another chapter in its development.

People were still very unsure, when the Wall came down in 1989, that they were witnessing the end game. They were still very unsure after the 1996 elections that communism had really stopped kicking in Russia. It would have been a safe pair of hands who predicted that the Soviets were in difficulty in the late 70s and early 80s and decided to turn the screws, keep the pressure on and finally put an end to the race on our terms. That was the role of the Missions in the 1980s, knowingly or unknowingly, to maintain the pressure in the best way that it could, to help write the penultimate chapter of the Cold War. The work of the Allied Military Missions right through to 1990 and beyond enabled Western administrations to say, look, the Soviet Union is still a threat, they are not dead yet, see what turned up this week in East Germany. And if people didn't like that, or thought it unnecessarily hawkish, then they simply needed to take a look at the overwhelming photographic evidence that we could offer. If people didn't believe that the Soviet Union would dare to strike pre-emptively in defence of its own security then they could also come and see, as we did, just how earnestly they practised for that role, even in the 1990s.

Brixmis and the other two Missions were a small but highly significant strand in the network of this Great Game with roles at all levels of the play, from the minutiae of tank armour construction, through a liaison function at executive level, to a barometer of the people at a national level. We were an invaluable thermometer stuck right up the backside of the Warsaw Pact which could be withdrawn, read at any time and reinserted for a different reading. Even so, I viewed our role at Brixmis as a constructive and positive contribution, however aggressively or furtively we carried it out.

Berlin changed that year from being smart, rich, affluent and clean to being forced to accommodate a darker side that it didn't care to acknowledge. Rich met poor and it was uncomfortable. They didn't like it and they found it difficult to deal with. The characteristic German traits of intolerance and arrogance against the weaker members of society began to emerge and the East Germans and other migrants bore the brunt of their frustration: from organised beatings, harassment and murder to simple impatience. I recall helping an East German Trabbie driver trying to negotiate an automatic car barrier just off the Kurfürstendamm in West Berlin. I thought he couldn't operate it and the traffic piling up behind, all of them West German (you could tell everything by number-plates), was becoming irate, hurling all manner of insults that basically implied he was stupid and should go back to East Berlin. I motioned the first one out and dragged him to the machine. It was broken.

These were alien characteristics to the average East German. They were rarely impatient, having learnt to queue all their lives and still be disappointed. They were neither arrogant nor pompous, rather very humble. They certainly weren't affluent, having had all their work, produce and earnings channelled into the state. The stark contrast between the two nations was revealed for all to see. What the Missions had been observing for many years was now on show for everyone. As 1990 progressed, there was enormous sympathy for the Easties. All they had come through on the more difficult side of the coin made it easy to side with the underdog.

Within three or four months of 9 November 1989, West German resolve to rebuild East Germany, which they had fought forty-four years to be given the privilege of doing, seemed dispirited at grass roots level. It was soon commonly joked by former West Berliners, if not most of West Germany, that the sooner the bloody Wall went back up again the better. Taxes rose in 1990 to accommodate the demands of putting the Easties back on their feet. West German companies, particularly encircled West Berlin companies, went out of business in the competition with their new partners. They couldn't match the low-wage Easties. Waifs and strays from all over Eastern Europe converged on West Berlin for handouts. Gypsies from Romania, cigarette sellers from Poland and black marketeers from Russia gave us a glimpse as early as 1990 of the state of the Eastern Bloc economies. 'Mauerkrankenheit' or 'Wall-sickness' became an excuse for things going wrong. It seemed as though forty-four years were about to come round full circle. So slow to learn and so quick to forget.

The market set up near the site of Hitler's railway station where he once dispatched the dispossessed to their final solution in the concentration camps, became the area for trade to take place between the plastic bag sellers, the cigarette carton sellers and the purveyors of various items of military equipment. Such was the sell-off of equipment in the markets and bazaars of West Berlin that the Mission coordinated shopping trips to establish the legitimacy of the claims that you could buy any item of military hardware you wanted. We were actually able to fill in pieces of the intelligence jigsaw puzzle that we had not been able to do by other means.

It was another channel of information and another change to the way we toured. We could not yet buy tanks and personnel carriers but that would come in time as both vendor and purchaser became more adventurous. In April 1990 I was able to purchase an RPG-7 quite openly from one of these stalls. Soviet soldiers taking time off in West Berlin, once confident enough to do so, would openly sell their shapkas and fur hats, now a most treasured fashion accessory in the West. What had previously been tradable for bottles of whisky after liaison meetings at SERB was now openly purchased on the streets for hard currency. The gypsies would camp outside Aldi supermarkets ready to bulk-buy as the shop opened, stripping it bare before the Westies got there. Beggars arrived on the streets to compete at the Blue Church with the drunks, drug pushers and prostitutes.

Now it became necessary for the Allied Powers to provide a calming and secure influence, not only officially on behalf of the Soviet Forces as they began their difficult and dangerous recovery home, but also unofficially on behalf of East Germans as they made their journey into reunification with the country they had been split from in 1945.

The Soviets had expected something like this to happen one day but it seemed inconceivable to many of our contacts that it could happen for this generation at least. Their basic miscalculation had been to assume that the economy of East Germany was much stronger than it was. However much the Soviets wanted to preserve two German states for their own ends it was not going to be feasible. They became resigned to the inevitability of German unity in fairly short order, not least because events already seemingly out of control on the streets of East Germany should appear to be under the control and direction of the four Allied Powers. What they had created in 1945 they needed to dismantle publicly and carefully. Free and fair elections, the movement of economic help from West to East together with the four Allied Powers combining with the two Germanies in the 'Four plus Two' talks, ensuring a sensible and calm transfer were the acknowledged keys to future stability. The Soviets were partly led, partly encouraged and partly resigned to it. Unification with West Germany was East Germany's only hope. Where the politicians and diplomats feared to tread, the economists led the way. Monetary union with the West D-mark sealed the change on 2 July 1990. On 18 July the Four plus Two talks signed away all Allied rights in Germany and on 3 October the two Germanies were reunified.

On all sides the future would lie with the younger generation, those, who despite indoctrination and years of suffering under communist rule, would emerge capable of learning something new while still flexible and energetic enough to do so. When Western companies expanded with great enthusiasm into the former Eastern Bloc in the early 1990s, one thing they learned very quickly was to concentrate on the young, those under thirty-five years old. Anyone older was an economic waste of time. They were so ingrained in their ways that to retrain them would have taken forever and cost too much. The longer the experiment with communism went on, the deeper and more invasive the surgery to correct it would have to be. The fact that they are in such a mess now is due to the perpetuation of the error for such a long time. East Germany has only forty years of communist rule to correct and that with the help of the most economically powerful nation in Europe. Russia has over seventy years to recover from. The surgery is still going on and we in the West have our own illnesses, caught as a result of exposure to the Cold War: problems as loosely connected as acid rain, nuclear fallout, arms exports turning up to be used against us, continued weapons testing and so on. All of these have to be treated as well.

The real tragedy has been the complete waste of time the world has endured while resolving the problem. It has taken over fifty years to begin to get the world back on course through the ridiculous sideshow of the Cold War. There have been no real winners, only lost opportunities. One could argue that the Cold War produced more technical advances and created a longer peace in Europe than we have ever known. That is irrefutably so. The spin-offs from research into nuclear, chemical and biological weapons have been considerable and the benefits of the space race phenomenal. One can only wonder what might have been if we had directed those resources more positively? Only now are we beginning to tackle more important issues: the developing countries, the environment, disease, how we live and what sort of future we can create. The Cold War diverted valuable resources away from these real issues to a rather selfish indulgence in a phoney problem dominated by one half of the planet. One can only hope that the lessons we have learned from the experience will help us craft the future. Will we be able to see when we are going wrong again or will we rush headlong down another blind alley? A close look at the way the Western world has organised itself over the last thirty years might suggest that we have learned nothing, as we fight for resources and energy, blindly follow what has come to be known in the civilised world as the rat race, while leaving the rest of the developing world behind. All this was condensed for me by the posting into SERB of Lieutenant Colonel Demchenko in late 1990. He openly talked to us about his opposition to nuclear weapons. He had worked for three months in the aftermath of what was the Chernobyl disaster. His wife had been pregnant at the time and lived only 100 kilometres away. He was deeply worried. For me he really rather summed up where we had got to.

By September 1990 it was clear that the Mission would stand down. The Soviets had been pressured into making a complete phased military withdrawal from East Germany and had agreed to the reunification of the two Germanies. Nearly a year on from the Wall falling it would be untrue to say that the elation felt at the time had lasted to the first anniversary. The Soviet military were withdrawing to certain poverty and decline. Like a cornered animal it was still a dangerous beast. Fears of a reaction led by the military were all too real. Removing the wounded animal to Russia only made the problem go away. It was by no means treated. West Germans were becoming aware of the awesome burden they had undertaken and the dire economic consequences of it. Their own booming economy was itself showing signs of faltering. East Germans, once drooling over the riches of the West, had become quickly disenchanted by the promises of unification. Employment fell and they had become second-class citizens in their own country. Suspicion and hatred were as mutual between them as they were between Soviets and Germans. Russians had been brought up on a diet of the Great Patriotic War and the struggle against fascism, Germans under the yoke or threat of communism and the crushing brutality of the Soviet Red Army at the end of the Second World War. These were still pretty irreconcilable differences for people of thirty, let alone anyone older. Soviet politicians, who had fought strongly against reunification, were now having to contend with their most hated enemy, the Germans, complete once more.

Additionally ethnic, religious and local grievances were spreading like a plague, all across the Soviet Union. Independence would come rapidly to many of the former satellite states during the next two years. Some, like Chechnya, were still being disputed in 1996. Western governments were drawing up the promised cuts that would make up the peace dividend, only to be surprised in late 1990 by events in the Middle East. In 1992 the crisis in Yugoslavia, a cauldron of religious hatred built up and contained for many years, erupted with some of the worst atrocities witnessed in Europe for fifty years. Its ferocity masked the seething discontent further east and across the whole of the former Soviet Union. British armed forces personnel were informed that they had been made redundant from their jobs while serving there. Precipitous action for a fast buck. It was not as though governments had little warning that difficulties around the world would still necessitate armed action and intervention. The Gulf War in 1991 should have been sufficient warning that the demise of the Cold War, far from reducing problems, simply revealed many more throughout Eastern Europe, the Middle East and Africa.

I undertook only six tours in September 1990. Even at this late stage of our existence they were still not without incident. At Retzow ranges on 3 September, together with Roger Bannister and Graham Heaman, we observed a Hip and Hind helicopter live firing programme that netted many new side-numbers the Mission had never seen before. New attack helicopters were clearly still coming into the DDR. We observed 21 GMRD deploy on their autumn exercise practising, as normal, their drills and tactics for a move west. Similarly, in the British Army in 1990, the enemy were still known as the 'red' forces – the national colour of the Soviet Union.

On 9 September, together with Peter Owen-Edmonds, one of the new tour officers that summer, and Pat Fryer, we observed, uninvited, the withdrawal by train back to the Soviet Union of the whole of 12 GTD. I felt particularly sorry for Peter and Will Stamper, the other new tour officer that year. They had given up nearly two years of their career to complete the Russian language course, German language course and finally Special Duties course to arrive in late June 1990 and be told in September that it was unlikely they would see a full two-year tour with the Mission. It was Peter in 1988 who had helped me get through the Russian language course. While I was studying the advanced interpreter's course during the day, at night I was going through the basic and linguist courses with him in order to catch up the twelve months I had missed. It is no coincidence that among the many ex-members of the Mission both Peter and Will went to work for joint West European and Russian ventures in the former Soviet Union within two years of the Mission closing, thus pioneering an entirely appropriate and more modern spirit of cooperation. In many ways it was a very real extension of the liaison role that they had been trained for, with different rules and in yet another wholly different phase of the West's relationship with the Russians.

On 11 September two Mission vehicles were involved in a very serious car accident at night, near Adamsdorf. The first vehicle had been run into by an East German civilian car. There were minor injuries to the civilians but nothing serious. The recovery vehicle and trailer that went out to get it was then also run into (while parked) by an extremely drunk East German driving with no lights. His car burst into flames and he had to be rescued from it by the two crews now out on the ground. The second G-wagon became unable to tow the trailer after the crash but was able to get back to Berlin. I was dispatched with Ernie Wilson as the second standby crew to recover the trailer and the first G-wagon. By the time it was all sorted out, it was nearly 7 a.m. before we started for home. As luck would have it we caught up a BTR-80 column that had just left barracks on a driver-training run. BTR-80 was still relatively new, with many technical features still unrecorded. We ran the column from behind with me in the back seat, curtains drawn, taking photographs and only Ernie in the front pulling the trailer and spare G-wagon behind him. The Sovs waved like mad. We had become a friendly face.

The last Mission, present for the last tour, 2 October 1990. Together with their sister Missions, this group of men and its predecessors monitored the 300,000 plus Soviet ground, air and naval troops stationed in the DDR, 365 days a year from 1964 to 1990.

On 13 September, with Ian Comerford and Pat Fryer, we observed 21 MRD and 94 MRD out on driver training, in the midst of which we obtained the very latest imagery of the BTR-70 'Gardelegen' variant complete with its satellite and aerials fully exposed. It was a great scoop for the Mission given that this vehicle was a key command and control element of a divisional communications system.

On 17 September, again with Ian Comerford and Dave Walton, a new driver, we observed the complete orbat of SA-10B on the Berlin–Rostock autobahn. This was the vehicle I had spotted over a year ago in Storkow that had caused so much concern to the director of the US Air Force (and potentially now to the head of the Turkish Air Force) because it wasn't supposed to be in East Germany. It hadn't been seen for a year since that date and ironically I saw it for the second and last time, only now it was being retrieved from the NVA rather than being handed over. They didn't leave anything like that to the Germans this time. Having seen that we continued our journey to Rostock where for the first time I managed to gain access to the docks and container yards by bluffing my way past the civilian guards. There were thousands of Sov vehicles on the hard standing, waiting to be shipped back to the Soviet Union. We dodged the patrolling UAZ-469 in and around the tightly packed columns of vehicles. It was very useful collateral for those watching the withdrawals from on high. The same picture emerged at the Mukran ferry on Rügen Island where we ignored the PRA restrictions to take a closer look at the ferry and installations that had featured so regularly in the history of the Mission.

On 24 September, with Martin Brain and Pat Fryer, we observed the withdrawal of NVA troops back into barracks off exercise. In June we had already stopped routine tasking against the NVA. The rumours that they would be disbanded post-unification were already rife, if not being prepared for. We spoke to some of the commanders. They were very despondent, saying that West German officers were already at the barracks telling them how it was going to be in the future and that all NVA officers above the rank of major would no longer be required. We had already seen evidence of West German vehicles in East Germany as they started their recce untactfully early. It was almost as if the West Germans, successors to all we surveyed, were becoming the focal point of all our frustration and anger at having to come to terms with what had been a very dangerous but thoroughly understood game. The change was clearly irrevocable now and it was very sad in a thoroughly selfish way because it had been one of the best jobs the British Army had to offer.

The last mission took place over 1–2 October 1990. Every single vehicle and every single tourer on pass went out. It became known as the unification tour. Some of the crews met on the first night to have an impromptu barbecue, something we had done down the years for departing tourers and Chiefs of Mission. The next day we all RV'd in broad daylight at Klein Behnitz for the official final barbecue, where we were joined by many of the remaining Brixmis staff able to get into East Germany. The Robertson-Malinin agreement was formally suspended that day. From there we proceeded to the Mission House for a last public entertainment engagement with SERB. Several very moving speeches were made, gifts exchanged and the evening finished off with the lowering of the Union Jack to the accompaniment of the bugler from 1st Battalion the Royal Welch Fusiliers playing the Last Post. All the East German staff were present. Their alleged long years of service to the Stasi, informing against us, now appeared hollow as they were, without exception, crying their eyes out in the realisation that we really were leaving. The emotion of the occasion was very deep. The Soviets were very sad to see us depart. The local Potsdammers had lined the streets from the Mission House to the Glienicke Bridge to wave goodbye.

We left the Mission House in convoy, beeping the horns in acknowledgement of the crowds who had come out to see us off. It was like a triumphal march into a relieved city except that we were leaving and the inhabitants were very unhappy to see us go. The crowds on the bridge were enormous. Only Special were there to film the occasion. There was no press. It was a private farewell between the people of Potsdam and ourselves. For the second time in a year I crossed the bridge with tears in my eyes as the last Mission paraded back into Berlin and into history. We left as we came, unnoticed and unremarked, a truly successful intelligence operation.

Epilogue

Brixmis was officially disbanded on 31 December 1990. Many of its members were rapidly dispatched for duty in the Gulf. A few stayed on under the auspices of the Joint Intelligence Section, Berlin. Soviet withdrawals were closely monitored, new equipment was still observed and 'contacts' with Soviet personnel were pursued. The rules of the game were significantly altered until Soviet troops eventually withdrew from East Germany and British, French and American troops bade farewell to their former Berlin garrisons.

What had we achieved, what had we learned and what could we usefully use to help in the future?

To understand what we learned we need to understand what the problem was. To fully understand the problem is to try and understand the Russians: their long and proud history, their geographical and ethnic makeup. For an emergency course in the long and complex history of Russia one needs to know three things. First, the country covers a huge area of the world's surface spanning several time zones, encompassing weather systems and terrain that range from difficult at one end of the spectrum to awkward at the other. Second, there exists in Russia an enormous variety of different cultures, religions and languages, which in their own right create a most complex communications and leadership challenge. As we attempt a closer financial and political union of member states of the European Union we may well learn something from their experiences alone. Third, the Motherland has been invaded throughout the centuries from all sides and from a variety of nations. The perceived betrayal by Hitler during the Second World War was the final straw. Stalin vowed that it would never happen again. On top of all that the latter half of the twentieth century saw the Soviets' own ambitions emerge to worry and threaten the rest of the free world.

The emergence of communism and its explicit export created a global anxiety, which came to a head in Germany, its epicentre Berlin, at the end of the Second World War and manifested itself in the events of the Cold War. An enigma, wrapped in a mystery, clothed in a riddle was Churchill's explanation of Russia. Why have they always craved a warm water port? Not just for trade but for launching naval forays. Why did they contribute to the Second World War and then almost turn on the West as soon as it was over? Because they didn't trust anyone other than themselves to stop an invasion happening yet again. They would put as much distance between Moscow, Leningrad and their border with Western Europe as they could. Why did they get so involved in the space race, stealing a march on the Americans with the first manned launch of Yuri Gagarin. Because it was a show of strength, externally provocative and internally strengthening. Why did they invade Hungary, Czechoslovakia and then disastrously Afghanistan? Because they were a threat to their own internal stability so delicate to maintain and so ferociously fought for. Why did they never invade

Romania? Because it wasn't a threat, it possessed enormous raw material deposits that the Soviet Union could not do without and furthermore, situated behind Bulgaria, Yugoslavia and Hungary, it wasn't considered necessary to incorporate it into the buffer states that cushioned them from future invasion. Why were Berlin and Germany divided like they were? Because the Russians got there first and dictated the terms to suit their own ends. Would we have done it any differently? It wasn't necessarily to spread communism first and foremost but if it was in with the package and you wanted to keep control then impose a system similar to your own . . . sure, why not? In short Russia is xenophobic and enigmatic.

Communism wasn't a good export because it wasn't a particularly good buy. The Soviet's inability to see that at home was their big mistake. Communist China does not pose the same physical threat: it has its local difficulties with Taiwan, Hong Kong, Nepal, Bhutan (and for that matter Russia), but there are as yet no universally perceived pretensions to expand beyond their borders. Furthermore, they have incorporated many Western ways, technologies and ideas into their culture in order to progress. Maybe they are just watching and waiting as many doom prophets suggest. 'An optimist studies Russian, a pessimist studies Chinese' was a saying I recall hearing at Ashford.

The implicit threat of the export of communism engendered the Cold War and the threat was issued over Germany. Everything flowed from that one flawed idea; what was good for them was good for everyone else.

Ironically, the beginning of the collapse was rooted in Stalin's desire to match the West in the arms race. Stalin's decision to upgrade the Soviet military capability to that of the West in the 1940s was followed by Khruschev in the 1950s and compounded by the onset of the space race. Whatever the justification at the time, the Soviet Union simply couldn't afford it. In retrospect it appears that the Soviet Union was inevitably doomed to economic failure thereafter. It was already hinted at by Khruschev himself in 1958. When referring to the nuclear arms race he said: '(it gives) our adversary an opportunity to exhaust us economically, without war, by forcing us to compete with them in a never ending arms race.' The Soviet Union took a severe dent in 1962 when Kennedy stood up to Khruschev over Cuba and forced Cuba to back down. What was good for Cuba was good for Germany and the Eastern bloc, but not for another twenty-seven years. It floundered badly on the rocks of the Afghanistan War between 1979 and 1985. Vietnam had taught the Americans the dangers of solitary intervention in another country's affairs. Communications were making the world a smaller and more informed place to live in. Even the Soviet Union, technically advanced yet socially and economically bankrupt, was unable to restrict the news from Afghanistan. As in Vietnam with the US, the military might of the Soviet Union ultimately proved ineffectual against guerrilla warfare. The cost, in terms of prestige and casualties, was difficult to recover from. Motivated once again by the desire to impose Soviet influence on another buffer state, the adventure turned out in practice to be a fundamental error of judgement. Poland and 'Solidarity' had already shown the way the world was moving between 1979 and 1981. Reagan's strengthening of the US Armed Forces and the tantalisingly realistic 'Star Wars' project forced the Soviet Union to pour even more resources into a final arms race that ultimately led to the economic, social and political collapse witnessed by the Mission right up to the end of 1990. Gorbachev attempted to paper over the cracks with glasnost and perestroika but they served only to contain the collapse and prevent it from being a bigger disaster than it might otherwise have been. The edifice of communism, represented so graphically by the Berlin Wall, finally began to crumble. However, it would have taken a clever man in the 1980s to spot the Soviets panting for breath, a brave one to broadcast the view and probably a certifiable one to predict the end of communism, let alone plan new defence budgets and strategies accordingly.

The superpowers and their respective blocs had taken themselves to the brink of mutually assured destruction and back in the space of forty-five years. If you had set out to invent the Cold War you couldn't have done it. The whole thing was absurd. If it is conceivable to summarise the rationale behind the Cold War then in my opinion it was very simply a lack of trust. That the Mission had played a very important role in bringing us back from the brink of disaster by building confidences and trust was clear and very rewarding to know. As I crossed the bridge for the last time I was content that the Mission's long and significant involvement with the Cold War had provided a most positive contribution to bringing about its end and that I had been part of it.

If any one person played a more than average hand in unravelling the spiral of mutually assured destruction and brinkmanship, then for my money, it was probably Mikhail Gorbachev and indirectly running a close second was Willy Brandt. Undoubtedly it was Gorbachev who decided enough was enough in all the satellite states of the Soviet Union, not just East Germany. It was Gorbachev who stood up to Honecker and the other satellite states and pulled the rug from under their feet. Most importantly it was Gorbachev who took the biggest risks with regard to the West and it was he who had the most to lose. He had to blink first to allow everyone else to blink with him. It was a huge play to undertake, an enormous gamble to run with. He had to trust what the West was saying to him. On a lesser scale, but no less critical, it was Willy Brandt who unravelled the stalemate of the Germany question and covered much of the important groundwork that Gorbachev would expand upon later. He had learned from his time as Mayor of West Berlin how to play the Soviets at their own game; salami slicing and bit by bit gains by stealth. In his policies of 'Small Steps' and 'Ostpolitik', he reduced the Germany question to manageable chunks to be dealt with one by one. Where the Allies saw total solutions he saw stages. Where the Allies saw final agreements he saw temporary measures. He understood compromise, he maintained integrity and he sought trust for both sides. He understood that unravelling the Germany question would have a knock-on effect.

Trust was something sorely lacking throughout the Cold War. Trust could only emerge after a lengthy period of confidence building. The Missions played their part in that process from 1946 onwards. The legacy of trust rebuilt through Gorbachev has been and is being rewarded with cooperation and a new relationship based upon compromise and attempts to understand respective problems.

It is not surprising that there are many ex-Brixmis, US and French Mission personnel working within the former Soviet Union today. Some are working openly and legitimately as business leaders in their own right, furthering the liaison side of the business. Others are engaged on the observation side. Both continue to contribute to furthering cooperation and confidence. Intelligence gathering remains part of a mutually acceptable and understood 'checks and balance' system. That it remains is to be regretted because it implies a lack of trust and that in turn implies that we may have progressed nowhere. But while one side cannot fully trust the other, such activity continues to be a legitimate way to establish the truth by other means and as such should be regarded as something healthy rather than anything sinister.

What did we learn from the Mission's experience to help us with the future? Probably what we already knew and practised; liaison and observation. We constantly underlined the need to keep talking as well as try to find out what challenges we were up against. What are we up against today? Russia in the late 1990s is still a potential flashpoint, not directly to us in an implicitly military way but indirectly because of its poor economic prognosis and its links with organised crime. On the other hand it is strategically situated between the Far East, particularly China, and the rest of Europe. Maybe one day, if not already (the Soviet Union was at open war with China by 1969 and both had the H-bomb), we should be very grateful for that. Now that ex-Warsaw Pact countries such as Poland have successfully applied to join Nato, the threat has been refocused. We are at last able to see the wood for the trees. If anything the Cold War has been a red herring, creating a myopic view of the world's real problems. Unfortunately, what its disappearance reveals is a much more complex and global network of threats that, hitherto, have been avoided by an almost total preoccupation with the Cold War.

There are now many potential flashpoints around the world and they come in various disguises. Terrorism in all its forms, inspired by minority ideologies, financed by drugs and with access to more terrifying and destructive technologies is now prevalent. For the first time the United States and Russia are having to contend with it at home. Drugs have become an insidious disease amongst the young on an international scale. Society, most notably in the Western world appears to be slowly breaking down; its moral values, community spirit and sense of purpose shattered by the necessities and vagaries of modern economics. Religious and other forms of extreme fundamentalism represent a new threat, which is of great concern to the West as it tears the Middle East apart. Then there are two truly global challenges that we will sooner or later have to face up to. First, the challenge of the information age, or to put it in a phrase that Cold War warriors might understand: the information war. Second, there is the ultimate challenge of the environment. The former would be a wasted opportunity if not tamed for global mutual benefit. The latter will tame us if we don't adjust. To deliberately misquote Bill Clinton; 'It's the environment, stupid.'

Though the Cold War is over, these new threats pose even greater challenges. Fortunately the demise of the Cold War, at last, allows us to identify, manage and control them.

Finally, there is the question of when the Cold War really ended. The fall of the Wall, as magnificent and global a piece of high drama that it was, did not define the conclusion of the Cold War but was simply another important landmark along its route. The Wall coming down produced as much tension, as much mistrust and as much uncertainty as any other phase. Marcus Wolf, head of the East German Stasi, himself subscribes to the 'cock-up' theory, that the Wall came down by accident rather than design as a result of Schabowski's incredibly unprepared press conference to the world on 9 November 1989. Soviet withdrawal from the DDR and the reunification of the two Germanies were certainly not on anyone's agenda that night but were forced to the table as a result.

The fall of the Wall certainly marked the beginning of the end and was the biggest hope for a resolution of the Germany question for forty-five years. But its fall was replaced with nothing more concrete than a vacuum, one set of rules hastily abandoned in favour of really not very much. It was not until the 27 May 1997 and the signing of the Founding Act on Mutual Relations, Co-operation and Security between Russia and Nato that we have witnessed the first, profound step towards reincorporating Russia permanently back into the Western world. That Russia no longer targets its nuclear warheads at any of the Nato countries is comforting but irrelevant. Both sides now have sight of, and a voice in, each others decision-making process and most importantly, the first tangible and meaningful effort to introduce trust back into the equation has been taken. This is the end of the Cold War and hopefully the beginning of a 'long peace' in Europe.

Reflections

I have said it before, and I say it again; it is the purest delusion to suppose that because an idea has been handed down from time immemorial to succeeding generations, it may not be entirely false.

Pierre Bayle (1647–1706)[1]

This additional chapter was written in the summer of 2011, some twenty-two years after the iconic fall of the Berlin Wall in November 1989. More significantly, it is two decades since the demise of the Soviet Union and the death of Stalinism. This chapter is intended to be a more scholarly examination of life after Brixmis and the broader intelligence function after the Cold War. Equally, it is a reflection upon contemporary times, the intelligence function's relationship with power, and what now passes for politics in Western societies. For those who thought that this additional chapter might include some new revelation about Brixmis daring-do, you should 'look away now'. That role is for other former Mission members and their associations to undertake. Better still, historians and political scientists might care to reflect objectively and independently upon the Missions as the number of former Mission members steadily declines and only a few personal memoirs emerge.

The author has also 'changed' since the original text was written. The intervening years have seen him leave military service, enter and then leave the private sector, and, for the last eleven years, engage with the academic world via a PhD in Intelligence Studies. As lecturer at Cranfield University, Shrivenham, the focus has been on what we think we understand by the concepts of risk, resilience and security. Indeed, since 1989, ideas of risk, resilience and security have become popular; trumping the examination of traditional concepts of intelligence and thoroughly eclipsing long-held notions of defence. It is telling in itself that societies which can wage war on an abstract noun – terrorism – and offer degree courses in others – risk, resilience and security – might themselves be suffering from an acute lack of self-confidence in their own projects if not desperately seeking meaning and purpose to their own existence. Thus, this changing context is worthy of investigation.

The contemporary fascination with these concepts might usefully be dated to the English publication of Ulrich Beck's *Risk Society* in 1992. The then remnants of the political left applied his thesis of 'reflexive modernity' – scientific and technological development creating humanity's own destruction – to health, consumer safety and

---

[1] The French philosopher Bayle encapsulates the prevailing sense of crisis in seventeenth-century Europe that called into question old historical certainties, received wisdom, and self-evident accepted traditional truths. The toleration of criticism of widely-held beliefs is vital to a construction of the truth.

the environment. This fascination was compounded, and a political circle completed, by the intense and readily visual events of September 2001 (9/11) in the US that allowed the old political right, as well as the author, to join in the application of the 'risk society' thesis to the arena of security. Yet, 9/11 created both 'easy' and superficial perceptions; a lazy analysis by which to explain and blame their occurrence on an 'obvious' enemy. The resultant accepted and received wisdom, reflected in the meaningless rhetoric of 'the global war on terror', attracted critical and considered contestation from the start. However, the rhetoric was quickly followed by an equally banal analysis encapsulated in phrases like 'the world has changed forever', 'an increasingly uncertain world', the embarrassing '7/7 – this is our 9/11', and the devastatingly simplistic 'it's not if but when'. These declarations belie how much we have erred towards a moralising rather than reasoned view of the world.

Moreover, the response to 9/11 has come to reveal more about 'us' than the events themselves said about its perpetrators. Indeed, post-Cold War, and specifically post-9/11, politics reflects the more pessimistic and misanthropic post-1960s America that began in a 1950s dalliance with liberalism, until the civil rights movement cemented a hard-line neo-conservative response, and finished with the assassination of President Kennedy and the demise of the Apollo space programme. These early Cold War experiences left America uneasy with itself at home, coercing its own population through fear in the repeated invention of 'bogeymen' – liberalism, Communism, and South American drug regimes – abroad. Fortunately, the same passage of time and the intervention of more thoughtful and clearer assessment have all come to challenge the early movers and their certain pronouncements of today's bogeyman – fundamentalist terrorism. Sceptical observers – Devji, Furedi, Malik, Neiman, Ormerod, R.D. Putnam, Ridley, Runciman, Tallis, Taleb, and Zakaria amongst others – have all, from different perspectives, argued that something far deeper and more fundamental has come to pass that defines contemporary context; beyond simplistic explanations of an enemy abroad constructed by intelligence and security communities in league with their political masters at home. Yet, the traction of their ideas with a public saturated by the easier negative mood is limited. The shorthand for this change includes: a disengagement from politics; a narcissistic focus on the individual rather than social solidarity; and, the absence of an enlightened purposeful ideology around which to coalesce.

This struggle for the correct narrative is important. Thus, this chapter contemplates three broad issues pertinent to the pursuit of intelligence matters post-Brixmis and post-Cold War. First – a broader assessment of contemporary context, power and politics that might usefully inform the prevalence of these new and dominating concepts of risk, resilience and security. Second – some more specific thoughts on intelligence and the intelligence function in contemporary times by contrast to the Cold War period that Brixmis operated in. Third – an evaluation of the contribution of Brixmis in relation to intelligence and context.

Understanding Contemporary Times

It is politics that defines the times. An enlightened view of politics can be summarised as the public search for a common good; people organising in order to achieve something beyond individual desires – to change things for the better. Today, Western politics is being hollowed out in exchange for the stability of what Isaiah Berlin famously called 'negative liberty' – a freedom from restrictions rather than a positive freedom to change things for something better. It is this negative ideology that has set the attitude today for decision-making across all aspects of society, let alone intelligence. Recognising this context at all might be an intelligent intelligence function's most useful role.

The Real Cold War Legacy

Adam Curtis, in *The Trap*, describes how the 1950s presented an opportunity for Western governments to release their societies, not only from the tyrannical spectre of fascism abroad, but also from the greedy self-interest of capitalism at home. Political elites, in those early years of the Cold War, determined that this vision – individual freedom for all – could be delivered through the central regulation and management of the economy. The economist Friedrich von Hayek disagreed and, in his *The Road to Serfdom*, argued forcefully that, however bad you imagine self-interested capitalism to be, an economy regulated by governments would be far worse. He argued that self-interested individuals maximising gain for themselves, absent of altruism, would ultimately deliver the greatest good for society as a whole. The regulated economy – constantly 'tweaked' by Keynesian governmental intervention – he argued, would only lead to paralysing control and tyranny. The post-1917 Soviet Union precisely exemplified his warning. However, Hayek's theories and fears were dismissed. Keynes's commanding role for government in economic affairs won the day (until an alternative form of governmental intervention – Monetarism – took over in the recession of the 1970s). Governments began to intervene in the public interest through the ethos of public service – politicians and civil servants acting altruistically for others.

Yet, ironically, it was intelligence's success in managing the Soviet nuclear threat, masterminded by the US Research and Development (RAND) Corporation, that convinced political elites and business alike that Hayek's self-interest theory might have been right all along. The constant feed of multiple intelligence surveillance data into powerful American computers revealed minute-by-minute warnings and indicators of Soviet nuclear intention. Thus, through computerised mathematical modelling, the uncertain intentions of two nuclear opponents suddenly became clear. And, a simple sufficiency of weapons on both sides guaranteed that an equally devastating response would visit either side initiating an attack; fear of the consequences prevented either side from beginning such an exchange. Mutually assured destruction (MAD) – based upon RAND's self-interest theory – became the cornerstone of Cold War strategy. This theory contributed to the greatest intelligence success of the Cold War – the prevention of it going 'hot'. Yet, it also generated the seeds of today's ideological dysfunction.

The notion that strategy could be played out by numbers – gaming and computer modelling – was to become the desultory and depressing ideology for all of society's activities to the present day. Arguably, it was a loss of faith in humans expressed in the demise of politics that led the search for alternative models. Also gone were the long-established decision-making philosophies based upon the ideas of Aristotle, Kant or Bentham. The self-interest idea at the heart of the strategy of nuclear stalemate was to be transferred to every other aspect of societal activity – justice, education, health and defence – by the time the Cold War came to its own demise. The theory formed the basis of a new political control, from advertising to psychology, convinced that all of human activity could be understood by mathematical models and equations. Its most depressing manifestation today is government's moralising intervention in every aspect of private life – drinking, eating, leisure, health, children – that would have been unconscionable just thirty years ago. The brilliant, paranoid-schizophrenic, and Nobel Prize-winning mathematician largely responsible for this development, John Nash, called it 'Game Theory'. The underlying assumption of Game Theory was that a fearful and suspicious human being would always be inclined to maximise self-interest over any alternative altruistic, collective or collaborative action. The sum of these individual self-interests would in turn create a fearful equilibrium – control – across society that out-weighed the alternative – chaos.

Late 1970s Britain, and the incoming Thatcher administration, experimented further with the idea of fearful, rational, self-interest as the single explanation of human behaviour. Notions of self-sacrifice, common goals and public service became illusory, disingenuous and hypocritical. The Blair-Brown governments of the late 2000s argued that political freedom could be handed back to the people through the marketisation of all aspects of society – the conferring of monetary value and price upon all products and services in education, health and even defence. Everything could be controlled and explained through mathematical computer-based calculations and systems theory; including notions of individual freedom. Today, rather than interfering so explicitly in private life, the Cameron-Clegg coalition utilises pseudo-scientific behavioural economics, neuroscience and 'nudge' politics to implicitly direct individual decision-making through notions of genes and neurons trumping freewill. They want individuals to come to the correct decisions by themselves; provided, those decisions coincide with what the Government predetermines! Far from fulfilling the rhetoric of getting out of people's lives, government continues to make itself more indispensable. Similar to the false contrast between hard and soft power, libertarian paternalism (nudging), like authoritarianism, is still telling you what to do – with or without force. Thus, the singularly most important ideological goal of all twentieth-century political elites – freedom – has become reinterpreted as 'public choice', 'marketisation' or 'nudge politics'. This interference with individual moral autonomy – the ability to make your own choices, including bad ones – was based upon the dark and dismal Cold War notion of self-interested people responding only to targets and incentives. It was compounded by an imploding political left incapable of true political activity in the sense of acting together in a common cause beyond selfish opportunism. Indeed, the very notion of the public – a self-conscious body operating in a cohesive and collective interest – became redundant.

Yet, many proponents of Game Theory themselves recognise the limitations: simplistic assumptions about human nature; a wilful dismissal of free will; and, stubborn acts of unrequited altruism, philanthropy and self-sacrifice all served to defeat the predicted outcomes of Game Theory calculations – the management of human beings by numbers continues to preside over a rise in inequality and the diminution of social mobility within Western societies, rather than liberate them. The idea that, through the pursuit of targets, league tables and pseudo-science we could become free from bureaucratic elites, free to choose our own lives, and free from the constraints of class, income, privilege or socially pre-destined roles, proved to be a fantasy. And despite November 1989 and the 'end' of the Cold War offering politicians what appeared to be yet another new era, a new beginning for geo-politics, the real legacy of the Cold War was not the prevention of it going hot – that was intelligence's achievement alone – but a political ideology that articulates a narrow view of what we want by way of human freedom. This negative freedom is based upon the Cold War paranoia for secrecy and the exploitation of mistrustful, suspicious, self-interested and isolated human beings constantly strategising against themselves for their own gain; defined at its outset by the computerised management of the arms race. Today, just like the unending supply chains of Cold War Soviet defence procurement, it has become difficult to turn off an idea so thoroughly ingrained in society. This new interpretation of so-called freedom and liberty has merely entrapped us in a vacuous and meaningless world content to normalise a heightened state of security as the reason for being. This absence of meaning and purpose is nowhere better caricatured than in the world of risk management.

The Banality of Risk Management

By far the most pervasive form of contemporary decision-making is risk management. It has found powerful expression in health and safety, the formalisation of governance, transparency, sustainability, corporate social responsibility and the more recent 'securitisation' of much of life. This management of risk, as distinct from an understanding of the concept of risk, has come to stifle and smother all efforts at pursuing progress and prosperity. Subservience to the rigid bureaucracy of risk management constitutes the biggest challenge to the long-tried and tested virtues – judgement, toleration, discretion, argument and moral autonomy – necessary to achieve prosperity and progress. The intelligence function implicitly, if not explicitly, deals in risk; yet, it too has come to be dominated by the processes of risk management rather than the support of meaningful political purpose.

Risk management has become hubristic shorthand for the regime by which future uncertainty can be predicted and controlled by shallow decision-makers. It has come to transfix governments and institutions alike with a powerful, hypnotic reason for being. That uncertainty can become 'knowable', 'measurable' and 'modelable' is itself incredible. It is as though the very word uncertainty has been stripped of its original dictionary meaning. Worse, and miraculously, because it is given a pseudo-scientific number, it somehow gains objective meaning. Still worse, it rejects any moral and political autonomy to decision-making on the basis of this so-called evidence; being allowed to be 'wrong' is one mark of a tolerant society. In fact, this deceitful reduction of entirely subjective issues to objective quantities is a meaningless and simplistic slight-of-hand that shifts any genuine effort to understand or pursue the truth yet further away. The effort to manage uncertainty becomes an organising concept in itself and devoid of any higher meaningful outcome. Thus, the reason for being becomes – similar to the interchange of purpose and process – the management of risk as an organising principle in its own right.

This bureaucratic decline into mediocrity is being pursued across many institutions and disciplines. Higher education is measured by rafts of commercial jargon that do anything but recognise the value of education for its own sake. The re-interpretation of league tables and waiting-lists for what it means to be well in the UK's National Health Service jeopardises the essential nature of care. In business, the 'risk management of everything' finds businessmen reluctant to declare profit-making as a principal goal. Rather they have succumbed to reputation managers, corporate social responsibility consultants, environmentally-friendly mantras, and any number of other abstract and objectively meaningless nouns – governance, compliance, transparency, accountability and sustainability – that reveal little about what they do, but much about the lack of confidence with which they do it. Public services forget what they are for: the police, fire and ambulance services now couch their roles in terms of public safety rather than upholding the law, putting out fires or emergency first aid. Similarly, the public have lost confidence to intervene when plain wrong-doing stares them in the face. Like institutional solidarity, citizen solidarity is shattered by the fear of consequential litigation, insurance claims and suspicion from those same public service organisations interpreting intervention suspiciously. Nowhere is this more powerfully and cripplingly expressed than in the cultural apartheid we have created between adults and children. The once understood direction of authority in that relationship has been stood on its head. Politicians, Anglo-Saxon politicians in particular, are so devoid of an ideological backbone, or too frightened to exhort anything remotely ideological, that they content themselves with an infantilising and patronising managerialism that simply interferes in how the rest of us wish to conduct our private lives. Worse, the rest of us, so unconfident in sorting out our own private lives, demand that these same so-called politicians intervene and regulate them on our behalf with ever-increasing shrill moral panic. Similarly in the scientific and technological world a growing 'complexity' narrative argues that the very scientific advances invented and developed by human-beings will somehow be responsible for humanity's downfall. This 'risk society' logic, in which modernity becomes reflexively responsible for our future demise as a species, forgets that science and technology have solved many of our problems to date, delivered much of what is deemed 'progress', and might continue to do so in the future. The change in attitude from 'can-do' to 'too difficult' has had a most debilitating impact upon prosperity and progress for all, as well as the most enduring feature of the last 100 years – the struggle to define and deliver freedom.

Undoubtedly, so-called 'new risks' have emerged, and the perceptions of some of the consequences of these new risk sources – GM food, nanotechnology, artificial intelligence, climate change and globalisation – can be ambiguous and alarming. However, it is worth remembering that some of these so-called new risks have been with us for a very long time: piracy and the slave trade are old examples of trans-national crime; crops have always been manipulated to improve productivity; and, we have always managed to adapt to, and exploit, climate change. Furthermore, some challenges like smallpox have been eradicated. So, these 'new risks' are merely new to us; relatively no less challenging than their predecessors were to our predecessors and no more 'risky' than those faced down in the past. What seems dangerously new is an unwillingness to meet them head-on. Perceptions of their impact are formed more out of fear and dread than by reasoned means. They are explained in terms of biology, psychology or the environment, rather than interpreted for meaning through our own political attitudes. Regrettably, today, our attitudinal and political response reflects a deeply misanthropic and unconfident approach to confronting life. Cynicism replaces scepticism, caution becomes precaution, risk aversion eclipses risk taking, victimhood trumps heroism, bureaucratic regulation extinguishes wise judgement, and sustainability suppresses progress.

To confuse risk for uncertainty is mistaken. To equate the source of a risk with its possible consequences is disingenuous. To conflate the perception of a risk with its reality is disabling. To then use that illogical reality of a risk as a basis for decision-making absent of human intervention is to deny genuine resilience and to wilfully mismanage risk. To invoke the precautionary principle as first response to uncertain, unknowable or marginal events is to invite the unintended consequence of the response proving worse than the original fear. Similarly, the pursuit of the 'what-if' or the 'not if but when' of risk, as exemplified by the 2004 US WMD Commission metaphors 'the failure of imagination' or 'a failure to join the dots', is a dangerous game. Where we spend finite resource should be decided by hard evidence rather than a surfeit of imagination. There is no end to the what-if game of risk management. Any astronomer will tell you that, when you look up at the night sky, there are countless ways of joining the dots. Knee jerk reactions combined with a desire to be seen to be doing something are fear-based responses not reasoned ones.

The overall and debilitating effect is not the explosion in risk, but the explosion in everything being interpreted as risk. Absent of meaningful objectives, values and principles, Western society increasingly and mistakenly utilises the management of risk as ends rather than means to ends. In this process, institutions are turned inside out; the marginal becomes normalised and the normal is marginalised. Contrast the extraordinary resource, time, and panic exhausted globally on so-called SARS, avian flu, or vCJD pandemics versus malaria, cholera or dysentery. The former have yet to happen and the latter still devastate populations; considerable resource is wasted on the treatment of an unlikely marginal impact. Organisations betray the moral and political vacuum of risk management – paralysis in the present merely waiting for the future to happen. This crisis at the heart of contemporary decision-making is not explained by malevolent scientific and technological progress. Rather, it is the absence of purpose to put such technological progress towards.

The political response to terrorism post-9/11 is a case in point. Western societies have been complicit in placing so-called 'Jihadi' terrorism upon a pedestal it does not deserve. The reality of terrorism is that it is an irregular mode of warfare for political purposes. By this definition alone any strategic meaning to Al Qaeda, 'jihadist' or 'islamist' violence can be dismissed. The pseudo-ideology of this present expression of extremism is devoid of meaningful and achievable political aims. Yet, considerable resources of the state are being thrown against it as though it represented an all-consuming political challenge to what we believe in, rather than straightforwardly criminal action. In reality it is a strategic and ideological mismatch of our own making. If the perpetrators of 9/11 had any grand ideological or political substance to their actions, then it is we in the West who endowed them with it. We condoned, if not enhanced, their actions with the response of a 'global war on terror', and we dignified their impact with strategic and existential significance by sacrificing values and principles that underpin our own strategy and ideology.

Part of that confusion derives from a misunderstanding or misreading of context. If context is misunderstood then purpose is equally misguided. If purpose is misguided, then many institutions, not least intelligence, are similarly blown off course in the operational conduct of their business. Yet, polities on both sides of the Atlantic flounder when it comes to articulating purpose, values and principles. Indeed, it is not just politicians engaged in a frustrating search for meaning. The middle-class, British-born, relatively well-off, young, male suicide bombers that brought carnage to London in July 2005 may very well have claimed – mistakenly – a pious devotion to Islam; but their acts could equally be interpreted as being motivated by a nihilistic sense of 'lashing-out' at a society that gives them no sense of purpose or identity; curiously unlike their 'first generation' parents, who consciously bought into the Western liberal democratic values of freedom, democracy and equality by coming here. The diminution of those attractive values in their lifetime must be galling. The so-called English riots of August 2011 similarly reflect a nihilistic action on the part of violent shoplifters absent of community solidarity; only out-done by the depressingly incoherent and unconfident response of the police. The wearing of veils (or crucifixes) might similarly be viewed as a desire for social solidarity – to 'belong' – in societies that decreasingly offer these things beyond the narcissistic celebration of self, celebrity and the individual. How ironic, if not hypocritical, that we can condemn acts of depravity in the handling of prisoners of war, when similar acts can be witnessed at home on 'reality' TV. Furthermore, this need for meaning and belonging is not exclusively ethno-centric or religious. It can be found in the environmental movement, animal rights activism, anti-war protests, anti-Americanism, and, bizarrely, the invention of illness. They all display a profound lack of confidence in authentic Western values and purpose. The danger is that arcane belief systems – religious to environmentalist – together with an unrivalled media become persuasive ideology if there is nothing to challenge or temper them.

When means are misinterpreted as ends, and institutions seem absent of purpose, one might interpret that as evidence of the emergence of an existential crisis of confidence. Indeed, it may very well be – similar to new risks – more in the perception than the reality. In the same way that the fall of the Berlin Wall in 1989 is often described as 'world-changing', so too is 9/11. Yet, 1989 and 9/11 were culminating events – dénouements – signposts of an already changed context influenced by the historical narrative that preceded them, rather than points of origin for new narratives. It is we that turn them into departure points for new stories rather than recognising them as ends of old ones. We further compound this misunderstanding of context by instantly converting these new stories into things we are against. Because we have no pre-existing purpose of our own to coalesce around, the bumps and knocks of seemingly awful events easily deflect us. Rather than bat them away in pursuit of a greater goal of our own, we turn to face them as though they were truly existential, and their resolution the true purpose.

The Intelligence Function

In Search of a Theory

This author has been studying the intelligence function for some eleven years now, rather than merely practising it for a short spell some twenty years ago. Almost on day one this change in perspective was guided by two giant scholars of intelligence studies – Michael Herman, formerly of GCHQ and the Joint Intelligence Committee (JIC), and Loch K. Johnson, Regents Professor of Political Science at the University of Georgia. Michael, through the Oxford Intelligence Group, introduced most academic luminaries specialising in intelligence, many practitioners leading their various intelligence agencies, and those within the legislature and civil service responsible for its oversight and governance. Doctoral research involved meeting and talking extensively with senior and directing intelligence practitioners slightly further down the 'food-chain' from agency heads. Lecturing and academic responsibilities enabled day-to-day contact with those more junior 'do-ers' of intelligence at the sharp end of the intelligence function, including Iraq and Afghanistan. All of these sources have collectively come to fashion the author's interpretation of what this thing called intelligence really is.

Johnson raised two important paradoxes inherent to intelligence and its relationship with power. First, a key feature of democracy: that any civilised society worth the title of 'good' will of necessity display and encourage a degree of 'friction' between its principle constitutional structures. The legislature and the judiciary should contest each others deeply held convictions and beliefs. Law-enforcement organisations should be held to account by the citizenry, directly or indirectly, through legislation, oversight and the press. Similarly, the Armed Forces and intelligence and security communities cannot simply do what they want absent of public approval and consent. Thus, it is the very existence of such friction that marks a civilised and liberal constitution from despotic or authoritarian ones, where little or no dissent – friction – is tolerated. Herman makes a similarly crucial point about the role of intelligence agencies and the type of power they represent: broadly, authoritarian states use intelligence and security agencies to enforce their policies, whereas liberal constitutional states use them to inform policy. Where that leaves traditionally Western democratic states post-Iraqi WMD remains to be seen. Juries – inquiries – continue to pronounce; the verdict does not look promising.

Second, the necessity for intelligence scholars to develop a 'theory of intelligence'; a framework, akin to those developed in sociological, economic and international relations studies, by which to describe and examine itself. It is a grand call. It seems more useful, to practitioners of intelligence at least, to understand the significant influences upon their decision-making processes, particularly the analytical element, than divine a potentially illusive grand framework that itself smacks of a discredited Game Theory. The phenomena that influence how intelligence is done – philosophy, history, human factors, information theory and ethics seem sufficiently robust, extensive, and worthy of study for any student or practitioner of intelligence. Thus, this author parts company with the notion that any self-explanatory theory of intelligence exists in the same way that there are management, economic or international relations theories (which themselves might be subjected to a similar critique). However, *how* it conducts itself can be interpreted, in part, through other well-established theoretical frameworks – cultural, psychological, political and social. Equally, it can be described, in part, by conceptual metaphors, for example the idea that intelligence is the interpretation of data for decision-making purposes is a fair description of the intelligence function. There is even a model of how the intelligence process works – the intelligence cycle – but it is so flawed in reality that even its practitioners are variously embarking upon new ones. Yet, notwithstanding these frameworks and models, it is simply not possible to explain intelligence in its own terms. The greatest expression of this problem for intelligence scholars – an absence of any grand method by which to examine itself – is reflected in the fact that there is still no clear definition of precisely what we mean by intelligence. Most intelligence studies conferences will inexorably descend into discussion about definitions. Indeed, From France to China there is no word to distinguish information from intelligence. The French use the word *renseignement* – inquiry – as their word for intelligence; while the literal Chinese translation for intelligence is 'news'. It is difficult to proceed with its evaluation if we cannot agree a definition of what we are trying to evaluate in the first place.

However, there is one rule of thumb that we can adopt from international relations theory to guide the interrogation of intelligence matters: distinguish the nature of intelligence from its character; its purpose from its processes; why it is done from how it is done. Then, the ultimate validity and usefulness of intelligence – how effective it is perhaps – is simply dependent upon its rigorous testing against reality.

There are at least three other important features of intelligence to bear in mind. First, and possibly the most important, is its special and privileged relationship with power. No other function, including the media, shares such an exclusive, influential and trusted access to decision-making than the intelligence community. That alone is sufficient reason to interrogate its activities and its efficacy. Second, it is no more, no less than just one more information working practice, in the same way that journalism, academic research or weather-forecasting are. The processes of information-working are quite simple: organisations actively seek data in order to answer specific questions so that decision-making masters might be better informed about actions they might come to take. A crucial step is knowing what questions to ask in the first place. But, the originating spark for the entire effort is defining purpose at the outset; otherwise, what questions would you ask and what data would you collect. Specifically, and perhaps offering some superficial distinction from other information-working activities, intelligence data are difficult to obtain by routine or transparent methods (not unlike journalism), most of the questions are usually about forecasting options for decision-makers in the future (not unlike the weather), and the pressures of time or circumstance in which this activity is done usually add an additional degree of difficulty (like most organisations). However you choose to characterise it, intelligence simply consists of a combination of information and interpretation. Whether its subsequent output is effective resides in whether or not it can recognise external socio-political moods, new contemporary contexts, and apprise policy-makers accordingly. Third, it is also necessary to examine what we think we understand by the commonly used term – 'intelligence failure'. In contemporary times, we might be forgiven for thinking primarily about the Iraqi WMD debacle in the run up to the 2003 invasion of Iraq. Interestingly, we rarely talk of the intuitive opposite – intelligence success. The recent tracking down of Osama bin Laden is, arguably, a testimony to the efforts of human intelligence that it was accomplished in ten years. Nor do we recognise that when something 'bad' is prevented from happening, it can either be causally linked to an intelligence intervention, or merely correlated. Second, where precisely does intelligence fail? Richard Betts, an authority on intelligence failure, acknowledges that failure can occur at each and every stage of the intelligence process. It may be that raw data is inaccurate, that the analysis is biased, or that final intelligence product is not distributed to those who need to know. But, Betts's most severe criticism of intelligence failure lies externally with policy-makers. Their handling, interpretation, direction and understanding of intelligence, together with recognising the limitations of what it can and cannot do, need to be established and managed accordingly. It cannot predict the future as some very senior practitioners still claim.

The conduct of intelligence is easy to understand. How it is done changes with the times, specifically the technology of the time. Indeed, given the historical evidence, one might confidently suggest that future technological development will change its conduct and character still further. But, the nature and purpose of intelligence – support to decision-making – will likely remain constant, however it is conducted. As Frank Webster argues in *Theories of the Information Society*, we may have 'informatised' data in the same way that we industrialised the means of production; but, a quantitative shift in the volume of data through digitised information combined with mobile communication technologies does not infer any qualitative shift; and, more information does not imply better interpretation. The availability of virtually unlimited data sources, in what is euphemistically called the 'information age', seems overwhelming. Ed Murrow, the American broadcaster who famously held Senator Joseph McCarthy to account in 1954, put it best: 'The newest computer can merely compound, at speed, the oldest problem in the relations between human beings, and in the end the communicator will be confronted with the old problem, of what to say and how to say it.'

Moreover, these same technological advances also deliver solutions: new attitudes to collection – just in time rather than just in case; new information processing techniques – data mining algorithms, visualisation software; and, distributed forms of analysis – social networks. These techniques are all emerging to cope with the data deluge as the data themselves expand. Furthermore, thanks to the Internet, the World Wide Web, satellites and mobile telephones, this information – the same information – is available to anyone equipped with a personal computer and an appropriate connection. Whether this democratisation of information leads to a better truth remains to be seen.

Precisely What Does Intelligence Do?

Where any significant change is most discernible lies in what the intelligence function now does. What it does has changed considerably since the end of the Cold War; particularly by the perceived significance of the events of 9/11. Thus, today, the UK intelligence system engages in three distinct roles: as producer of traditional strategic assessments via the JIC; as 'global policeman' through monitoring terrorist and criminal networks; and, the capacity building of other countries' efforts to defeat terrorist and insurgency groups. Counter-intuitively, perhaps, it is the first role that is least useful. The use of secret single source intelligence reporting drawn from individuals selected principally for their willingness to share secrets – as Iraqi WMD ably demonstrated – is not the best way to analyse contemporary challenges such as climate change, energy supply, financial stability, food provision or security itself. The JIC and its Assessments Staff may be drawing on too narrow a range of reporting to compete with increasingly sophisticated expertise of the more open private sector, academia and NGOs. Moreover, the JIC has less impact on policy than is often imagined. The second task of global 'spanner' is better suited to the intelligence community's ability to combine human intelligence with communications intelligence and bulk data gathering. It is producing results. The third task of helping other countries to enforce the law and resist insurgency is proceeding on an *ad hoc* basis with occasional successes; but, it requires co-ordination across Whitehall so that improvements in the capabilities of other countries' intelligence services are accompanied by improved police and justice systems, and enhanced oversight.

Similarly, persistent problems in the preparation of assessments have never been fixed. The 1982 Nicoll Report assessed the JIC's failure to predict the 1968 Soviet Invasion of Czechoslovakia, and both the Chinese invasion of Vietnam and the

Soviet invasion of Afghanistan in 1979. The report said: 'In several of these studies, it has appeared that the JIC made up its mind very early, and either did not change it at all (as with USSR/Czechoslovakia) or only later, in the face of very strong evidence of military preparations'. The report added: 'there has been a tendency to assume that factors which would weigh heavily in the United Kingdom would be equally serious constraints on countries ruled by one-party governments and heavily under the influence of a single leader'.

These cognitive biases and analytical failings are well known in the field of psychology. Furthermore, they have been recognised and incorporated into intelligence-practitioner scholarly writing. Yet, these same criticisms, repeated in Percy Cradock's examination of the JIC in *Know Your Enemy*, the 1982 Franks Inquiry into the 'run-up' to the Falklands War, and the 2004 Butler Report into the intelligence debacle surrounding Iraqi WMD, all show little sign of being addressed by the Government, either now or over the past quarter of a century. The 2008 IISS Strategic Survey states: 'The problem [of Iraqi WMD intelligence failures] was not so much one of intelligence analysis as of the inability of the UK's analytical community to put themselves into the minds of those whose behaviour they were analysing.' In the same vein, no effort was made by the JIC or policy-makers to think radically about the pre-invasion failure of the UN inspectors to find militarily significant quantities of WMD. At no point did anyone consider that absence of evidence might in fact indicate evidence of absence; or, as Donald Rumsfeld might say – those things we don't know we don't know, we don't know because they don't exist! Following Butler's recommendations, some progress has been made towards establishing a UK analytical community; a Professional Head of Intelligence Analysis has been appointed in the Cabinet Office. However, the position commands little resource, has no line-management responsibility, and can only advise and seek to exercise influence. Additionally, courses now exist in intelligence analysis at King's College, London, to provide consistent methodology and standards. Yet, there is little evidence within the Assessments Staff, that a permanent cadre of analysts is becoming established.

If these problems have not been addressed in twenty-five years, then maybe they are simply not important problems to the Government. The memoirs of senior politicians rarely mention a JIC assessment being influential in their decision-making such that there remains doubt as to whether JIC papers are regularly read by senior ministers at all. Thus, it is possible that we overestimate the extent to which policy decisions are based on intelligence, and underestimate the extent to which ministers are influenced by their own political agendas, personal contacts and 'DIY' assessments. It would be a naïve politician who gave less weight to a JIC assessment than to a barrage of tabloid headlines; yet, the assumption of the high significance of that assessment in decision-making may be equally naïve.

So, How Intelligent is Intelligence?

There are at least three reasons why intelligence seems not to be behaving intelligently in today's context.

First – the notion of politicisation. The intelligence community has, in recent times and specifically in regard to Iraqi WMD, allowed itself to be misled by power. Harry Hinsley, the historian and WWII Bletchley Park cryptanalyst, argued that the role of intelligence is to tell truth to power and to then leave the policy-makers well alone in their decision-making deliberations. By contrast, Robert Gates, the former Director of the CIA and latterly Secretary of State for Defense in the US, argues that analysts must consider policy-makers' concerns, understand their objectives, and provide analysis relevant to their context. Thus the debate about where the policy-maker/analyst relationship should reside on this spectrum is irresolvable; although notwithstanding Iraqi WMD, the tendency today is strongly toward the Gates doctrine. In regard to Iraqi WMD, the season of inquiry that followed 2003 suggests that not only did they not tell truth to power and leave well alone, but that the cycle went into reverse such that policy-makers (not just politicians) told the intelligence community what truths to tell back to them. In part this was due as much to 'cock-up' as conspiracy: a change of leadership at the top of the UK Defence Intelligence Staff (DIS) – a key all-source analysis asset during 2001/2002 immediately preceding the crucial decisions that led to the 2003 invasion; and, the illness of the lead technical intelligence specialist for WMD did not help. Additionally, the then head of the Joint Intelligence Committee – the UK's ultimate analytical body – was a human intelligence (Humint) collector by trade, expert at running agents, rather than a thoroughbred analyst. Arguably, he failed to judge the weight and import of the counter-analysis emanating from the DIS WMD group against his own inevitable bias towards familiar SIS Humint sources. Moreover, the same head of the JIC was not at the end of his civil service career as had been customary for such a crucial position, but still in line for one more promotion. Thus, he became easy prey to the accusation of manipulation in the face of political pressure emanating from Prime Minister Blair's Downing Street office. Indeed, the entire intelligence community appeared spineless in allowing itself to be manipulated away from the Harry Hinsley dictum of telling truth to power. However, also in part, there was some conspiracy – opportunism maybe – within the senior policy-maker/ intelligence-director level relationship. A very defensive SIS was looking to shore up its position against a decade of cuts and reductions post-1989. The Iraqi WMD question was an opportunity to 'advertise' its unique access to secret foreign intelligence; an opportunity not missed by the then Chief of SIS.

Second – internal and systemic cultural barriers. Notwithstanding the quality of its people and the resources available to its agencies, the intelligence community, like any large organisation, struggles to overcome systemic and cultural barriers to efficient and effective working. In addition to the usual decision-making flaws of confirmation bias, mirroring and group-think, it suffers from the ambition of egos, the pursuit of careers, the paralysis of two-year appointments, the need to be seen to be doing something, stifling bureaucracy and office politics. This is made worse in the UK intelligence community, unlike the US intelligence community or the UK Defence community, by the fact that *there is no single community*. In particular, there is no joint school of intelligence where practitioners can learn or study their trade together. But, the most pernicious and permeating feature that hinders both the efficiency and effectiveness of the intelligence function is a security classification system reflecting the paranoia of the intelligence function. Notwithstanding recent exhortations of 'need-to-share' versus 'need-to-know', this principal barrier – extensively case-studied from Pearl Harbor to 9/11 – remains constant. This cultural 'gatekeeper' to the passage of information is still being circumvented by 'water-cooler conversation'; informal rather than formal methods of communication. The system has become so nonsensical that the US Congressional

Research Service is forbidden to use any of the recently released WikiLeaks documents because they were once classified. Yet, they can all be freely and openly retrieved from the Internet. How can their analysis be optimal if some of the more useful and relevant information available to them in plain sight is denied them by their 'own side'?

Third – coping with a changing context. Specifically and contemporarily, the intelligence community remains challenged by two key global contextual changes of the last three decades. First, although they are equipped with the modern tools of the digital world, they have not yet all adapted culturally to the implications of the transformation in ICT, or at least not adapted their own requirements for secrecy to the inevitable openness of present-day information-working. Those people currently in charge or at the senior directing end of intelligence agencies are roughly aged 55–65 years old. Yet, those aged 51 in 2011 will have most likely missed out on the digital mobile ICT transformation during their childhood/student education. Second, worse still, these same people who missed out on 'second-nature' IT will probably have cut their teeth, become institutionalised, and politically inculcated by everything Cold War. And today they are in charge just as the world is undergoing a mobile digital transformation and the Cold War ethos of secrecy no longer applies. They have also struggled, as a whole, to react to the change in context from the Cold War intelligence war to the present-day terrorist threat. While the Iraqi WMD fiasco certainly seems the most unintelligent thing that the intelligence community has done in recent times, scholars of intelligence studies argue that the failure to respond proportionately to the terrorist threat of the late 1980s remains the more significant.

Furthermore, allowing our respective politicians to portray a terrorist threat as an existential challenge to contemporary Western liberal democracies is significantly more unintelligent. The failure to alert policy-makers to the slippery slope of meaningless security alert states, the suspension of habeas corpus, the removal of trial by jury, the criminalising of so-called hate speech, the near instigation of thought-crime, and be complicit in the use of rendition and torture have all been massive 'hits' on the very founding values of what a liberal constitution strives for. Arguably, we have completed much of the work of the so-called terrorists for them. It is we who have changed our society. It was an unintelligent intelligence that failed to recognise and interrogate these deeper implications further in order to prevent them becoming today's lazy assumptions and received wisdoms. Some did, but they were not heard. Ironically, this third unintelligent response to a changing contemporary context will probably be resolved more quickly and naturally than either the more endemic politicisation or systemic cultural barriers. These people have to retire or pass on at some point in the not too distant future! However, whether the next generation will recognise the deeper Cold War legacy of vacuous ideology remains to be seen. It may be that we simply engage in one more iteration away from an Enlightenment project as new echelons of intelligence personnel become seduced by their relationship with power and political elites.

The usefulness or effectiveness of intelligence is probably only best validated by rigorous testing against reality. But, how do you do that? Like the contested definition of intelligence, evaluating its effectiveness is also a perennial problem for practitioners and customers alike. Surely there are league tables, targets and balanced scorecards that can convey a measure of effectiveness through Game Theory or systems analysis? All of these approaches – like risk assessment matrices – merely confer an air of pseudo-scientific objectivity upon essentially and intrinsically subjective uncertainties. There is a more simplistic, time-honoured rule of thumb that is guaranteed, probably, to get you to the right answer in your gut at least. If it walks like a duck, and talks like a duck, then it's probably a duck! There is still no better answer for negotiating the grey areas of the usefulness, or otherwise, of intelligence. The challenge is to recognise the duck that you are looking at, and determine whether or not it is the one you wanted.

If political elites do not know what they are for, but simply stumble from one crisis to another or, worse, address crises precautionarily before they ever materialise, then the intelligence function, at the wrong end of that yo-yo, will suffer accordingly. It is in this more fundamental way – an inability to think intelligently about contemporary times, to be unaligned to an ideological purpose, and to be tethered to decision-makers who are themselves all at sea – that inevitably makes the deliverers of intelligence product appear unintelligent to the rest of us.

Brixmis Revisited

How does a new understanding of context and intelligence change any view about Brixmis? Superficially, it changes little. The intelligence contribution to preventing the Cold War going hot remains extant; and, Brixmis's contribution to that outcome was important. Indeed its contribution was judged sufficiently important to both justify the money spent on it, as well as support its continuing role precisely when wider political tensions were most acute.

Brixmis was principally interested in dispositions – numbers – and thus capability. We attempted an educated assessment of intention, but just as the computer modelling underpinning MAD was flawed, our ability to 'predict' what the Soviet military might do with their equipment was similarly unrealistic. We could merely observe and report the factual happenings at the desperate edge of uncertainty's here and now. We could not be sure of their intention untill they happened. While Game Theory assumed super-rational self-interested behaviour, we observed motivated military people, who appeared reasonable, reasoning, and – like us – in the service of their political masters.

The nagging curiosity was how their political masters could wreak such havoc at home yet their representatives appear so reasonable and reasoning upon contact with Brixmis abroad. Our political ideology was so obviously 'right' by contrast. The answer lies in the fact that both systems – capitalist and communist - had much in common. They both originated in the West and both pursued liberation and freedom for its people; the one by ruthless tyranny in order to achieve a so-called glorious and greater good, the other by control to achieve stability as a goal in itself. The brutality of the Communist revolution in 1917, the reaction to it, the reaction to the reaction, and the subsequent regime of Stalinist terror had common cause with the violence of the French revolution(s) post-1789. Left and right were merely two routes to the same thing. Yet, the contrast between the two approaches – violent versus controlling – reveals a bleak and disconcerting ideological distinction. Their violent struggle for freedom – that ended in tyranny – at least believed in something; the version of freedom we pursued in the West was empty of purpose.

So, while Brixmis 'counted tanks' – capability – and did it very well, others predicted human intentions on an entirely false premise that computer modelling could reveal them. Thus, the intention part of the threat equation was falsely constructed.

Policy-makers had already decided that the coercion of society through the portrayal of a frightening and exaggerated view of the 'other' abroad, combined with a control through self-interested individuals at home, would be the necessary tools of power. Simultaneously, while much wool was being pulled over many eyes, the same political elites in the West pursued their negative version of freedom – control – entirely devoid of a positive purpose and entirely opaque to those who thought they were conducting a genuine existential struggle. So, while Brixmis was 'fighting' one seemingly honourable struggle for freedom abroad, there was a more complex fight against an alternative, twisted version of freedom being concealed and avoided at home. The paradox and hypocrisy is yet more stark for today's intelligence communities, as the purpose behind recent conflicts is increasingly being revealed as hollow.

Part of an early realisation that things are not always as they seem began in Brixmis itself. It was then conventional and received wisdom among Cold War military circles that the Soviet Union's armed forces, while being massive in number, were deficient in technical capability, and, that their personnel were short on initiative. Yet, many who worked intimately with this supposedly flawed machine saw a paradox: equipment was not necessarily technically inferior, but ruggedly simple; simplistic and inflexible command and control structures were ruthlessly and rapidly manoeuvrable at will. The AK-47 is not the weapon of choice merely because it is cheap to produce, but also because it is simple and reliable to use. And, the history of Soviet military action and political ideology is replete with the reckless abandonment of huge quantities of manpower in pursuit of a clearly defined and existential purpose to succeed. Compounding the paradox amidst the rather feverish days of East European liberation was the Mission-observed appearance of increasingly sophisticated Soviet military equipment arriving in East Germany throughout the early 1990s. In part this was due to long supply-chain timelines that characterise military procurement all over the world, and in part due to the innate and relentless ability of Soviet scientists to innovate and develop technologies. Yet, to those operating on the ground, notwithstanding the economic haemorrhaging of the Soviet Union at home since the late 1970s, the date of the Soviet demise could not be firmly set for 1989. Additionally then, and continuing to this day in other areas of intelligence activity, there was a growing realisation that the paranoid secrecy of intelligence work ends up doing most harm to its own side – fellow practitioners and citizens alike. This manifests as simple barriers to the passage of information or the somewhat more childish internal one-up-man-ship of security clearances. But, the most significant consequence is the stifling inability to recognise the context of the day.

Similarly, there are some things once done in Brixmis days that are less likely to be repeatable on operations today. There is less chance, for example, that you could have 'fun' undertaking somewhat dangerous intelligence work! This is more a reflection of an unconfident sense of self and mission across society as a whole than any change in the gravity of today's intelligence work. Similarly, the autonomy with which young officers and junior NCOs were allowed to operate has also changed significantly. Aged 25–35, Brixmis personnel were expected to recognise the diplomatic and international significance of their action behind enemy lines and balance the consequences of getting things 'wrong' with the gains of success. Yet, formal risk-assessment procedures simply did not exist. Assessments were forged by experience and judgement, often instantaneously, and 'in the head'. Indeed the objectives of the organisation were so clear and dominating that any discussion of risk was subordinate to the achievement of those objectives. Planning (assessment) was conducted in order to maximise their achievement rather than minimising 'unwanted' consequences. It was intuitively understood that you did not want to make mistakes; but, also understood that accidents and mistakes did happen, and that they would be dealt with when they happened rather than anticipated as though they would happen. Today, the equivalent unit might be expected to check its proposed actions against some risk management matrix and a lawyer. Thus, the entire direction of intent is questioned and questionable from the outset as the focus intrinsically shifts away from the pursuit of goals and towards the reduction in any risk associated with those goals. What once passed for the application of informal commonsense amongst trusted adults has become a distrusting infantilising of similar adults. Having selected, trained and dispatched people to do incredibly grown-up and dangerous things, what they are in fact saying to them is we do not trust you to do them and we do not trust ourselves to stand-up for you when accidents occur or mistakes are made.

In the same way that the Cold War intelligence effort was entirely aligned with the ideological struggle of the day, so too Brixmis was purposefully oriented – it knew what it was doing and why it was doing it – and it was successful. That it might have been aligned with a deeper philosophical misunderstanding of what freedom in the twentieth century was about – negative freedom, a freedom absent of purpose – is only obvious now. The result of that pursuit of a negative freedom is, today, a slavery to control by the latest bureaucratic elite, itself absent of political purpose and unclear about what it wants for its own society. The tragedy of the amazing work done by Brixmis and other Cold War intelligence efforts was that it was operating under the negative freedom assumption, the depressing theory of self-interested Game Theory, a hollowing out of proper politics such that it is difficult to conclude anything other than the Cold War was a giant historical cul-de-sac where all enlightened efforts at producing a good society were suspended. It is cruel to think that the sham was so well constructed as to be impervious to the intelligence community that inadvertently supported it. Worse, it is still going on today – the Enlightenment project was abandoned early in the Cold War precisely because of intelligence's success at managing it, and remains abandoned today in favour of banality and control.

To a degree, the ending of the Cold War, and the closing of Brixmis in particular, also represented a loss of meaning at a personal level if not at a collective national level. A 50-year reason for being – purpose – had been removed at a stroke for many individuals, the Armed Forces, and from the nation as a whole. Indeed, it might be said that this loss of purpose also precipitated a wholesale loss of the identity that had been crafted out of the ideological struggle of the Cold War. Yet, this release from the 'great game' also revealed some of the myths and mysteries that had been kept from us – deliberately or sub-consciously. In part, the Cold War was a useful construct for power to contrive a connivance, or what has been called a culture of fear, by which power retains power. Since this loss of purpose and identity, Western society has itself wandered incrementally, imperceptibly, and unrecognisably into something else that only the opportunity to reflect upon can now begin to reveal – purposeless pragmatism and managerialism as cover for the absence of direction let alone transcendence to a real understanding of the contemporary context.

The disarray at the end of the Mission's life, and the ensuing self-destruction within the Joint Intelligence Section that took on Brixmis's work, might be ascribed in part to the uncertainty of the time: were the Soviets really going to leave; would German unification succeed or even proceed; could the BND take on the role of the Missions; why were new types of Soviet equipment still arriving in the former DDR; and, just what did the August 1991 coup in Moscow signify? Equally in part, it can be ascribed to a rapid break-up of the Mission team in response to new global events: some were dispatched to the 1990–91 Gulf War; others became engaged in the conflicts marking the split of Yugoslavia; while yet more became involved in wider arms-control and weapons inspection teams. All of these new missions reflected the extraordinary, transferable skill set and knowledge built up over forty-six years of Mission life. But in part the somewhat hasty, undignified and testy disintegration of the Mission was intrinsically due to the absence of mission itself. Procedural wrangling, political in-fighting, and an unravelling of the cohesion that only authentic ideological or moral purpose can give swelled as Brixmis's originating political purpose dimmed. The microcosm of contemporary society was being reflected precisely then in Brixmis's final moments. Metaphorically, the writing was on the wall for the author to see all along. Apart from the 'five rules of touring' quoted at the front of this book, there was one other mantra that Chiefs of Mission used to 'calm down' tourers taking too many risks: 'There's nothing out there worth dying for'. Actually, there was; but, no longer!

In his 1946 classic work – *A History Of Western Philosophy* – Bertrand Russell argued that the greatest question philosophical thinking should address is how to derive the balance between a sufficiently enforced social coercion that gets things done for all in society and a sufficiency of individual liberty for each of us to live a good life. Too much coercion – regulation, bureaucracy, nationalisation, conscription – ossifies societies into a fearful paralysis prohibiting innovation, experimentation and progress. Conversely, too much liberty leads to anarchy, a free for all and societal breakdown.

Abdicating any effort to address this fundamental philosophical question, it has become received wisdom to say that the single most important role of government is the defence of its nation. This author disagrees. The single most important role of a government is to know precisely what it wants for its nation that is worth defending in the first place. In 1969 Robert Rathbun Wilson, the then Director of America's Fermi National Laboratory (Fermilab) and responsible for ground-breaking research into particle acceleration, was summoned by the US Congressional Joint Committee on Atomic Energy to explain how the cost and output of his laboratory contributed to the security and defence of the nation. Wilson replied: 'You misunderstand. My research has nothing to do directly with defending our country except to make it worth defending.' It is a society's values and purpose – what it is for – that make a society worth defending. Until recent times, an Enlightenment project – freedom of speech, a free press, equality of justice under the law, trial by one's own peers, freedom of religious expression, and the pursuit of prosperity and progress for all – was a project worthy of purposeful and wilful politicians. Today, the most problematic challenge that the intelligence community has to contend with is that its own political masters, and a political class more generally, do not know what they are for. Politicians fail to articulate, beyond sound-bites, what their vision of a 'good society' project should look like and how to get there. Thus, they have little to defend beyond the empty rhetoric of claiming the right to defend. They trample upon, that illusive balance between collective coercion and individual liberty that Russell alluded to in 1946.

Appendix I

THE ROBERTSON-MALININ AGREEMENT

AGREEMENT

REGARDING THE EXCHANGE OF MILITARY LIAISON MISSIONS BETWEEN THE SOVIET AND BRITISH COMMANDERS-IN-CHIEF OF ZONES OF OCCUPATION IN GERMANY

In accordance with Article 2 of the Agreement of 'The Control Machinery in Germany' of 14th November 1944, the Soviet and British Commanders-in-Chief of the Zones of Occupation in Germany have decided to exchange Military Liaison Missions to be accredited to their respective Staffs in the Zone and to confirm the following points regarding these Missions:

1. The Mission will consist of 11 officers assisted by not more than 20 technicians, clerks and other personnel required for W/T. (wireless/telegraphy)

2. The Mission will be placed under the authority of one member of the Mission who will be nominated and termed the 'Chief of the Soviet/British Military Mission'. All other Liaison Officers, Missions or Russian/British personnel operating in the Zone will accept the authority and carry out the instruction of the Chief of the Mission.

3. The Chief of the Mission will be accredited to the Commander-in-Chief of the Forces of Occupation. In the case of the British Zone this means Air Marshal Sir Sholto Douglas. In the case of the Russian Zone this means Marshal of the Soviet Union Sokolovsky.

4. In the case of the British Zone the Soviet mission is invited to take up residence at or near Zone Headquarters (Bad Salzuflen area).

5. In the case of the Soviet Zone the British Mission is invited to take up residence at or near Karlshorst or Potsdam.

6. In the case of the British Zone the Chief of the Soviet Mission will communicate with the Deputy Chief of Staff (Execution) Major General Bishop or his staff.

7. In the case of the Soviet Zone the Chief of the British Mission will communicate with the Deputy Chief of Staff Major General Lavrentiov.

8. Each Mission will have similar travellers' facilities. Passes of an identical nature in Russian and English will be prepared. Generally speaking there will be freedom of travel and circulation for the members of Missions in each Zone with the exception of restricted areas in which respect each Commander-in-Chief will notify the Mission and act on a reciprocal basis.

9. Each Mission will have their own wireless station for communication with its Commander-in-Chief. In each case facilities will be provided for Couriers and Despatch Riders to pass freely from the Mission HQ to the HQ of their own Commander-in-Chief. These Couriers will enjoy the same immunity as Diplomatic Couriers.

10. Each Mission will be provided with telephone facilities in the local exchange at their HQ and given facilities for such communications (post, telephone, telegraph) as exist when touring in the Zone. In the event of a breakdown of the wireless stations the Zone Commander will give every assistance in meeting the emergency by providing temporary facilities on his own signal system.

11. Each Mission will be administered by the Zone in which it resides in respect of accommodation, rations, petrol, and stationery against repayment in Reichsmarks.

The building will be given full immunity.

12. The object of the Mission is to maintain Liaison between the Staff of the two Commanders-in-Chief and their Military Governments in the Zones.

The Missions can also in each Zone concern themselves and make representation regarding their nationals and interests in the Zones in which they are operating. They can afford assistance to authorised visitors of their own country visiting the Zone to which the Mission is accredited.

13. This agreement is written in Russian and English. Both texts are authentic.

14. The agreement comes into force the moment letters have been exchanged by the Deputies to the British and Soviet Commanders-in-Chief of the Zones of Occupation in Germany.

(Signed)

B.H. ROBERTSON Lt General, Deputy Military Governor, CCG (BE)
M.S. MALININ Col.-General, Deputy Commander-in-Chief, Chief of Staff of the Soviet Group of Forces of Occupation in Germany, Berlin 16 September 1946

Appendix II

TOUR EQUIPMENT

Tour equipment was geared firstly towards completing missions and secondly towards self-sufficiency. Inevitably the two were interdependent. There was no point going out into the DDR to undertake missions if you couldn't stay out there for up to six or seven days at a time or if when you got to your target you didn't have the right equipment to tackle it.

The range of conditions met and experiences to be dealt with over the years finely tuned the Mission's inventory. Temperatures ranged from a bone-numbing minus 30 degrees Centigrade and several feet of snow in winter to a sweltering plus 40 degrees and endless clouds of dust in summer. Targets varied from underground bunkers that required breaking into, to distant training areas only visible with the greatest magnification. Eating and drinking was for the most part conducted inside the vehicle. Ablutions were reduced to wet wipes. Shovel recces were carried out first thing or not at all. First aid included extensive training in dealing with trauma and accidents. First aid kits included morphine and plasma drips to cope with remote and difficult locations, a lack of two-way communications and slow or nil response from local emergency services. The last thing we wanted in the event of an accident was be carted off to an East German or Soviet hospital, not for safety reasons but for the appalling variation in standards of medical care from those one might receive in the West.

Self-sufficiency, together with the tools of the trade, were key. It all had to be transportable. Without doubt the most versatile, reliable and effective carrier was the Mercedes Geländewagen. It was the platform from which we launched the vast majority of all our missions, the shell in which we carried everything we needed plus items that we brought back from Tommy finds and unexploded ordnance to armour plating and chemical samples. Moreover it was invariably the first and last word in escape. Second only to the cameras, the G-wagon made the job possible.

VEHICLES

Mercedes Geländewagen: 1982–90.

Four-wheel or two-wheel drive option. Exceptional cross-country capability.
Spare 90-litre fuel tank.
Front mounted electric winch.
Stowed hand winch on turfor-jack.
Average distance of 500 kilometres travelled per day.

Opel Senator (3 litre): 1978–90.
Used only in preference to the G-wagon where speed was of the essence, low-profile was essential or if all the other vehicles were out on tour. Quite often used for local tours of Potsdam. It appeared less aggressive and more like a formal flag-waving tour.
Four-wheel or two-wheel drive option.
180-litre fuel capacity, 1,300 kilometre range.
Top speed in excess of 200 k.p.h.

All vehicles were under-armoured to enhance cross-country capability. They were rewired to isolate lights, horn etc. or configure them to replicate East German vehicles. IR spots and extra beams were fitted. Colour schemes were all-over drab olive green to replicate Soviet and East German military vehicles.

CAMERAS

Nikon F3 Manual – three bodies and motor drives made from a Kevlar-based material for protection.
85-mm, 180-mm, 500-mm mirror and 1,000-mm mirror lenses.
Doubler to extended focal length up to 2,000 mm.

Nikon F4 Automatic – one.
This camera was trialled with an 85–150-mm telephoto lens. It wasn't approved because it negated calculations for mensuration without knowing the precise focal length.

'Mickey Mouse' – one, usually AF 35-mm Canon.
A point and press camera in emergency. Very useful for underground work or when in a tight spot, it could be operated almost within the palm of the hand unseen.

FILM

All film was colour by late 1989.
100–400 ASA.
The 400 ASA could be up-rated or 'pushed' to 6,400 ASA for aircraft or low light work.
Colour slide for presentation work if time and memory allowed!
Film was the cheapest part of the operation and tourers carried what they thought would be necessary for their tour. Sometimes tours would return with two or three rolls, sometimes they would be conserving film after the first hundred rolls. Two spare packs of twenty 100 ASA and twenty 400 ASA were always carried at the bottom of the camera case for this eventuality. Film was stored in fridges back in Berlin to keep it as fresh as possible before use.

Some infrared photography was undertaken where circumstances warranted. It was rarely necessary unless flash photography would have alerted sentries or locals. It did not always produce fine enough detail.

Video camera – various including Olympus 303.
Extremely useful for the recording of training drills or our own training and operational requirements such as routes, OPs and going. Not always successful in capturing technical detail until frame speeds were increased and single frames from video coverage could be used for analysis.
Some videos could be fitted with Nikon lenses giving focal lengths up to 6,000 mm.

Modulux – one.
An image intensifying device used at night under ambient and artificial light conditions.
It was specially adapted to fit the Nikon F3. It could also be used with an adapter on the video camera.
Mini-Modulux – the successor to Modulux: half the size and half the weight.

There were three separate boxes for camera equipment. One for the cameras, one for the video and one for the Modulux. Each of them were tied on to the internal chassis of the G-wagon to prevent them being removed.

PERSONAL SURVIVAL EQUIPMENT

STOWED IN VEHICLE

Gore-Tex outer garments.
Snow boots (worn as overboots).
Gloves and hat.
Canadian parka.
Bed roll – Arctic or summer sleeping bag inside Gore-Tex bivvie bag, rolled up inside a Gore-Tex one-man hoop tent fitted with rubber mat base. The whole thing could be compressed into a manageable bundle no bigger than a rucksack – with practice! They could be pitched and occupied in seconds in the dark on virtually any terrain.

CARRIED ON PERSON AT ALL TIMES

Pen-knife, Magna-light red filtered torch and Silva compass all tied to clothing.
Wallet with East German currency and emergency telephone numbers always carried.
Simple Casio watch with alarm and timer.
Soviet Pass except for Operation Tomahawk.
Blood group details.

FOOD

Brew Kit – a simple construction of three coffee jars taped together containing coffee, sugar and powdered milk. The more elaborate had pouches for tin opener, racing spoon and tea bags. The brew kit was by far the most important item of sustenance carried. It not only provided liquid refreshment when cooking was inappropriate but it masked a thousand misdemeanours from the eyes of the Sovs and East Germans. The British drinking tea on the side of the road as a vehicle convoy went past was one of many eccentric pastimes. Six thermos flasks of boiling water were carried. They were refilled with boiling water every morning as part of the driver's duties. Enough food for the tour plus up to three days extra rations was carried. Breakfast and lunch were usually light meals. Dinner was cooked inside the vehicle on a 'bluey' in the evening while watching a railway line or road junction. Breakfast in my case consisted of porridge oats with boiling water added. Coffee was most welcome after that. Lunch was usually sandwiches pre-prepared at home. Dinner was luxury and a combined effort. One of the crew brought preboiled rice, sufficient for three nights, one member brought the meat and the other brought a tinned sauce and some vegetables. The last two were stewed or curried in the vehicle's tour pot, which was usually purchased from the East so that it would not be conspicuous if left in a hurry. Quite often the appearance of kit would necessitate dumping the evening meal, not recklessly but by opening the door and leaving it where we were parked to be retrieved sometime later.

TOURING EQUIPMENT

MAPS (CARRIED BY BOTH TOUR OFFICER AND NCO)

1:500,000 Soviet PRA map issued by GSFG/WGF.
1:500,000 PRA map issued by BAOR.

Strip map – consisting of eleven books of 1;50,000 OS maps cut and pasted together. The strip map was the main aid to navigation until on target.
Target maps – blank 1;25,000 maps used for close target recce. Both strip and target maps were unmarked for obvious reasons other than with OPs of which there were thousands.
Vehicle mounted EZB compass and kilometre tripmaster.
DDR fuel map detailing all petrol stations that would take our Soviet fuel coupons.

VISUAL AIDS (CARRIED BETWEEN THE CREW)

Binoculars – three pairs minimum, ranging in field of view, magnification and physical size. Usually Zeiss, not because they were manufactured in East Germany but because they were the best.
Snipers 'swift scope'.
PNG – two pairs minimum. One pair for the driver as situation demanded.

MISCELLANEOUS (CARRIED BETWEEN CREW OR FOR CERTAIN OPERATIONS)

'Black Banana' – long-range listening device and microphone.
Scanner – used by air tours to monitor air traffic control frequencies and aid positive identification of active airfields.
Thermal Imager – highly classified video apparatus operating in the far infrared end of spectrum.
Lock picking set – used by specially trained personnel as required.
Bleeper system – always checked before leaving and secured under dashboard inside glove compartment. Not carried on local tours.
Diamond scraper – for removing samples of armour as opportunity arose.

OTHER (CARRIED BY TOUR OFFICER AND NCO IN RAF NAVIGATOR'S BRIEFCASE)

Sony mini tape recorders – two.
Robertson-Malinin agreement in English and Russian.
Letter of authority in German and English.
Nark list – a list of known number-plates operated by the Stasi/MfS compiled by the Mission over the years.
Number-plate identification codes – these ranged from Diplomatic and Trade Missions to regional and city identifiers.
Unexploded ordnance *aide-memoir*.
Map revision cards.
Long stay/detention pee bottle.
Bribes – whisky, cigarettes, chocolate, sweets, newspapers, pornographic magazines, all manner of things.

CLOTHING

Tourers dressed down, that is to say as drab and as 'earthy' as possible. Olive green lightweights and an olive green shirt or jumper was standard rig. Black flying boots were issued. I used even lighter jungle boots. Berets were worn when crossing the Glienicke Bridge or in formal meetings with Soviets and East Germans as a result of detentions or chance meetings. Camouflage clothing was strictly prohibited in order to reflect the spirit of the Robertson-Malinin agreement for liaison missions. Camouflage clothing would have looked strikingly out of place in East Germany anyway. The only organised body wearing camouflage were Spetsnaz forces. Everybody else from farmers to East German and Soviet soldiers wore a variety of drab green. We were no exception. We wore badges of rank and Brixmis arm flashes unless on certain operations where their loss would have been compromising.

ABLUTIONS

Washing was a luxury rarely performed other than by the use of wet wipes bought in the American-PX (supermarket). Defecation was timed to perfection before leaving on tour and conducted on tour inconspicuously with a shovel to dig the hole necessary for burial. Teeth were cleaned dry. Other than that crews would all smell together!

Index